Support for the American Welfare State

Support for the American Welfare State

The Views of Congress and the Public

Fay Lomax Cook
Edith J. Barrett

Columbia University Press   New York

Columbia University Press
New York   Oxford

Copyright © 1992 Columbia University Press
All rights reserved

Library of Congress Cataloging-in-Publication Data
Cook, Fay Lomax.
    Support for the American welfare state : the views of Congress and
    public / Fay Lomax Cook ; Edith J. Barrett.
    p. cm.
    Includes bibliographical references and index.
    ISBN 0-231-07618-5 (cl.)—ISBN 0-231-07619-3 (pbk.)
    1. Public welfare—United States—Public opinion.   2. Public
opinion—United States.   I. Title.
HV95.C6478   1992   92-18654
                                                                    Cip

∞

Casebound editions of Columbia University Press books are Smyth-sewn
            and printed on permanent and durable acid-free paper.

                        Printed in the United States of America

                        c 10 9 8 7 6 5 4 3 2 1

We dedicate this book to our parents
with love and gratitude:

DeLeslyn Morgan Lomax Fleming,
the memory of Clifton Lamar Lomax,
and
Lucille Cramer Barrett and A. Delgado Barrett

Contents

Figures

Tables

Acknowledgments

As we send our completed manuscript to Columbia University Press and look forward to its publication, we also look back with deep appreciation to the people and organizations who made it possible. First and foremost, we are grateful to those members of Congress and the general public who took the time to speak with us. Without generous gifts of their time in interviews that averaged forty to fifty minutes, we would not have been able to write this book.

Equally important to our work was the funding necessary to do the research. We are grateful to the Ford Foundation and in particular to its Project on Social Welfare and the American Future for awarding the grant that enabled us to conduct the research. The vision that spearheaded this particular project at the Ford Foundation owes much to the intellectual leadership and commitment of both Franklin Thomas, president of the Ford Foundation, and Charles V. Hamilton, who directed the project. Staff member Alice O'Connor provided the enthusiasm, the organizational skills, and well-timed smart, probing questions to propel the project to completion. The members of the Research Advisory Committee on which Fay Cook served provided a lively forum for the discussion of social welfare policy issues and research questions, and she thanks Hugh Heclo, Edward M. Gramlich, Ira Katznelson, Alicia

Munnell, and William J. Wilson for creating an exciting community of scholars, even if it lasted too short a time.

The Russell Sage Foundation also provided important funding for this book. A year as a fellow for Fay Cook and a quarter year as a research associate for Edith Barrett gave us time to work in an environment rich in intellectual stimulation and generous in services. We are grateful to Eric Wanner, president of the Russell Sage Foundation, for the marvelous atmosphere he created for productive scholarship. To Theodore R. Marmor, special colleague and friend, we owe many thanks for his help in making the year possible by organizing a research group on social welfare policy, for his special knack of infusing excitement and vigor into even the most mundane academic discourse, and for his continued intellectual support.

At Northwestern University, the Center for Urban Affairs and Policy Research provided release time to Fay Cook for research and writing. Even more important, it has provided a supportive intellectual haven where interdisciplinary discussions and research can take place. For helping to create that environment, for the loan of books, and for critiques of chapters and articles over the years, thanks to Christopher Jencks, John McKnight, Dan A. Lewis, Jane Mansbridge, Wesley Skogan, and Burton A. Weisbrod. In the School of Education and Social Policy, Fay Cook acknowledges important support from Dean David Wiley and Professor Bernice Neugarten, the founders of the Graduate Program in Human Development and Social Policy.

Members of the faculty in the Department of Political Science and the Taubman Center for Public Policy at Brown University have helped Edith Barrett survive the first years of teaching while simultaneously completing the manuscript. Special thanks go to Thomas Anton, Darrell West, Nancy Rosenblum, and Michael Rich for their welcome criticism and steady support. Several undergraduate assistants at Brown have provided help; particular thanks go to N'Tanya Lee and Grace Lee, who have spent endless hours in the library searching for obscure statistics. We also extend our thanks to the University of Southern California's Institute for Health Promotion and Disease Prevention Research, where Edith Barrett's year and a half as a postdoctoral fellow allowed her to focus on data analysis and early work on the manuscript.

Many graduate students in Northwestern's Human Development and Social Policy Program have contributed to the research analyses that form the core of *Support for the American Welfare State*. In the important first years, these included Ernesto Constantino, Susan Popkin, and Julie Kaufman. In the equally important final stages, Anne Welch, Christine George, and Richard Settersten provided research assistance. Richard Settersten's help often went above and beyond the call of duty; for his role in constructing many of the figures, coding interview data, and thinking through conceptual issues, we will always be grateful.

Earlier versions of this book were reviewed by Robert Y. Shapiro and Benjamin Page. Their comments were invaluable. For helpful conversations and advice, we thank Kenneth F. Janda and Tom Smith. Our editors at Columbia University Press, Gioia Stevens and Jonathan Director, were wonderful supporters and advocates.

Finally, we are grateful to our families. Jeff Howard, Tom Cook, and David Cook have been wonderfully supportive. Jeff Howard was our ever-present source of expert advice on the fine details of grammar and syntax. Tom Cook was our ever-present critic whose comments sharpened our thinking and strengthened our analyses. David Cook was our ever-present reminder that this book was simply taking too long and would we just finish it, please. To these three, a special thanks for time spent together and for understanding the time spent apart.

1

Social Welfare Policy in America: The 1980s as a Crossroads

This book examines the state of the American welfare state from the perspectives of both the American public and members of the U.S. Congress. It describes how much support exists for programs of the welfare state and explains why members of the public and Congress hold the views they do about these programs.

Such an analysis is long overdue. In the 1980s and continuing into the 1990s, social welfare opponents and proponents alike have claimed that the welfare state is in the midst of a crisis—a financial crisis caused by the growing deficit and the mushrooming costs of social welfare programs, a demographic crisis caused by a growth in the numbers of people relying on social welfare programs, and a crisis of legitimacy caused by the purported unwillingness of the public and Congress to continue financing welfare state programs (OECD 1981; Stoesz and Karger 1992). This sense of crisis is reflected in many reports issued over the past decade addressing the state of the welfare state. Some reports came from the federal government (e.g., White House Domestic Policy Council 1986), others from state governments (e.g., California Department of Social Services 1986; Washington State Department of Social and Health Services and the Employment Security Department 1986), think tanks (e.g., American Enterprise Institute 1987), national nonprofit organizations (American Public Welfare Association 1986; National Governors Association 1987), and philanthropic founda- tions (e.g., Ford Foundation 1989).

These works look at the potential crisis in social welfare from a number of viewpoints but spend little or no time examining what the public and members of Congress think about social welfare programs in general or about the particular programs they are most and least willing to fund. We propose to take on that task. We describe the extent to which the major programs that constitute the current American welfare state are supported by the general public and by members of the U.S. House of Representatives (major programs include Social Security, Medicare, Unemployment Insur- ance, Aid to Families with Dependent Children [AFDC], Food Stamps, Medicaid, and Supplemental Security Income [SSI]). Armed with such knowledge, we are better able to probe the truth of reports of a so-called crisis of legitimacy. If a crisis in support does exist, the American welfare state is in serious jeopardy, and policy- makers must reconsider the role of governmental intervention in the social welfare domain. If, however, we find general support for the current welfare state intact and the crisis of legitimacy rhetoric unwarranted empirically, then the question arises as to why such crisis rhetoric arose in the first place. There is yet a third possibil- ity: we may find that some welfare programs are supported more than others. If this turns out to be the reality of American support for social welfare, then the oversimplified rhetoric of the 1980s should be brought to public attention and corrected.

Evidence of a true crisis of legitimacy in the American welfare state is sketchy at best. It is anecdotal and relies on media reports, interpretations of the electoral successes of Ronald Reagan, and conclusions from opinion surveys asking broad, general questions about "welfare," which in fact leave the definition of "welfare" unclear. To date, there is no study that directly addresses this crisis of legitimacy. To do so systematically, a study needs both a repre- sentative sampling frame and items that probe into beliefs about the broad range of programs and services that make up the entirety of the American welfare state.

It is not enough merely to describe the level of congressional and public support for particular social programs. It is also impor- tant to explain the bases for these beliefs. Until now, few empirical studies have systematically examined the reasons people hold certain beliefs about different social welfare programs, although there are numerous speculations in historical accounts, and various empirical studies on the reasons for political decisions in general. There are four schools of thought. The first is based on self-interest and assumes that individuals support those programs from which they directly benefit. The second explanation argues that people develop political predispositions in childhood that incline them to be Democrats or Republicans and to hold liberal or conservative ideologies, and that these general predispositions are then reflected in beliefs about specific policy issues, such as social welfare. A third explanation holds that Americans make support decisions on the basis of clearly demarcated beliefs about which people "deserve" support and which do not. The final explanation presumes that Americans perceive some programs as more effective in their implementation and outcomes than others and therefore support those they think are effective, irrespective of the "deservingness" of the social group targeted for assistance. In the chapters to follow, we first examine each of the four explanations separately and then combine them to see if a multivariate model does a better conceptual and empirical job in explaining patterns of support.

To describe and explain support for the major programs of the American welfare state, we will report on interviews with a nationally representative sample of 1,209 members of the public at large and a representative sample of 58 members of the U.S. House of Representatives. Our research questions include: To what extent does the American public support the current social welfare system? Are some aspects supported more than others? If so, which parts are most supported, and which parts least supported? Why? Do members of Congress feel the same way as the general public? How are the views of the public and Congress similar? How and why do they differ?

The Context

The twentieth century has been remarkable in many ways. From the automobile to the airplane, from the radio and television to the home computer, from the polio vaccine to organ transplants, our lives have been transformed by technological developments that few people could have envisioned when the century first began. The social developments have been no less sweeping. Where once higher education was the privilege of only the wealthy, it is now an option for nearly every American. Women and racial minorities have gained civil and political rights, workers are protected from the hazards of the workplace, and progress has been made to protect the environment.

Not the least of these social changes has been the development of the American welfare state. The United States has enacted and implemented programs to protect citizens from the economic and emotional trauma brought about by unemployment, long-term illness, work-related injuries, disability, and retirement. Some version of these welfare state programs to guard against such risks exist in all nations of the Western world. In fact, welfare states have become so prevalent that some commentators have referred to them as a "structural uniformity of modern society" (e.g., Coughlin 1980:3). Such a statement could not have been made of the society of 1900.

The American version of the welfare state developed during the Great Depression of the 1930s. In 1935 President Roosevelt signed the Social Security Act. This far-reaching piece of legislation is most notable for beginning Old Age, Survivors, and Disability Insurance (OASDI), a program now commonly referred to merely as Social Security. OASDI helped and continues to help the elderly cope financially in their retirement. The Social Security Act was also responsible for a number of other long-lived programs, including Aid to Dependent Children, the precursor of the Aid to Families with Dependent Children program (AFDC). From the years following the enactment of the Social Security Act until the mid-1970s, policymakers continued to expand the social welfare system with a particular interest in improving the network of social welfare programs.

From 1935 until the mid-1970s, most of the political debate concerning the social welfare system focused on the means for enhancing and enlarging social welfare provisions. Social welfare programs enjoyed a relatively secure position in the policy landscape of the United States, and their proponents did not fear for the system's collapse. However, the optimism that characterized those expansionary years began to dissipate in the face of the economic woes that dominated the United States in the 1970s. Feeling the pinch of declining industrial productivity, competition from other industrialized nations, and a seemingly insolvable oil crisis, policy-makers began to discuss cuts in domestic programs.

In the late 1970s and early 1980s, the policy debate underwent a transformation. Discourse about social programs became more critical than ever before, questioning whether the government should be involved at all in the private lives of its citizens. With the resounding victory of Ronald Reagan, cutbacks in social welfare programs became a pronounced theme of the early 1980s. Reagan promised to reduce the role of government in domestic life and proposed changes that would dismantle many social welfare programs (see Palmer and Sawhill 1982 for a full treatment of Reagan's proposals). Because Reagan had run a campaign advocating cutbacks in social welfare programs and reduction of governmental powers, his administration interpreted their electoral victory as a public mandate to drastically reduce social welfare spending, and they did not hesitate to begin acting on this charge. Thus the 1980s became a watershed in U.S. social welfare policy. After half a century of growth and development, social welfare programs were under attack and their future was now unclear. The welfare state was seen by many to be in a state of crisis—ideologically, politically, and economically (see, for example, OECD 1981).

Despite this serious challenge, the welfare state weathered the controversy and suffered few serious cutbacks (Palmer and Sawhill 1984; Greenstein 1991). Conventional wisdom aside, this fact is one on which both conservative and liberal analysts agree. Stuart Butler (1987) of the Heritage Foundation, a conservative think tank, notes, "The basic structure of the Great Society is still firmly intact. Despite the Stockman axe, virtually no program has been eliminated and most are still enjoying healthy growth. . . . The system as such has not changed significantly" (p. 3). Paul Peterson and Mark Rom (1988), fellows during the mid-1980s at the Brookings Institution, a liberal think tank, make a similar point: "Programs aimed at the poor, the needy, and the handicapped were spared major reductions during the Reagan years. Indeed, the cost of these programs reached new highs in 1982 when the recession forced more people to turn to social welfare for subsistence" (p. 226). Our own analyses of budget data on social welfare programs confirm these positions. For example, in 1980, the year before Reagan took office, federal spending for AFDC was $7,198 million (or $10,214 million in 1988 dollars). In 1988, Reagan's last year in office, federal spending for AFDC was $10,319 million—an increase of 1 percent in inflation-adjusted dollars. Similarly, federal spending on Food Stamps increased by 1.4 percent between 1980 and 1988 (from 9,083.3 million in 1980, or $12,889.6 million in 1988 dollars, to $13,071.1 million in 1988).*

How is it that welfare state programs survived the Reagan assault? We will examine one possible reason for the survival of the American welfare state—a strong reservoir of public and Congressional support.** We find that members of the public and, perhaps more important, members of Congress support the maintenance of the social welfare system and have little desire to dismantle it.

To reach this conclusion, we examine U.S. citizens' and policymakers' views concerning the major programs of the American welfare system and about the social groups that these programs target. We will also examine four major implicit or explicit theories of congressional and public support for social welfare—self-interest, political predispositions, recipient deservingness, and program effectiveness—and probe each to examine which better explains levels of support. Our analyses are based on telephone interviews with 1,209 members of the public (averaging 45 minutes in length) and personal interviews with 58 members of the U.S. House of Representatives (averaging 50 minutes in length). We will see that neither public nor congressional support for social welfare is unanimous or without reservations; yet it has been sufficient to enable the maintenance of welfare programs through a decade of turbulence.

This chapter lays the groundwork for our analysis of what the public and members of Congress think by presenting an overview of the American welfare state and an examination of the purported welfare state crisis.

---

* Our data on spending for AFDC and Food Stamps are from the two sources cited for table 1.1: the 1991 *Green Book* and the *Social Security Bulletin*. We converted the 1980 dollars to 1988 dollars using the Consumer Price Index from the *Statistical Abstract of the United States 1990*, p. 471.

** Piven and Cloward (1988; see also Piven and Cloward 1982) discuss another reason for the durability of social welfare programs in the face of retrenchment efforts. According to them, those welfare bureaucrats, professional organizations, and institutions with a stake in the welfare state opposed the Reagan assault on social welfare. Similarly, Smith and Stone (1988) argue that resistance also came from private, nonprofit organizations that receive government grants to deliver social services.

The Complex American Welfare State

The economic culture at the turn of the century was such that, as Robert Hunter (1904) described, ordinary workers might earn enough to live on while they worked but "should they cease, they are in destitution and hunger" (p. 4). As Hunter showed, "The slightest economic disturbance or rearrangement may precipitate them into misery. The margin of life upon which many of them live is so narrow that they must toil every possible hour of working time, and the slightest economic change registers its effect" (p. 59).

Hunter described poverty and the poor in 1900, a time when, much to the dissatisfaction of many political commentators (including Hunter himself), neither the government nor industry offered citizens any protection against the normal risks of life. Should ordinary workers become sick, disabled, unemployed, or even unable to work merely because of age, their families would be forced to live in poverty and to depend on charity. When Hunter and other early reformers during the Progressive Era suggested that the federal government should have some role in protecting citizens against the normal risks of life, they were met with skepticism, and sometimes ridicule. Many policymakers felt certain that neither the German model of social insurance nor those of other European countries could prove successful in the unique American economic system.

Hunter and his colleagues were not swayed, however. After an extensive description of the different groups among the poor and an analysis of the causes of poverty, Hunter concluded his book with an agenda for reform—including national systems of old age insurance, unemployment insurance, sanitation mandates for tenements and factories, maximum work hour laws, minimum wage laws, and child labor legislation. In 1904 his agenda seemed unattainable. Today we accept the reforms he advocated as the rights of every citizen.

The Rise of the American Welfare State

What Hunter was advocating in 1904 was a minimum standard of living for every American as a basic right of citizenship. He believed that no American should have to live in hunger and cold or without adequate shelter and clothing. Hunter's proposals for leg-

islation, however, fell on relatively deaf ears. At that time, a reso-
lute belief in states' rights—that all powers not explicitly granted
to the federal government through the Constitution rested with
state governments—precluded any role for the federal government
in offering social welfare programs. For example, in 1854, fifty
years before Hunter's research, President Franklin Pierce refused
to allow institutions for the mentally ill to be built on federal land.
President Pierce's veto sent a clear message concerning the role of
the federal government in social welfare affairs; the veto upheld
the historic responsibility of state and local governments and private charities in matters of social welfare (Axinn and Levin 1975).
The federal government exercised little power to force national
programs upon the country, and state governments, for the most
part, had neither a particular interest nor the financial resources for
large-scale programs, although many states offered financial assistance to poor widows with dependent children and ill-kept "alms-
houses" for other non-working poor, e.g., the elderly, young, disabled, and mentally ill (Patterson 1981). Until the 1930s, little
progress was made by the federal government toward meeting the
needs of the poor, and Hunter's proposals remained unaddressed.

In addition to the separation of federal and state powers so
adamantly maintained at the turn of the century, a second barrier
to governmental intervention in social welfare programming was
the prominent theory regarding the cause of poverty advocated at
that time. Most people holding positions of power maintained that
poverty was a self-inflicted condition that could only be overcome
through self-dedication and hard work (Bremner 1956). Government involvement not only would be of no use, but also would
symbolize the government's sanctioning of laziness and sloth.

It took the stock market crash of 1929 and the economic depression that followed to alter beliefs in the supremacy of states' rights
and in the individual responsibility for poverty. For the first time,
it became clear to both the public and policymakers that the overwhelming majority of the poor did not bring their poverty upon
themselves, and that social and economic problems crossed state
lines and could best be remedied through nationwide, federally
sponsored programs. After over thirty years of political debate, the
stage was finally set for the emergence of a national system of social
welfare programs.

The American version of the welfare state began with the passage of the Social Security Act in 1935. A landmark in American political and social history, it reflected a shift from local and individual responsibility for the care of the needy to the federal government. The Social Security Act created permanent programs out of the temporary programs of the Depression's Federal Emergency Relief Administration (FERA). By establishing these permanent programs, Congress accepted long-term federal responsibility for the social welfare of American citizens.

A Myriad of Programs

It is difficult to describe in a single paragraph, or even a single chapter, the U.S. social welfare system. With the Social Security Act of 1935, President Roosevelt transformed the notion of nationally funded aid to the poor into reality. Although the concept of national responsibility for social welfare was not new to European countries, up until the Great Depression of the 1930s, Americans had for the most part depended upon local governments, voluntarism, and philanthropy to help those in need. But in the 1930s the state of the nation had changed, and the generosity of a few could not be counted on to meet the needs of so many. Nor could the blame for destitution be easily placed on the shoulders of the poor themselves. The federal government had no option but to become involved in the welfare of its citizenry.

In its provisions, the Social Security Act retained some of the old-style programs that had previously been offered locally, but it also added new ones to the system. At the time of passage, many states offered some minimal coverage to the elderly, the blind, and poor widows with children. The federal act, working within the structure of these existing programs, created a group of national categorical non-work-related programs of assistance for the same target groups. For the elderly there was Old Age Assistance (OAA); for the blind, Aid to the Blind (AB); and for poor children there was Aid to Dependent Children (ADC). These programs were administered by the states but received their funding through joint matching grants-in-aid between the federal and state governments. New to the social welfare scene was a number of social insurance programs designed to meet the inevitable financial problems of old age and unemployment. These new insurance programs—Old Age Insurance (OAI) and Unemployment Insurance (UI)—were engineered specifically to cover those citizens with former or current workforce connections and, quite unlike public assistance programs, were financed through payroll tax deductions and employer contributions.

All these programs still exist, though each has subsequently evolved over the years. In addition, a patchwork of new programs has been introduced to create the present-day American welfare state. Between 1935 and the 1950s, Congress expanded OAI to include survivors (1939) and workers who were forced to retire because of disability (1956). The program, now officially entitled Old Age, Survivors, and Disability Insurance (OASDI), is referred to by most Americans simply as "Social Security." In 1969 and 1971, Congress passed legislation to increase Social Security benefits, and in 1972 indexed benefits to the cost of living (referred to as COLAS, or "cost of living adjustments"). The easy passage of the COLA legislation demonstrated the regard with which Social Security was held by members of Congress.

Another early program enacted by the Social Security Act of 1935 was Aid to Dependent Children (ADC). ADC provided cash benefits for children whose parent (for years two-parent households were not covered) was unable to financially support them. Funding for ADC was provided through both the federal and state governments on a matching basis: the federal government contributed $1 for every $2 spent by states. Perhaps the most significant modification in ADC occurred in 1962 when a dependent parent became eligible for benefits. Until that time, awards were given only to cover the child's expenses. The revised and newly named Aid to Families with Dependent Children (AFDC) also included a number of social services—employment assistance, vocational rehabilitation, child care, and basic adult education—designed to increase the likelihood of long-term employment among adults in households (Derthick 1975). Also in the 1960s, several states began to provide AFDC to families with unemployed fathers when unemployment benefits had been depleted. By 1986, half of the fifty states had AFDC-Unemployed Parent (AFDC-UP), and as of the end of 1990, all states offered AFDC-UP (as mandated by the Family Support Act of 1988).

AFDC is only available to families with dependent children. On the other hand, nearly every worker within the United States is eligible for Unemployment Insurance (UI). Designed to help the unemployed during spells of forced idleness, UI eligibility and benefits are based on past earnings and work experience, not financial need. The maximum duration of payments is normally twenty-six weeks, but in 1970 when the unemployment rate exceeded 4.5 percent for three consecutive months, Congress authorized an additional thirteen weeks of benefits (in 1981 Congress revised this legislation such that the unemployment rate must exceed 6 percent for the additional coverage to take effect). UI is funded through a mandatory payroll tax: employers pay 6.2 percent of the first $7,000 of an employee's annual earnings. Most of the money collected is returned to the states, and the states become the sole administrators of the program. They determine the eligibility of the covered worker and the duration and amount of individual benefits, and they distribute the funds. As a result of state-level decision making, individual state programs vary widely in their administration, although the tax rate is universal (Levitan 1990).

Retired elderly can turn to OASDI for assistance, but some elderly do not qualify for Social Security benefits or the amount they qualify for is too small to meet their minimum daily needs. Likewise, people with disabilities often cannot qualify for Social Security benefits because of their limited employment histories. To meet the special needs of these individuals, the Social Security Act of 1935 included Old Age Assistance and Aid to the Blind. In 1950 Congress instituted a new category of public assistance—Aid to the Permanently and Totally Disabled (APTD). In 1972, Congress passed legislation replacing these separate state-run programs with a federally administered program entitled Supplemental Security Income (SSI). Unlike state-administered AFDC and UI, SSI uses federal eligibility standards and, similarly to OASDI, the benefits are adjusted for inflation (Levitan 1990). The beneficiaries of SSI are divided primarily between the elderly and the disabled: in 1986, 47 percent were aged, 51.5 percent were disabled, and 1.5 percent were blind (*Social Security Bulletin* 1987b).

Most of the programs discussed thus far were originally established in one form or another under the Social Security Act of 1935. Medicare and Medicaid, incorporated into the system in 1965, are the two most important recent additions. Enacted through Titles XVIII and XIX of the Social Security Amendments, both Medicare and Medicaid address the health needs of the poor and disabled. Medicare covers most hospital and medical costs for persons aged

65 and older and for seriously disabled younger Social Security beneficiaries. It offers subsidized health insurance similar to that found on the private market (U.S. Department of Health and Human Services 1990), but is funded through employee and employer contributions based on a portion of the employee's salary (1.45 percent) up to a predetermined maximum level. Medicaid, on the other hand, receives its funding through federal and state budgets. Federal grants to states allow Medicaid to provide health care coverage to poor persons receiving AFDC and SSI (thirty-five states also extend Medicaid eligibility to people who do not qualify for AFDC or SSI but whose incomes are low enough to qualify them as "medically needy"; Levitan 1990:81). Each state receives federal shares of expenses ranging from 50 to 83 percent, depending on the state's per capita income, operates its own Medicaid program, and establishes its own rules within the parameters of federal regulations and guidelines.

In addition to these programs, most of which either the Department of Health and Human Services or the Social Security Administration oversees, there are many other programs within the American welfare state. Qualifying beneficiaries may receive food subsidies through the food stamp program, administered through the Department of Agriculture, as well as the occasional distribution of surplus foodstuffs (such as milk or cheese), also dispensed by the Department of Agriculture. Pregnant women and newborns can receive assistance for their special nutritional needs through the Women, Infants, and Children (WIC) program. States and cities, with the assistance of federal funds, support low-rent housing or rent subsidies. These are only a few of the myriad social programs offered by the federal, state, and local governments throughout the United States (see Levitan 1990).

Characterizing Programs

As should be clear even from the brief description thus far, the American welfare state is quite complex; social programs are different from each other in at least four key aspects that can be used to compare programs: their benefit structure, the goals they pursue, their beneficiaries, and the governmental level of their administration. These four program features are helpful for delineating the differences among social welfare programs, and will prove useful in later chapters when we discuss levels of public and congressional support for programs and the reasons for such support.

First, programs differ in the structure and form of the assistance they provide. Structurally, some are administered as insurance policies, requiring potential beneficiaries to contribute to the fund (OASDI, UI, Medicare). Others, the public assistance programs, are needs-based, means-tested systems and require no previous contribution as a stipulation for receipt, but do require that one's income fall below a specified level (AFDC, SSI, Medicaid). A second structural difference lies in the form of the benefit; some simply provide cash (OASDI, UI, AFDC, SSI), while others meet the particular demand directly through in-kind services, such as medical care, food, and housing (Medicare, Medicaid, Food Stamps).

A second way of characterizing programs is through the goals they implicitly or explicitly stress. For example, Social Security strives to assist the elderly and disabled in maintaining their long-term financial independence after retirement due to old age or disability. Unemployment Insurance, on the other hand, provides only short-term income support while the worker is between jobs. Head Start, a preschool program for poor children, attempts to improve the educational opportunities of underprivileged children. A number of programs address the health concerns of recipients, but again, each attacks the problem from a different angle. Medicare and Medicaid provide access to health services and are used most frequently when illness arises. Food Stamps and WIC, on the other hand, are preventive programs, offering their recipients nutritional benefits that may help prevent illness. Thus, some programs pursue long-term goals while others address only the immediate needs of their recipients.

A third defining attribute of programs is their beneficiary groups. While AFDC is targeted primarily at children but also assists the caregiving parent, SSI is targeted at the disabled and the elderly. Unemployment Insurance can be received only by those who have worked and whose employers have paid into the program. Work, monetary contributions, as well as old age are necessary conditions for receipt of Social Security (except for the survivor provision). Each program has its own audience, but beneficiaries often overlap at the intersection of eligibility for in-cash and in-kind assistance (for instance, recipients receiving AFDC may also qualify for Food Stamps and Medicaid benefits, and Social Security recipients also usually receive Medicare).

The final dimension that can be used to classify the diverse programs is the type and level of program administration. Social Security is administered entirely by the federal government; beneficiaries receive monthly checks sent directly from the Social Security Administration. Few programs, however, are administered as simply as Social Security. AFDC, for example, receives funding through the federal and state governments but is managed by district, county, or local agencies responsive to a larger state agency. AFDC recipients must appear in person at the local office to apply for grants, and individual records are kept at the state and local level. As would be expected, there is greater diversity in benefit levels within the programs managed at the state level than by those controlled at the federal level.

Our purpose for presenting these four principal defining characteristics is twofold. The American social welfare system is complex, and we find these dimensions useful as a framework to understand the intricacies of the system. Perhaps more important, however, is that these dimensions are also useful for understanding the types of programs that the American public and Congress support and why they support them.

This brief summary of the social welfare system has merely given an overview of some of the major programs that constitute the American welfare state. Other authors provide more comprehensive histories and summaries of the entire system (see Trattner 1989; Patterson 1981; Katz 1986; Levitan 1990). Although the American social welfare system is hardly the product of a well-developed philosophy of social helping, Marmor, Mashaw, and Harvey (1990) argue convincingly that it nonetheless embodies an implicit commitment to two broad goals—insurance to a broad stratum of the nation's population so that destitution is not the result of a breadwinner's loss of income (OASDI, Unemployment Insurance, Medicare); and assistance to those who are so poor they cannot provide adequately for themselves (AFDC, SSI, Medicaid, Food Stamps).

A Crisis in the Welfare State?

Throughout its relatively short history, the U.S. welfare state has seldom been without its critics. The Social Security Act of 1935 made monumental changes in the condition of social welfare in America, and its conception and accomplishments created opponents as well as proponents. President Roosevelt received criticism from both the right and the left when he introduced the Social Security legislation in 1935. The right, including the U.S. Chamber of Commerce and the National Association of Manufacturers, found the act a threat to the American way of life and individual liberty, asserting that it violated American concepts of self-help and individual responsibility. The left, on the other hand, argued that the act did not go far enough, providing no integrated, comprehensive, logical plan to ensure social security (Trattner 1989:265). Both arguments have been consistently repeated over the years in the debate over social welfare.

Thirty years after the enactment of the Social Security Act, President Johnson, who began his career in politics as a protégé of Franklin Roosevelt, announced that he would carry on where Roosevelt had left off. Johnson would wipe out poverty in the twentieth century (Patterson 1981:140). In 1964 he easily carried his Economic Opportunity Act through a supportive Congress. Following the vision of a "Great Society," government efforts accelerated to ensure the well-being of all citizens, to equalize opportunities for minorities and the disadvantaged, and to mitigate the social, economic, and legal foundations of inequality. Like Roosevelt's programs in 1935, however, Johnson's War on Poverty programs also encountered criticism. Some questioned the effectiveness of government efforts. Others condemned the Great Society for not doing enough or for magnifying the problems of inequity by helping only a small segment of the needy. Still others criticized the programs on philosophical grounds for interfering with the natural meritocracy and the process of free enterprise (Patterson 1981:145). Despite the objections, many of the Great Society programs have survived, including Medicare, Medicaid, Head Start, compensatory elementary and secondary education programs for the disadvantaged, and civil rights legislation.

President Richard Nixon, hardly a social liberal, received his share of criticism for proposing the Family Assistance Plan (FAP).

The FAP blueprint would have guaranteed a minimum income to all, but the plan was received by a less than enthusiastic Congress. Conservatives opposed the idea of a guaranteed income, claiming it would reduce the incentive for poor people to work, while liberals opposed the plan because they said the guarantee ($2,400 for a family of four in 1971 dollars, or roughly $7,280 in 1990) was too low. After Congress twice rejected the bill, Nixon gave up the effort and regained favor for a time with the dissenting right-wing Democrats and Republicans (Lehmann 1989). Nonetheless, out of Nixon's efforts on behalf of FAP arose Supplemental Security Income (SSI), providing a federally guaranteed minimum income to old, blind, or seriously mentally or physically disabled poor individuals. Furthermore, in 1973 Nixon approved the decision by Congress to raise Social Security benefits by 20 percent, and in 1974 he allowed for the indexing to inflation of Social Security and SSI benefits (that is, to allow for an annual automatic cost-of-living adjustment [COLA] whenever inflation rises by at least 3 percent). Nixon's support for federal involvement in social welfare programs was also evident in his approval of expansions to the food stamp program, including a mandate that all states offer the program (Trattner 1989).

There were fewer changes in social welfare during the brief presidency of Gerald Ford, Nixon's successor. However, with the incoming Carter administration in 1977, new ideas regarding social welfare began to emerge. Jimmy Carter proposed a two-track system, one for poor people able to work and one for those unable to do so. The poor who could work were to receive wage supplements, federal help in finding employment, or as a last resort, one of 1.4 million public jobs to be created at slightly more than the minimum wage. Those who refused to work would get no assistance payments, although they would still receive benefits for their children. Carter proposed combining SSI, AFDC, state-local general assistance, and Food Stamps into one unified program with a single eligibility standard. Except for those who refused to work, all those who were eligible would be assured a minimum benefit level ($4,200 for a family of four in 1977 dollars, or roughly $8,760 in 1990 dollars), and only half of their earnings would be subtracted from their benefits (Lynn 1977).

Carter's proposals ran into the same opposition that had defeated Nixon's Family Assistance Plan. Liberals maintained that the minimum benefit level was too low and were especially concerned about the linkage between work and welfare. Conservatives, on the other hand, believed the plan to be unnecessarily costly, and questioned the ability of the government to create 1.4 million public sector jobs (Patterson 1981).

But whatever the conflicts, the American social welfare system grew tremendously between 1935 and 1980. From Roosevelt to Carter, most presidents proposed reforms that would result in an expansion of both the number and costs of social programs. Even though not all of these changes were enacted, they were composed in an environment of ever-growing belief in the social rights of citizenship. The executive and legislative branches of government implemented programs that guaranteed improvements in the lives of Americans citizens, and people grew to expect these benefits. Thus, in spite of its many critics, the U.S. social welfare system survived and grew over the years.

While early attacks never truly threatened the welfare state, the assaults of the early 1980s jeopardized it much more seriously. This is because President Reagan's proposals were different than those of his predecessors. The cutbacks in programs proposed by his administration were seen as draconian. Responding to the proposed cuts, some observers presented a worst-case scenario: a historical regression back to the days of Robert Hunter. They feared, and even anticipated, a dismantling of the welfare state due to the impact of financial problems and the attack by ideological and political adversaries. Unlike previous criticism, the outlash of assaults during the 1980s seemed to be based on more than the voices of a few. At the time, there was a simultaneous growing national fiscal burden and a burgeoning number of poor. These two factors, plus a seeming public outcry for reform, led some in Washington to proclaim a war on welfare (Stockman 1986). In the words of David Stockman, Reagan's first director of the Office of Management and Budget, "The Reagan Revolution . . . required a frontal assault on the American welfare state. . . . Accordingly, forty years' worth of promises, subventions, entitlements and safety nets issued by the federal government to every component and stratum of American society would have to be scrapped or dramatically modified" (Stockman 1986:8).

According to some commentators, the welfare state in the 1980s was in a state of crisis (Murray 1984; Grace 1984; Mead 1986), and in the 1990s some say it still is (Stoesz and Karger 1992). For these authors and others (e.g., Taylor-Gooby 1985), it is possible to distinguish three types of crises, crises concerning fiscal and demographic issues and public support concerns. Some described a fiscal crisis due to the ballooning national deficit that had presumably been exacerbated by the level of expenditures for social entitlement programs. Others proclaimed a crisis based on shifting demographics, both a growing number of citizens falling at or below the poverty line and a growing number of elderly citizens. And yet others related the crisis to an alleged downturn in public support for social welfare—the same downturn that was supposed to have helped Ronald Reagan come to power.

The Fiscal Crisis

During the late 1970s and early 1980s, the strains of functioning in an increasingly competitive world market began to show in obvious ways in the American economy. Perhaps the clearest evidence of this was that in a few short years the United States lost its status as the world's leading lender nation and instead became the world's leading debtor nation. With the continuing rise of the national deficit, Congress passed legislation that had a major impact on the future of social welfare programs. The Balanced Budget and Emergency Deficit Control Act of 1985 (better known as the Gramm-Rudman-Hollings Act) called for mandatory cuts in domestic and military spending if certain reductions were not met voluntarily. In 1981 Congress had passed tax reforms (Economic Recovery Tax Act) easing the tax burden on the wealthy and, consequently, decreasing the total federal tax revenues (Trattner 1989). Thus, social welfare programs were in jeopardy not only because of the potentially devastating cuts demanded by Gramm-Rudman-Hollings but also because of dwindling federal resources.

Public spending on social welfare is not small. In 1988, federal expenditures for social welfare programs comprised 10.9 percent of the GNP (gross national product) and 49.1 percent of all federal expenditures (U.S. Department of Health and Human Services 1991). (As a referent, defense spending accounted for 6.3 percent of the GNP and 27.5 percent of all federal expenditures during that same year [U.S. Arms Control and Disarmament Agency

Table 1.1

Spending for the Nation's Social Welfare Programs, 1988
(in billions of dollars)

	Expenditures		
	Total	Federal	State & local
Social Insurance Programs	316	303	13
Cash Benefits			
OASDI	216	216	—
Unemployment Insurance	16	3	13
In-Kind Benefits			
Medicare	84	84	—
Public Assistance-Type Programs	123	81	42
Cash Benefits			
AFDC	19	10	9
SSI	15	12	3
In-Kind Benefits			
Vendor Medical Payments			
(Medicaid)[a]	61	31	30
Food Stamps	13	13	
Overall Total	439	384	55

[a]Vendor Medical Payments are made directly to supplies of medical care. This figure also includes the administrative expenses of the Medicaid program.

Sources: All figures except AFDC taken from Ann Kallman, "Public Social Welfare Expenditures, Fiscal Year 1988," *Social Security Bulletin* 54:7–10, 1991 (table 2, "Social Welfare Expenditures under Public Programs"). ADFC figures from U.S. House of Representatives, Committee on Ways and Means, *The 1991 Greenbook: Overview of Entitlement Programs: Background Material and Data on Programs within the Jurisdiction of the Committee on Ways and Means*, Washington, D.C.: U.S. Government Printing Office (table 17, "Total, Federal, and State AFDC Expenditures," p. 614).

1990].)*** Billions of dollars are spent annually to support the social welfare system, but the budget has always been disproportionately weighted toward social insurance programs and away from public assistance programs. As shown in table 1.1, of the seven largest programs in 1988, 72 percent of the dollars spent went toward social insurance benefits. Yet these programs have not been the targets of fiscal cutbacks; the principal targets are AFDC and Food Stamps, which make up less than 8 percent of total social welfare spending (see Marmor, Mashaw, and Harvey 1990).

Some observers argue that overspending on social welfare pro-

*** The corresponding figures for social welfare expenditures at the state and local levels are 7.6 percent of the GNP and 60.1 percent of all state and local expenditures. Total expenditures for social welfare programs (federal, state, and local figures combined) were 18.5 percent of the GNP and 52.8 percent of all government expenditures.

grams helped to cause the poor performance of the U.S. economy during the 1970s and 1980s. Though fiscal concerns are real in the United States, however, it is not at all clear that welfare state spending has hurt economic growth. Indeed, Marmor, Mashaw, and Harvey (1990), using data from the Organization for Economic Cooperation and Development (OECD), show that social welfare expenditures in Western industrial nations have had no consistent relationship to rates of economic growth. Nonetheless, despite the lack of clear evidence of a relationship between government spending on welfare and the nation's economic condition, policymakers continued to pursue cutbacks as a viable solution.

Although Marmor and his colleagues argue convincingly that welfare spending cannot be the cause of failed economic growth, their data do not rule out the possibility that the perception of a relationship between spending and growth motivated government officials to cut back on social welfare programs. Conservatives maintained that the welfare state had to be reduced because of the strain placed upon the government. Although these beliefs may have been based on faulty reasoning, they were nonetheless influential and, when added to the growing national deficit and the decreasing economic growth of the United States, helped exacerbate the atmosphere of fiscal crisis.

The Demographic Crisis

To some extent, the rhetoric of fiscal crisis had been precipitated by a change in the demands made on an already stressed system. In the 1980s, the United States witnessed an increase in the number of citizens potentially requiring some form of financial assistance either due to age or economic status.

A striking change at the population level has been the aging of our society. Since the 1930s, when the Social Security Act was written, the proportion of the population aged 65 or over has more than doubled, from 5.5 percent in 1930 to 12.6 percent in 1990 (U.S. Bureau of the Census 1991a). This change has occurred for two reasons. First, the birth rate has declined and been below the replacement level since 1973 (Siegel and Tauber 1986). Whereas in 1960 there were 118 births per 1,000 women, in 1988 there were 67 births per 1,000 women (U.S. Bureau of the Census 1991d:63). Second, Americans' life expectancy has increased. In 1900 the life expectancy at birth was 48 years, whereas in 1988 it was 71.5 years for males and 78.3 for females, and by 2010 it is projected to be 74.4 for males and 81.3 for females (U.S. Bureau of the Census 1991d:73).

The continued aging of the nation has major implications for the stability of the social welfare system. Funds for the maintenance of the system come from both income and payroll taxes and therefore demand an active labor force. As the population ages, fewer people are left in the workforce, while at the same time more people become beneficiaries. A historical look at changes in the dependency ratio demonstrates this point. In 1960 there were 16.8 persons over 65 for every 100 working-age people (ages 18 to 64); in 1990 this ratio increased to an estimated 20 to 100, and the ratio is projected to increase to 29 to 100 by the year 2020, and to 44 to 100 by the 2080 (U.S. Bureau of the Census 1989). The fear of an insolvent social insurance system, whether valid or not, has caused many young adults to believe that Social Security will not be there for them when they retire (Goodwin and Tu 1975).

A second demographic trend that has been cited as contributing to a fear of impending crisis is the change in the composition of the poor (Ehrenreich and Piven 1984; Ellwood 1988; Bane 1986). Before President Johnson's War on Poverty in the 1960s, the elderly made up a disproportionately large segment of the poor. With improved Social Security benefits, the addition of Medicare and Medicaid, and SSI, the well-being of the elderly has improved dramatically. Unfortunately, as the income of the elderly rose, their place at the bottom was quickly filled by a growing number of children in poverty. Figure 1.1 demonstrates the shift of poverty among the elderly to poverty among children. In 1966, 28.5 percent of elderly people were poor as compared to 17.6 percent of children. By 1990 the proportion of elderly persons in poverty had dropped to 12.2 percent, well below the poverty rate for children, 20.6 percent of whom lived in poor families (U.S. Bureau of the Census 1991b).

Children in female-headed households are more likely than those in two-parent households to live in poverty. In 1990, for example, 53.4 percent of children in female-headed households lived below the poverty line, compared with 10.2 percent in two-parent families (U.S. Bureau of the Census 1991c). The number of children living with a single, female parent has changed dramatically in the

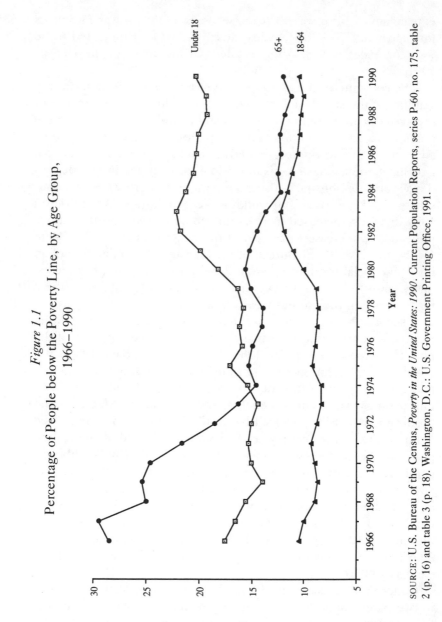

Figure 1.1

Percentage of People below the Poverty Line, by Age Group,
1966–1990

Under 18

65+

18-64

Percentage Below Poverty

Year

30

25

20

15

10

5

1966   1968   1970   1972   1974   1976   1978   1980   1982   1984   1986   1988   1990

SOURCE: U.S. Bureau of the Census, *Poverty in the United States: 1990*. Current Population Reports, series P-60, no. 175, table 2 (p. 16) and table 3 (p. 18). Washington, D.C.: U.S. Government Printing Office, 1991.

last thirty years. In 1960 only 6 percent of white children and 16 percent of black children lived solely with a female adult. By 1990 these percentages had more than doubled to 16.5 percent and 55.4 percent, respectively (U.S. Bureau of the Census 1991b). There are many reasons for the increase in female-headed households— new divorce laws, more societal acceptance of unwed motherhood, and the high unemployment rate for males. There are also many reasons why female-headed families are poorer than other fami- lies—the lower wages earned by women, the lower labor force participation of women, and the poor enforcement of child support regulations. Whatever the causes, the feminization of poverty has very real consequences for children and has the potential to influ- ence the state of the social welfare system dramatically (see Ell- wood 1988 for a detailed treatment).

A final demographic change that has its effects on the social welfare system is a phenomenon referred to as the "vanishing middle class." As Levy (1989) shows, the buying power of incomes has decreased considerably since World War II. From 1947 to 1973 income for all people increased and more were able to live the middle-class lifestyle. After the mid-1970s, however, the buying power of money decreased, and those who had previously been able to afford a house, a new car, or their children's education found themselves no longer able to do so. Once a high school education was enough to provide an adequate standard of living; but by the 1980s workers with high school diplomas suffered de- creases in their income (in constant dollars) not experienced by those with higher levels of education. In 1973, the average income of a thirty-year-old man with a high school education (in 1987 dollars) was $24,338 while a thirty-year-old man with a college degree earned an average of $28,157 (Levy 1989). Thirteen years later, the numbers had decreased in both groups, but dispropor- tionately so: the thirty-year-old man with a high school education earned an average of $18,257, while the thirty-year-old with a college education earned $27,309. This demonstrates a widening income gap. In 1973, a college education increased an individual's expected earnings by roughly 16 percent, but by 1986 those returns had expanded to 50 percent. Levy interprets this as evidence of a disappearing middle class, a situation that does not bode well for the future of a tax-supported social welfare system.

Demographic changes have caused many to lament the rise in

the number of those requiring assistance while the great middle class of financial contributors seems to be decreasing. The compounding effects of an aging nation and a nation with a decreasing proportion of workers lead many to question the continued strength of the social welfare system.

A Crisis of Public Support?

Both the fiscal constraints and the demographic changes are real, regardless of whether they present reasons for alarm. The authenticity of a public outcry to reduce welfare spending is less clearly established empirically. Commentators claim that public support is necessary for the maintenance of a viable social welfare system and that contemporary social welfare programs have very little support from the general public. As Flora (1985) points out, "The Western welfare state is based on the political consensus produced in the democratic mass polity, and its structure must reflect the basic nature of this consensus" (p. 13). Many believe that this consensus has broken down and that the American public is not willing to support the social welfare system. The crisis is more than one of affordability; it is one of values. Members of the public, it is argued, do not believe tax dollars should be used to aid the poor.

For the past twenty-five years, researchers have been tracking what many interpret as a growing public distrust of government intervention in private affairs. Lipset and Schneider (1987) present evidence from a number of large social surveys that show that Americans continue to be dissatisfied with their leadership—most strikingly of nongovernmental leaders but also of government leaders. Social welfare programs, financed and managed by the government, have been said to be primary targets of public disdain. According to Esping-Anderson (1983), "To both popular and scholarly commentators, the voters have not only rejected flawed and expensive programs, they have renounced the very idea of the welfare state. It seems an outdated and naive vision whose idea has come and gone" (p. 28).

Evidence from a variety of sources seems to point to a lack of perceived legitimacy for social welfare programs. For example, a book on the history of social welfare policy in the United States begins with the claim, "Nobody likes welfare" (Katz 1986:ix), while the introduction to another book on social welfare policy begins even more strongly, "Everyone hates welfare" (Ellwood 1988:4).

Does everyone "hate" welfare? As we discussed earlier, there is no single "welfare" program. Social welfare programs are a diverse assortment of social insurance and public assistance programs; some provide cash while others offer in-kind assistance such as medical care or food. The question is not "Does everyone hate welfare?," but "Does everyone hate the concept of welfare, or are specific programs disliked?" To answer this question one must explore support for individual programs.

Until now, data on support for specific programs have rarely been gathered. Instead, support has been measured through global, nonspecific questions, such as the one asked by the National Opinion Research Center (NORC) in its General Social Survey: "Do you think we are spending too much money, too little money, or about the right amount on welfare?" If support is operationalized as saying we spend too little money on welfare, then it is true that very little support exists. From 1973 (when NORC first asked the question) to 1989, the average percentage of respondents expressing great support for welfare has been 20 percent. Even when we include those who say we spend the right amount on welfare in our measure of supportiveness, we do not find overwhelming support for welfare. As figure 1.2 shows, public supportiveness for welfare has hovered around 50 percent throughout the past two decades. In comparison to government spending on such things as alleviating crime, improving and protecting the environment, and improving and protecting the nation's health, spending for welfare receives a low priority.

If we were to argue that there has been a crisis in public support for social welfare, then we would need to demonstrate that opinions about welfare during the 1980s were more negative than those of previous decades. Again, looking at figure 1.2, we see that when President Reagan was elected in 1980, support for welfare was at a low. There was an increase in support shortly after the Reagan victory through his first years in office. By 1986, support was higher than it had been a decade earlier. Because the referent in the question is unclear (what exactly is "welfare"?), we cannot conclude that there was no crisis, but neither can we determine that there was a crisis of legitimacy.

To learn whether support would be similar if other phrases were

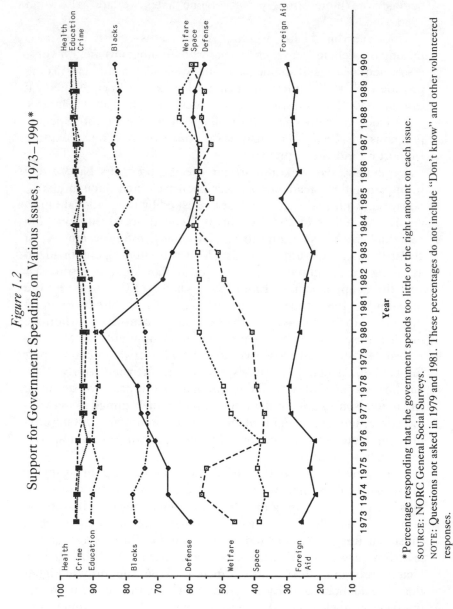

Figure 1.2

Support for Government Spending on Various Issues, 1973–1990*

Year

*Percentage responding that the government spends too little or the right amount on each issue.

SOURCE: NORC General Social Surveys.

NOTE: Questions not asked in 1979 and 1981. These percentages do not include "Don't know" and other volunteered responses.

substituted for "welfare," NORC conducted an experiment in their 1984 survey, using the term "welfare" for one-third of the respondents but substituting the term "assistance to the poor" for another third and "caring for the poor" for the other third. On average, support for "assistance to the poor" was 44 percentage points higher than for "welfare," and support for "caring for the poor" was 39 percentage points higher than for welfare (Smith 1987b). These findings demonstrate that the term *welfare* has a negative connotation, and thus does not give us any clear indication of a crisis in support.

Indeed, even in the 1930s, most members of the public recognized and accepted the role of the government to provide assistance for the truly needy, but the majority preference centered around work relief rather than cash payments. In fact, 90 percent of those interviewed in a 1930s poll stated that they would rather have the government provide jobs than directly offer cash. Nonetheless, when respondents in a large nationally representative survey conducted in 1938 were asked, "Do you think the government should provide for all people who have no other means of obtaining a living?" 68 percent answered yes. When the same question was asked in 1946, 1947, and 1948, those answering yes ranged between 72 and 73 percent (Shapiro et al. 1987).

During the time of social welfare expansion in the 1960s, the public expressed support for social welfare. A poll taken in 1961 demonstrated that the majority (60 percent) favored additional funding for the needy. Similarly, surveys in 1981 through 1986 consistently showed a majority (at least 63 percent) supporting spending increases to help the poor (see Cook 1986 for a review of the survey questions). A similar question in a *Los Angeles Times* poll conducted in April 1985 showed that 59 percent of the public favored increased federal spending on "poverty programs." In general, over the years the public has supported programs to help the needy (although not for "welfare"), and this support does not appear to have diminished, even in recent years.

There is, however, another way of estimating a potential crisis in legitimacy. We can observe how Americans speak out publicly about welfare programs and proposed legislative cuts. During the decade from 1978 to 1986, a number of letters to the editor focusing on social welfare were published in newspapers. Shortly after Reagan took office (in January 1981), he announced his intention to reduce the federal budget. The Omnibus Budget Reconciliation Act of 1981 (OBRA) was by far the most sweeping anti-welfare legislation up to that date. It proposed financial cuts to many social welfare programs, and its effects are still being felt more than ten years later. From figure 1.3, which shows the number of letters concerning social welfare spending appearing in the *New York Times* and the *Washington Post,* we can see that the public did respond

Figure 1.3

Letters to the Editor for and against Proposed Cuts to Social Security and Public Assistance, 1978–1986

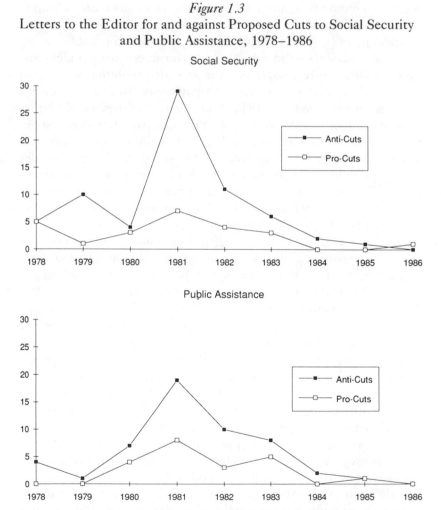

NOTE: Frequencies refer to letters to the editor between 1978 and 1986 appearing in the *New York Times* and *Washington Post.* Compiled by the authors.

vocally to the proposed cuts. There was an increase in 1981 both in anti-cut and pro-cut letters to the editor, but the largest increase was by those opposed to cutbacks. These anti-reduction letters continued to be printed through the early years of Reagan, but they decreased in number. By 1983 the number of letters appearing in these two newspapers opposing Reagan's cutbacks were nearly equal to those in support.

These figures demonstrate two things. First, they show that not all citizens were willing to see the social welfare system dismantled. Some who were in support of the proposed cuts wrote letters. But in the early years, the majority of the letters expressed dislike for the proposed legislation. We must, of course, keep in mind that newspapers can choose which letters to print. Thus, what is printed is not a representative sample of public opinion nor even of the opinions of all people who write. Furthermore, had we chosen other papers we might have seen a slightly different pattern. We specifically chose to document the numbers of letters appearing in the *New York Times* and the *Washington Post* because these are the papers read most frequently by leaders in Washington.

The second observation from these figures, however, brings up once again the issue of a lack of public support for social welfare. Clearly, the newspapers printed many more letters objecting to OBRA than supporting it. On the other hand, public reprimand of legislation quickly died down, despite the fact that the legislative issues continued. The legislation that followed was perhaps not as large and sweeping as OBRA, yet it still threatened major changes to social welfare. For example, in 1982 the Job Partnership Training Act (JPTA) replaced CETA (Comprehensive Employment and Training Act). Both offered job training, yet the new JPTA, unlike CETA, was to offer no financial stipend for participants—undoubtedly a decrease in the service provided. We did not find evidence of a public outcry in the letters. The numbers of letters expressing negative views toward cuts in public assistance quickly became equal to those expressing pro-cut views. Looking at the direction of the letters, we fail to see any clear consensus about programs and proposed legislation.

The findings we have presented so far concerning public opinion demonstrate an ambiguous picture of public support. The public does not favor "welfare" but is willing to "assist the poor." We see the public writing letters to newspapers against OBRA, but not against later proposed cuts. Was there a crisis of public support? Clearly the Reagan administration believed itself to have a public mandate to "reform," and it attempted a major dismantling of federal domestic programs. As Palmer and Sawhill (1984) and Greenstein (1991) document, it has clearly not succeeded. Why?

The Role of Congress

One reason why changes were not as drastic as they could have been involves the role of Congress. Each member of Congress is elected to represent the best interests of his/her constituency as well as the concerns of the nation as a whole. By understanding the opinions of the American public, we can better gauge whether there was a breakdown in public support. But to interpret how the opinions of the American public play into legislative decisions, we need to explore the views of members of Congress.

Political scientists have examined the voting behaviors of legislators (see for example, Clausen 1973; Jackson 1974; Kingdon 1981; Bullock and Brady 1983; Miller and Stokes 1963; Poole 1988). These researchers have paid close attention to how legislators' voting behavior is influenced by their constituency, fellow Congress members, party platforms, interest groups, and the administrative branch. An additional factor not often included in political research, however, is the role played in decision making by Congress members' own personal attitudes and beliefs. The work of Miller and Stokes (1963), and later of Poole (1988), has been particularly influential in showing that the personal beliefs of Congress members have a direct influence on their final votes and thus the shape of policy. Recently, Wilson and Caldwell (1988), using a number of psychological measures of attitudes to predict voting behavior among members of the European Parliament, discovered that personal attitudes are just as influential as party affiliation on a number of voting issues. A study conducted by Barrett and Cook (1991) also provides direct evidence on the role personal attitudes play in legislative decision making. Thus, as we try to understand why changes were or were not made to social welfare policy in the 1980s, it may prove especially useful to pay close attention to the opinions of the policymakers themselves.

Congressional Leadership

Every member of Congress votes on policies affecting the social welfare system, but some representatives are more closely involved than others in the construction and oversight of social welfare. These representatives—principally leaders of committees and subcommittees dealing with social welfare issues, that is, chairs and ranking minority members—play a special role in the process. Matthews and Stimson (1970) find that committee chairs and ranking minority members influence congressional voting behavior. Committee leaders have power both within and outside the committee's boundaries. To a large degree, committee leaders are responsible for setting the direction of the political debate (Smith 1989). Leaders not only promote, neglect, or crush legislation within their committees, but also give advice regarding voting to Congress members outside of the committee. For example, in his analysis of the Senate passage of the Trade Agreements Act of 1979, Jerome (1990) outlines the power wielded by committee leaders and demonstrates how the desires of committee and subcommittee leaders were largely responsible for its final policy outcome.

Because the direction that the committee takes is influenced largely by the desires and politics of its leaders, the opinions of committee leaders can be an important factor in congressional decision making. To understand the legitimacy of the crisis rhetoric and to comprehend why social welfare legislation has taken the shape that it has, we must likewise understand the beliefs of significant congressional leaders. In our study of members of Congress, we will pay special attention to the beliefs of leaders of social welfare committees and explore how these attitudes reflect those of Congress as a whole.

Congress and Public Opinion

We now turn to the relationship between congressional and public preferences. Does public opinion, whether it be for or against a policy, have any effect whatsoever on the decision-making process or the eventual policy outcome? Political scientists have addressed this question as an issue of legislative-public representation and have examined the strength of both "dyadic representation" and "collective representation" (Weissberg 1978). Dyadic representation considers the extent to which a particular legislator represents the views of his or her constituents and thus focuses on the relationship between one representative and one district. Collective representation, on the other hand, refers to the extent to which Congress members as a group represent the American people and thus focuses on the preferences of the public as a whole and on the votes or the preferences of members of Congress as a group. Thus, the dyadic perspective asks how well members of Congress represent their particular districts, while the collective perspective asks how well Congress as an institution represents the American public.

Much of the political science research on dyadic representation stems from the work of Miller and Stokes (1963). They conclude that although the relationship between congressional actions and constituency desires is not simple and direct, the constituents do have some influence over their elected officials. Specifically within the social welfare domain, Miller and Stokes discover the best communication between representatives and their constituents is manifest through shared party membership. Members of the public are most assured of appropriate representation by electing their party's candidate. For other issues, such as civil rights legislation, Congress members look to the specific opinions held by residents of their district. Regardless of how the link is made, Miller and Stokes argue there is a relationship between the behaviors of elected officials and the opinions of those they have been elected to represent.

Weissberg (1978, 1979) argues that Miller and Stokes miss the clearer similarity between general public opinion and overall congressional activity by looking only at this narrow definition of representation. He says that the views of constituents should be represented by Congress as a whole and may not necessarily correspond to the views of any specific individual within the legislature. Using this collective measure of representation, Weissberg (1978, 1979) and later Hurley (1982) find the actions of Congress more in tune with the desires of the public as a whole and thus present evidence of a collectively representative Congress.

Similarly, Monroe (1979) found a significant level of consistency between public beliefs and policy outcomes. The outcomes Monroe reported showed that in more that 60 percent of the issues examined, the policy was consistent with the views of the interviewed public. The degree of congruence was greatest (75 percent) when members of the public favored the status quo. Yet even when change was preferred, the relationship was still significant. Although the level of agreement between policy and public opinion was lower for social welfare issues (57 percent) than for other policy areas (for instance, foreign policy [92 percent] and Vietnam [71 percent]), the relationship cannot be ignored. It should also be mentioned that other studies show less congruence on redistributive issues as well (see Shapiro and Jacobs 1989). Monroe demonstrated that public opinion does correspond cross-sectionally with policy outcomes; but he was unable to show that the members of the public actually influenced the policy outcome.

Page and Shapiro (1983) and Shapiro and his colleagues (Shapiro and Patterson 1986; Shapiro and Jacobs 1989; Shapiro and Young 1988; Farkas, Shapiro, and Page 1990) have described and demonstrated a causal link between the beliefs of the public and changes in public policy. Examining public opinion and policy data for the United States over a forty-year period, they find that changes in opinions measured in a given year corresponded to policy changes one year later, implying that policymakers responded to the desires of the public. Page, Shapiro, and their colleagues argue that not only does public opinion lay the foundation on which social welfare policy decisions are made, it also is often responsible for motivating the adjustments made to existing policies.

Other researchers have strengthened the evidence of a causal relationship through the use of case studies. For instance, Burnstein and Freudenburg (1978) discovered a relationship between Senate roll-call voting and public opinion concerning Vietnam. Rochefort (1986) followed state government decisions concerning mental health care policy and demonstrated the congruence between policy changes and public opinion. The evidence depicting an important association between public opinion and policy is plentiful and spans many policy areas, from domestic social welfare to foreign policy. Thus, public opinion is certainly relevant to the fate of the welfare state in the United States today. (For a more general discussion of public opinion research, see appendix A).

During the 1980s, the future of American social welfare was in jeopardy. It was a watershed period for all the programs that up until then had only experienced expansion. Facing major budgetary constraints, a rise in the number of potential beneficiaries, and questionable public support, the U.S. social welfare system was under serious attack. The election of Ronald Reagan as president and the policies he pursued were seen as the embodiment of this threat. Yet despite the verbal assaults, fewer cutbacks were implemented than might have been anticipated. By focusing primarily on public and congressional opinions, we will explore some of the reasons behind the unexpected turn of events.

In chapter 2 we introduce several explanations for public and congressional support for social welfare. As mentioned earlier, very little is known about support for specific programs within the system. When we dissect the system, do we find that some programs are more supported than others? If so, why? Chapter 2 introduces some reasons why we might expect differences in support for various programs.

To answer these questions, we examine the opinions of 1,209 members of the American public expressed through telephone interviews. We also look at the opinions of 58 members of the U.S. House of Representatives. Chapter 3 examines the level of support among members of the general public and of the U.S. House of Representatives for the system of programs that comprise U.S. social welfare. The chapter probes specific beliefs about program recipients and program effectiveness. Chapters 4, 5, and 6 take the issue of support one step further and explore why people hold the beliefs they do. In these chapters, we test the explanations suggested in chapter 2. Chapter 7 offers a summary of all the results and speculates on the future of social welfare in America.

According to Lane and Sears (1964), a political system is shaped and guided by what its members believe. Obviously, personal beliefs and attitudes are but one component in the complex decision-making process that leads to social welfare program expansion or contraction. Yet such attitudes are often overlooked. Researchers tend to focus on the role of economics, international relations, and politics in shaping policy decisions. We do not want to argue that such factors are of no importance. Instead, we argue that the intricacies of preferences should not be ignored. Knowing the opinions of all involved in policy-making can provide useful insights into the policy process and potential policy outcomes. By exploring attitudes, we can likewise investigate the legitimacy of the social welfare crisis rhetoric and, equally important, we can gain insight into the correspondence between congressional action and public beliefs.

2
Explanations of Support for Social Welfare

Why do members of Congress and the public choose to support particular social welfare programs and not others? There are at least four major explanations. The first two are implicit in historical and current analyses of the social welfare system, and we label them recipient deservingness and program effectiveness. The other two—self-interest and political predispositions—have been examined by scholars outside the field of social welfare as general theories about political preferences rather than as specific theories about social welfare preferences.

The recipient deservingness explanation of support focuses on the recipients of social welfare programs rather than on the programs themselves. It has to do with judgments about which groups of recipients are deserving of help and which are not. According to this explanation, if we learn respondents' answers to the question "*Who* should be helped?" we will be able to predict which programs those respondents will most strongly support. Thus, recipient deservingness, a theory that we find embedded in both the historical literature and current discussions of the American welfare state, contends that support is influenced by personal attitudes and opinions concerning those who participate in the programs. Individuals who believe the targeted recipients of particular programs are worthy of assistance will be more supportive of those programs than individuals who see little deservingness among beneficiaries.

A second explanation focuses on the programs themselves and sees support as deriving from perceptions of program effectiveness. Ask citizens "Which programs *work?*" and we will be able to predict which programs they will support. Like the recipient deservingness theory, the program effectiveness theory is implicit in much of the literature as an explanation of why Congress and the public are or are not willing to support certain social welfare programs. Program effectiveness contends that Americans favor programs they perceive as achieving intended goals with minimal waste, fraud, and abuse. Conversely, the theory suggests that Americans dislike programs that they perceive to be mismanaged and wasteful. If programs are seen to be effective, they will be supported.

Both recipient deservingness and program effectiveness suggest that support for social welfare is driven by attitudes specific to the particular program being evaluated. We therefore classify them as being program-based explanations of support.

Two other explanations suggest that support depends more on the personal interests and concerns of those making the decisions about support, be they members of the public or the Congress, than on features of the programs themselves. The self-interest theory of support asks, "Is something in it for *me* if I support this particular social welfare program?" If so, then one should support the program; if not, support should be lower. Thus, support for a program is directly related to its utility to the individual reviewer. It stands to reason that those who can gain the most from a program will be its most ardent supporters.

The final explanation relates level of support to respondents' political predispositions, often gained through the experiences of childhood and adolescence. Political predispositions might include ideological self-designation as a conservative or a liberal, and party identification as a Democrat or a Republican. The theory postulates that if we ask someone, "Do you consider yourself a Democrat or a Republican?" and "Do you think of yourself as liberal or conservative?" we will be able to determine the respondent's level of support for social welfare programs from the answer.

Recipient Deservingness

Notions of deservingness must be nearly as old as human history. Recorded discussions of deservingness in the context of social welfare provisions date back to the 1601 Elizabethan Poor Laws in England. Among the ideas Americans have inherited from Elizabethan legal traditions, separating those deserving and undeserving of public assistance is clearly one of the most salient (Stein 1971; Macarov 1978; Axinn and Levin 1975). Macarov, in fact, contends that deservingness has been, and continues to be, a "controlling concept of social welfare" (p. 98). Distinctions concerning those who are deserving are firmly grounded in the individualistic tradition of American life, a tradition founded in early political, religious, and secular thinking (Leiby 1978).

But what exactly is "deservingness"? What qualifications must a recipient hold in order to be deemed "deserving"? From the scholarly literature on the subject, we have uncovered five major attributes of this concept. First, and most important, Americans usually think of the level and extent of the beneficiary's need. Social psychological studies have shown through experiments that the perceived level of a person's need largely influences the likelihood that another will offer help (e.g., Berkowitz and Conner 1966; Krebs 1970). Moreover, the greater the intensity of the need, the more likely it is that someone will provide assistance (Schwartz 1975). Survey results from a sample of Chicago residents have replicated these earlier experimental findings. Cook (1979) found that Chicagoans reported a greater willingness to help disabled people as the severity of the disability increased. She also found respondents more willing to help those who were demonstrably poor than those who were not, but she did not find increases in support as the severity of poverty increased.

Need alone, however, may not be enough for a person to be considered deserving of help. It may also be important for the public and members of Congress to believe that no alternative sources of help exist to meet the need. For example, some researchers (e.g., Cook 1979) have speculated that the elderly might receive more support than children and young adults because the latter two groups have alternative sources of help, i.e., children are seen to have parents who should help them and young adults are seen to have the option to work (Axinn and Stern 1985).

A third attribute of deservingness is cause of need. Stein (1971) suggests that needs must be seen as legitimate for a person or group to be considered deserving; in other words, as not self-inflicted. Deserving individuals, says Stein, are those not perceived to be at fault for the situations in which they find themselves. According to Ellwood (1988), holding people responsible for their actions follows directly from a central American ethic—the autonomy of the individual. Ellwood argues that this tenet is the underpinning of much of the philosophical and political rhetoric concerning American social welfare policy. If it is true that people are autonomous and have control over their lives, then it follows that people ought to be held responsible for their actions.

Poverty, then, can be perceived as resulting from an individual's character and personality, or it can be perceived as being the result of circumstances beyond the individual's immediate control. People perceived as needy because of their own doing are likely to be cast into the "undeserving" category, while those perceived as poor because of external circumstances are likely to be considered "deserving." This distinction has had important policy consequences throughout U.S. history. When the Charity Organization Society workers of the late nineteenth and early twentieth centuries were deciding who they should help, they asked themselves: "What is the cause of the distress?" (Woodroofe 1962:36). If the destitute individual was perceived as causing his or her own plight, he or she was immediately considered "undeserving" and denied aid by the society. More recently, President Reagan in his January 1987 State of the Union address made a similar point: "We will never abandon those who, through no fault of their own, must have help" (quoted in Daeley 1989:187).

Social research gives weight to this definition of deservingness. Cook's survey (1979) of Chicago residents included an experiment that presented respondents with vignettes of individuals needing assistance. The vignettes varied the responsibility for the individual's situation of need. The results strikingly show that people who are seen to cause their own plight receive far less support than those whose condition was caused by some external force.

A fourth component of deservingness is that the individual strive toward independence and self-sufficiency, and not passively accept a destitute situation. The historic distinction between the deserving and the undeserving includes the individual's "desire for independence." Stein explains it this way:

> Roughly, the deserving poor are those who are dependent through no fault of their own, and who need help because they cannot avoid their status or could, with some assistance, become independent. *Also included are those who, although poor, steadfastly strive to maintain their independence.* Such persons are thought to be the proper objects of public sympathy; others are not. (pp. 47–48; emphasis added)

Leiby (1978) agrees that the perception of the deserving poor, both now and in the past, is one of people who are "trying, despite their handicaps and disappointments, to escape dependency and become self-sufficient" (p. 33), while the undeserving poor are those who are "willing to take advantage of others to escape their own responsibility" (p. 33).

A fifth attribute of deservingness concerns how recipients are seen to use their social welfare benefits. Macarov (1978) argues that to be considered deserving of aid an individual not only must be seen to be in dire need of help but also must be perceived as using his or her benefits prudently: "Those who are adjudged to be unable to use the help properly or well may be refused it" (p. 204).

Thus, we conceptualize recipient deservingness along five dimensions. We argue that individuals—both members of Congress and the general public—consider these dimensions when deciding whether to support particular social welfare programs. According to the recipient deservingness theory of support, then, five criteria must be met in order for an individual to support social welfare.

1. Those individuals worthy of help from a program must be perceived to be truly in need.
2. Not only must individuals lack the particular resource being offered (whether it be cash or an in-kind service), but individuals must have no other possible resources available to meet that need.
3. Those individuals helped through a program must not be seen as being at fault for their particular situation. That is, the condition must be perceived as due to forces beyond the control of the recipient.
4. Those individuals helped through a program must be perceived to possess the will to be independent. They must be seen as

trying to help themselves, but because of insurmountable external barriers that prevent independent living (whether they be
physical handicaps or social impediments), they have not been
able to manage adequately.

5. Along with these other characteristics of "good citizenship" (not
at fault and a desire for independence), the recipients must also
be perceived to use their benefits wisely. That is, recipients
must not be seen to abuse their limited resources or to spend
recklessly.

The underlying theme behind the deservingness explanation is,
therefore, that society should help only those worthy of its assistance. The definition of "worthy" centers around being a good
citizen—participating in those activities the American culture values (e.g., work and saving). When a program helps worthy citizens,
this suggests that the program will receive substantial support. In
contrast, programs that target individuals who do not meet these
five criteria of deservingness will receive less support. Although
the discussion so far has focused on beliefs of the general public,
there is no reason to suspect that members of Congress are immune
from similar influences. We hypothesize that the same criteria that
affect public opinion likewise influence congressional support.

Program Effectiveness

While a discussion of deservingness focuses on the worthiness of
the individual recipients, the program effectiveness explanation
spotlights the merits of the program itself. According to this perspective, members of the public and Congress are more supportive
of those social welfare programs that they believe are effective.

Historically, debates over the effectiveness of social programs
have followed fast on their enactment (Katz 1986), but the most
dramatic increase in the emphasis on program effectiveness came
in response to the announcement of an all-out effort against poverty
in 1964 and Lyndon Johnson's plans for his Great Society (Haveman 1987). The War on Poverty and Great Society programs played
major roles in the rise of policy analysis and evaluation research.
So, too, did President Johnson's 1965 executive order establishing
the planning-programming-budgeting system (PPBS). Both policy

analysis and evaluation research can be understood as efforts "to understand the effects of the activities of government on its citizens" (Haveman 1987:156).

But what exactly is program effectiveness? The policy analysis and evaluation research literature are replete with attributes (see, for example, Haveman 1987:91). From this literature, we take four attributes that specifically apply to social welfare programs and define an effective program worthy of support. The first addresses what a quality program should not do: it should not encourage dependence on government assistance. A number of critics accuse welfare programs of forcing dependence upon their recipients by not demanding obligations in return for assistance (Mead 1986). Without obligations, they argue, welfare programs perpetuate dependency and recipients never learn the importance of work. Murray (1984) argues that poverty is maintained because the generosity of programs does not motivate recipients to become independent. Critics such as Murray oppose social welfare programs because they believe that poverty is caused not so much by some inherent characteristics of the poor but is "promoted by public programs that assist the poor, negating the discipline of the marketplace" (Harpham and Scotch 1989:45).

A 1985 survey of 2,444 respondents by the *Los Angeles Times* found that 59 percent believed that welfare made "poor people dependent and encouraged them to stay poor" while only 19 percent believed it gave them a chance to "stand on their own two feet and get started again" (Lewis and Schneider 1985). Public opinion polls from the 1970s found over 60 percent believing that welfare programs actually encouraged women to have children before marriage. Mitchell (1970) describes the paradox of programs that are counterproductive in their efforts to help: "From the welfare recipient to the conservative businessman, almost everyone believes that existing welfare programs are in a mess. They are an insult to the recipients and do not make able-bodied people productive. . . . They are a continuing source of conflict" (p. 338).

A second attribute of program effectiveness is the active encouragement of independence. People have differing opinions on exactly what the goals of social welfare programs should be, but most would agree that whenever feasible, programs should strive to help recipients become self-sufficient. Ellwood (1988), for example, says that "the ideal social policy system would encourage self-support and independence through work [and] make people responsible for their actions" (p. 17). Haveman (1987:91) lists the "encouragement of self-sufficiency" as one of the key goals of an effective social welfare system.

A third characteristic focuses on mismanagement, fraud, and abuse. Despite good intentions, programs may be unable to achieve their intended goals because of fraud and abuse. Although no empirical evidence exists, we contend that programs that the public perceives as plagued to a greater extent than others with problems of abuse receive less support from the public and less political backing from legislators.

In his assault on fraud and abuse, President Reagan attacked not only abusive welfare recipients but also lax management by program administrators and poor law enforcement by states (Matt and Cook 1991). Reagan told Congress in his first State of the Union address on February 18, 1981: "One government estimate indicated that fraud alone may account for anywhere from 1 percent to 10 percent—as much as $25 billion—of federal expenditures for social programs" (Reagan 1981:B8). Later, in his 1983 address, the president strengthened his rhetoric: "The truly needy suffer as funds intended for them are taken not by the needy but by the greedy. For everyone's sake, we must put an end to such waste and corruption" (Reagan 1983:A12).

The public has long been keenly aware of the potential for fraud in social welfare programs. A poll taken in 1964 demonstrated that 61 percent of the respondents believed "some" welfare recipients had cheated in order to qualify for benefits, and an additional 7 percent believed most had. The same question asked again in 1984 showed 72 percent believed some of the people on welfare qualified through dishonest means, and an additional 17 percent believed most on welfare used dishonest claims to qualify for benefits. Feagin (1972) questioned 1,017 people and learned that 71 percent of them believed that many welfare recipients are not honest about their needs. A 1978 Gallup poll examined the proportion of recipients the public felt were "chiselers." The majority of respondents (60 percent) felt at least 20 percent of the recipients cheated. Further, 57 percent claimed to have seen someone using food stamps "inappropriately." A 1984 poll showed that 54 percent of the respondents believed recipients getting more than they deserved was a bigger problem than those getting less than they deserved.*

A fourth attribute of program effectiveness is directed at program importance—larger societal benefits. Kinder (1981) shows that people are guided by "sociotropic" evaluations when assessing policies and policy leaders—that is, they weigh the impact of policies on the nation as a whole and these evaluations are more important than their own personal "pocketbook experiences" when they assess their support for the president (p. 17). Thus, in order for programs to be considered effective they must be seen to benefit society at large. For example, Ellwood says that Social Security was "brilliant" in conception "for it managed to reinforce the values of autonomy, work, family, and community" (p. 27). It not only helps the elderly in their retirement, but also the adult children of the elderly who might otherwise have to assist their parents financially. Social Security provides retired people with independence, but that independence must be earned. Social Security benefits are only offered to those who have worked and made contributions. Finally, Social Security brings the community together since every worker contributes to the well-being of the elderly. Thus, Social Security can be perceived by many to benefit society as a whole: it helps nearly all elderly citizens and motivates the young to work.

Although we can describe an inefficient program in exhaustive detail, it is more difficult to describe an effective one. Because of the differing needs of target groups, any definition of effectiveness likely varies with the particular programs and the specific population being assisted. For example, numerous commentators argue that, when trying to help working-age, able-bodied adults, the public prefers programs that motivate recipients to work and save (Butler and Kondratas 1987). Coyle and Wildavsky (1986) say that since the public sees independence as the route out of poverty, programs should be designed to promote self-sufficiency. On the other hand, when programs for the elderly are considered, striving for independence becomes less of an issue—maintaining an acceptable quality of life may be more important. Programs that strive for an accepted goal may not only be the most effective but also the most preferred by the public, for many people agree with Jacob

---

* Recipients are not the only ones perceived to get more than they deserve. Physicians and other health care professionals have also been accused of defrauding Medicare and Medicaid (e.g., GAO 1976, 1983).

Riis when he wrote in the late 1800s, "It is money scattered without judgement—not poverty—that makes the pauper" (Riis 1892:277).

The following attributes apply to a program effectiveness explanation of support for social welfare—criteria that entail personal beliefs and are presumably important to Congress members as well as the public:

1. A program that is perceived to force dependence upon its recipients will not be supported.
2. A program will be supported when it is seen as actively helping recipients gain their independence and self-sufficiency. The efficient program promotes the skills or motivation necessary for recipients to help themselves.
3. Fraud and abuse should be at a minimum. Supported programs are those that assist qualified recipients but are not indiscriminately handing out benefits.
4. Favored programs are seen to be important by benefiting not only individual recipients but also society at large. These benefits might include private concerns, such as relieving the family of the burdens of caring for aging relatives, or more global concerns such as a satisfaction in knowing no citizen is involuntarily hungry.

As we look at the impact on opinions of program effectiveness, we should not assume that all evaluators see only the negative aspects of programs. Schwarz (1988), in fact, tells of the triumphs of social welfare programs, describing the success of post–Eisenhower era programs in reducing the percentage of Americans in poverty. Schwarz maintains that, though "the government's programs to attack poverty [were] at times seriously flawed," they "frequently were effective" (p. 49). In chapter 4, we will test the notion that perceptions of a program's effectiveness influence public and congressional support for the program.

Self-Interest

A great deal of literature explores the question of self-interest in political and social actions. Early Roman philosophers, Christian thinkers of the Middle Ages, Thomas Hobbes and his eighteenth-century contemporaries, Adam Smith and the writers of the American Constitution, and, more recently, academic social scientists

(Downs 1957; Mansbridge 1990; Sears and Funk 1990; Kelman 1987, to mention just a few) have grappled with the dialectic of human selfishness and altruism in society. Despite centuries of inquiry, the degree to which human attitudes and behavior are motivated by a desire to improve personal position remains controversial. Up until the mid-1980s, it appeared that self-interest was the dominant explanation of political and personal behavior. However, a lively debate has surfaced recently, and self-interest theory is currently under attack (see, for example, Mansbridge 1990; Reich 1988).

Unlike the program-based explanations of support discussed earlier, the self-interest theory of support is far more dependent on the characteristics of individual respondents. As it implies, self-interest is personal and can only be defined in terms of the specific person or group concerned, since a behavior that is in the best interest of one might simultaneously have deleterious effects on another. Similarly, attitudes and behaviors of all citizens, whether they be the voting public or decision-making legislators, may potentially be driven by private desires.

Researchers studying voting behavior among the public and in Congress have investigated whether citizens are motivated to vote for candidates and referendum choices that would be to their own personal benefit. Some find evidence supporting this hypothesis (Campbell et al. 1960), while others encounter conflicting results (Wilson and Banfield 1964). The outcomes of research on self-interest in other areas of congressional decision making are also not conclusive. Downs (1957) and others (Buchanan and Tullock 1962; Mayhew 1974; Fiorina 1977) present evidence of a rational Congress, of a group motivated by the desire for reelection and acting accordingly. This conclusion is unsatisfactory to some, who see members of Congress as often seeking to construct the "best" possible public policy with little thought to their own careers (Kelman 1986; Quirk 1988; Sen 1977; Wilson and Banfield 1964). Thus, prior research on both Congress and the general public are contradictory with respect to the role self-interest plays in shaping attitudes.

Self-Interest in the Public

The fate of California's Proposition 13 provides an example of self-interest-motivated public voting behavior. The 1978 binding referendum gave citizens the opportunity to express their opinions on the rising state tax rates. In the wording of the proposition, voters could choose to lower property taxes, while in exchange for payment reductions, government services, such as police and fire protection, would also be cut back. The high voter support for Proposition 13 demonstrated that taxpayers favored reductions, a finding many interpret as evidence of self-interest-motivated behavior. The argument is made even stronger with the findings by Sears and Citrin (1982) that, while homeowners felt confident their taxes would be reduced, most doubted that services would actually decline. In voting to reduce property taxes, citizens felt they were improving their financial well-being (by lowering their taxes) without really sacrificing the services to which they were accustomed. Those voters dependent on government aid, that is, those who had the most to lose with the new legislation, were not driven to oppose the proposition because they, too, did not believe services would actually be reduced. The voter reaction to Proposition 13 gives strong evidence that individuals will, at least sometimes, act to help themselves even at a potential cost to society as a whole.

Cigarette smoking in public places is another social issue that has been used by researchers to demonstrate the power of self-interest. Through opinion polls of smokers and nonsmokers, Green and Gerken (1989) found that self-interest seems to drive people's attitudes about smoking restrictions. They discovered that non-smokers were far more likely to favor smoking restrictions than were smokers; and light smokers were more supportive of restrictions than heavy smokers. When asked about increased taxes on cigarettes, personal income and ability to pay had little effect on whether nonsmokers favored taxes. But among smokers, those better situated to pay higher taxes were less opposed to increases, while smokers who were poor were most adamantly opposed to increased cigarette taxes. Furthermore, the higher the proposed taxes, the greater the disapproval among smokers, regardless of their personal income. That smokers were more opposed than nonsmokers to restrictions, both physical and financial, is evidence that self-interest is at play.

As both of the above examples demonstrate, self-interest appears to be strongest when there is a clear outcome expected for the respondent (e.g., decreases in property taxes, increases in cigarette taxes). Green and Gerken (1989) used data from 1984 and

1987, a time when public acceptance of smokers was at an all-time low. The respondents no doubt had reason to believe the suggested restrictions would come to pass. A similar survey conducted in the 1950s or 1960s, when smoking was more acceptable, might have yielded less strong results. When issues are vague or unlikely, self-interest is less likely to play a role in one's actions. In this case, factors like personal ideology or internal beliefs (symbolic politics), seem to become more important (Sears et al. 1980).

A number of researchers are far from convinced of the importance of self-interest in political activities. The basic concept of self-interest is easy enough to understand in theory: people hold beliefs and make decisions such that their own goals or interests are served. In practice, however, the concept is far more complicated. For instance, how can a researcher distinguish between self-interest and firsthand knowledge? If we were to find that the poor are the most supportive of public assistance programs, can we assume that this is because they would be the most affected by reductions? Or might it not be the case that their support is driven by a knowledge of what it means to be poor and without assistance?

Similarly, in defining self-interest we also need to predict what respondents might consider their long-term gains as well. While it is easy to see that the elderly have personal concerns in supporting Social Security, it is important to note that nonelderly adults also benefit. Without a program such as Social Security that distributes the burden across an entire society, working-age adults might have to pay more to subsidize the well-being of their parents or other older relatives. And of course there is the argument that every working citizen will eventually receive benefits from Social Security, so all have some direct self-interest even though the benefit is not immediate. Thus, although the self-interest hypothesis is easy to consider, it is much more difficult to study empirically.

According to Kluegel and Smith (1986), the most popular view of the forces underlying policy attitudes is that they reflect individuals' views of their own self-interest: "How will the policy in question affect me?" (p. 144). They interviewed a nationally representative random sample of 2,212 Americans in 1980 regarding their beliefs about inequality and found that African Americans, low-income respondents, and those not self-employed were more supportive of welfare spending than other groups, a finding they call a "straightforward effect of apparent self-interest" (p. 161).

However, Kluegel and Smith go on to show that general beliefs about opportunity and inequality are more important in determining views on redistributive policies than self-interest and personal experiences.

Shapiro and Patterson (1986) examined results from past national surveys on public issues in light of the self-interest hypothesis. They conceded that some self-interest is occurring, but they were unable to determine how much. For the most part, they found that measures of self-interest cannot be separated from group interests. They found it difficult to separate group interest from group knowledge of the issue. In one case, Shapiro and Patterson suggest that African Americans tended to be more supportive of social welfare not only because of the costs-to-benefits ratio that favors them individually, but also because they, as a group, share similar experiences of discrimination and unequal opportunities. Shapiro and Patterson also found that women tended to be more supportive of government assistance. This suggests that heightened support by females might be brought on not by self-interest but rather by a feminine social consciousness, a greater sensitivity to people in need resulting from differences in the upbringing of women as compared to men.

Social welfare programs provide a public as well as a private good, and one's support for programs may be directed by a personal vision of society as well as by a heightened sense of community. American democracy has its roots in a belief in community action. In his treatise on American democracy, Tocqueville (1848 [1969]) wrote that U.S. economic prosperity stemmed from a combination of both individual self-interest and a strong sense of community. Indeed, he reports observing citizens acting to better themselves by improving their communities and the lives of every individual within their community.

Deciding who has a personal interest in social welfare is not an easy task. To test the theory of self-interest, we have selected four groups that could possibly be so motivated. Citizen support is considered to be motivated by self-interest in the following cases:

1. Support will be highest for all programs among those who are currently receiving benefits or who have recently received them. These individuals have the most to lose from program cutbacks and the most to gain through expansions of funding.

2. Individuals who have close family members or friends presently receiving benefits will be especially interested in the programs. These individuals not only are likely to share similar characteristics with recipients, but they should support programs in defense of their family.
3. Support for the public assistance programs will be low among the affluent and high among the poor. Low-income respondents pay little in taxes and stand to gain from social welfare programs, whereas high-income respondents pay more in taxes and stand to lose if benefits are increased.
4. Young families who are poor and have children or are in their childbearing years will be particularly supportive of the AFDC program. Although the vast majority will never need the benefits provided, it is in their best interest to assure that the program exists should they ever need it.

Congressional Self-Interest

As elusive as public self-interest may seem, classifying congressional self-interest is even more difficult. Representatives are individual citizens and as such should behave as other members of the public. But what about their self-interest as elected officials? Weiss (1983) argues that policymakers make their decisions based on three criteria: ideology, interests, and information. In addition to seeking reelection, legislators also desire to gain access to positions of greater power and authority. Thus, actions that would yield these benefits could be construed as directed by self-interest. On the other hand, Congress members following the desires of their constituents may be doing so not in order to be reelected, but because it is what they believe to be the correct role of an elected representative or because they happen to share the same values as their constituents.

Are Congress members motivated to help themselves first? Stigler (1971) argues that they are. In regulation policy, Stigler notes, both politicians and the public behave from a self-interest-driven perspective. While the public is concerned with its own economic well-being, politicians likewise act to better themselves—in this case, to pursue legislation that they perceive will get them reelected. In his notable study of Congress, Morris Fiorina (1977) argues that the search for electoral security motivates many federal distribution programs.

Tufte (1978) presents a notion of policymaker self-interest from an analysis of political campaigns. By manipulating benefit and tax increases, politicians are able to lead members of the public to believe that their tax and financial concerns are being addressed. Playing on the self-interests of the public, politicians believe the voters will elect the official responsible for those benefits. In his analyses, Tufte found that increases in Social Security and veterans' benefits tended to occur right before elections (nine out of thirteen in his analyses from 1946 to 1975), while increased taxes for Social Security were likely to come at the beginning of the year following the election—that is, the year after the increase (about two-thirds of the times in the same thirty-year period). The idea, of course, is that the public will not remember the tax increase by the next election but will attribute benefit increases directly before election to the incumbents.

The desire to be reelected is suggested to be most salient among junior members of Congress, and not surprisingly, Dodd (1977) found that junior members are more attentive to their constituents. As experience in office increases and reelection leads to job security, awareness and direct actions on behalf of the constituency decreases, according to Dodd's findings. However, the results from Dodd's work do not appear to be universal. Parker (1986) failed to find any effect of seniority on attentiveness to district concerns. In fact, he found that long-term incumbents spent more time in their districts than others. Despite polls that show strong public acceptance and satisfaction, Parker suggests that favored incumbents still lack a feeling of reelection security. They continue to seek affirmation from their districts and to behave in ways most likely to result in reelection.

In addition to manipulating voter response through direct financial gain, politicians seeking reelection also spend more time in their districts. Constituencies are more satisfied when their representatives spend time in the district and are more likely to reelect such officials. Legislators' actions are to a large degree, according to Stigler (1971), in response to the demands of the public.

How can we define self-interest among Congress members? A desire to be reelected is no doubt self-interest-motivated. But can we necessarily say that a representative who votes according to the desires of his or her district or in a way that brings financial betterment to the area is doing so out of a desire to be reelected? Could it not also be interpreted as the desire to be a literal voice of the people? Quirk (1988) suggests that policymakers act upon what they believe to be the public's beliefs. Is this self-interest, or is this public responsibility? Quirk does not suggest that they do so solely out of a desire to represent the public and ignore their own self-interest. He implies that behavior is guided by many things, including gaining the respect of other political elites and appearing to act independently and responsibly when needed. Quirk also asserts that politicians act on behalf of their larger constituency and not just on behalf of those who are affected by the policy or who are well-organized.

As with the public, defining self-interest among Congress members is difficult. How interests are defined depend on the amount and kind of information the policymaker has, and new information can easily change the perceptions of self-interest. Two hypotheses fit the theory of self-interest driven behavior among elected representatives:

1. Congress members from high-income districts will be less supportive than those from low-income districts of public assistance programs. High-income districts pay the taxes to fund programs yet few constituents are beneficiaries.
2. Congress members from districts with a large proportion of elderly will be more supportive of Social Security and Medicare than those with a younger constituency.

As these hypotheses demonstrate, congressional self-interest is determined almost solely in terms of the needs of the district. Any given individual representative no doubt has personal concerns that motivate behavior as well (for example, the desire to be on a coveted committee), but the limitations of the survey prevent us from addressing this factor.

Political Predispositions

We have offered thus far three explanations as to why people are more or less supportive of social welfare and why they might choose to help particular groups above others. The final explanation we call the political predispositions theory. It holds that members of the public and Congress support social welfare programs because of political preferences they learned early in life. These preferences, or predispositions, include political party identification (Republican or Democrat) and self-reported political ideology as liberal or conservative.

Sears and his colleagues (Sears 1975, 1983; Sears et al. 1980) call the use of political preferences to guide decisions "symbolic politics." They argue that, when confronted with a decision, people look to "symbols" in the new decision similar to those held within their preference schemes. Taken out of context, making each new decision may be a daunting task. Yet by relying on values and past decisions to guide the process, the selection is simplified, and the decision maker is more confident. By using predispositions (or "symbols") to lead to the new decision, the process is shortened and responses retain relative consistency with one another.

The Public and Political Predispositions

Perhaps the most common political decision-making predisposition is party affiliation. The origin of party identification is not entirely understood. Children tend to adopt party affiliations similar to those of their parents or other significant adults. Early socialization plays a significant part in determining affiliation, but adult experiences can also alter one's political identity. One piece of evidence supporting the effects of adult experiences is the propensity for women—especially in the past, but even still today—to adopt the party of their husbands; this is chiefly the case with women who are exclusively homemakers (Darcy, Welch and Clark 1987). We also know that Democrats and Republicans differ demographically, with the working class predominantly belonging to the Democratic party and the wealthy predominantly Republican. Once party affiliation is established, however, it remains relatively stable throughout one's adult life (Abramson 1983; but see Cavanaugh and Sundquist 1985 for a recent shift in this general trend as a larger proportion of formerly Democratic southern whites have begun to identify with the Republican party).

The two major parties of the United States, the Democratic and Republican parties, endorse different tactics for addressing the problems of poverty and the role of government in supporting social welfare programs. The Democratic party is more likely to endorse increased government spending to address social welfare issues. It readily backs government-sponsored education and job training programs, as well as the child-care centers necessary to enable poor parents to attend these programs. The Republican party, on the other hand, asserts that the best means of meeting the challenges of poverty are through a strong independent economy. Although the Republican party does not expect nor even promote the elimination of the welfare system, its preferred solutions include such options as economic enterprise zones to motivate business growth in high unemployment areas, and stimulation of the economy, so that benefits will "trickle down" to the poor. It is not difficult to predict, therefore, that individuals who identify with one or the other party will hold differing levels of support for social welfare programs.

Party affiliation is important in distinguishing a number of public attitudes and a considerable amount of voting behavior. Pomper (1972) noted a large increase during the 1950s and 1960s in the relationship between opinions on issues and party identification. More recently, some pollsters report that differences *between* self-defined Democrats and Republicans are small on such social issues as abortion and sexual norms, while differences *within* each party by education and social status are large. Nonetheless, many political commentators think Republicans and Democrats continue to be most sharply divided on the broad issue of the proper role of government in national life (Ladd 1985).

Although we know that social and economic variables correlate with party identification, we cannot easily determine whether they are causally connected. Some researchers argue that self-interest, motivated by the needs of the social class, influences party support (see Abramson 1975). So, for example, the poor, who have the most to gain from the liberal programs of the Democratic party, are more apt to vote for the Democratic ticket. The well-to-do, who have the most to lose from any increased taxation, are least likely to be Democrats. Business leaders who are likely to receive benefits from policy motivating production and manufacturing would be most likely to join the Republican party. It is likely that the relationship between self-interest and party affiliation is correlational rather than causal. People have a predisposition toward particular party membership through social class, background, and adult experiences; and as personal beliefs and interests strengthen, they too influence the membership decision.

A second form that political predispositions take is ideology as defined by liberalism and conservatism. Embedded in the labels *liberal* or *conservative* are beliefs about political issues such as equality and the role of government. Individuals hold certain values as important and these form a relatively consistent ideological foundation upon which decisions are based. Political ideology tends to be closely related to party affiliation, but the two measures are not identical. Sixty percent of Republicans interviewed by NORC in 1983 reported themselves to be conservatives while 26 percent of Democrats called themselves conservatives (Ladd 1985). Although few Republicans would identify themselves as extremely liberal, within both parties there are gradations of liberalism and conservatism.

Verba and Orren (1985) found that people's views about equality varied depending upon their self-defined ideology; self-described liberals were more likely than conservatives to favor income gap reductions. Carmines and Stimson (1989) show that racial issues have been defined in ideological terms since the 1964 presidential election, which pitted Lyndon Johnson, who favored federal activity in civil rights, against Barry Goldwater, who opposed it. According to Carmines and Stimson, race is a "prominent, if not dominant" connotation of the ideological labels *liberal* and *conservative:* "If we ask simply, what do we know if we know someone avows a position on the liberal-conservative continuum? we answer that more than anything else we know that person's views on race" (p. 133). Because of these and other similar findings, we expect ideology to affect support for social welfare.

According to the political predispositions explanation of support, the following criteria would be necessary for the explanation to remain viable:

1. Individuals who identify themselves with the Democratic party will be more supportive of social welfare programs in general than those who identify with the Republican party.
2. Individuals who consider themselves liberals will be more supportive of social welfare programs than those who consider themselves conservatives.

The relationship between political predispositions and public opinion toward social welfare is an interesting question. Does one first decide social welfare programs are worthy of support and then identify oneself as a Democrat and a liberal, or is one a Democrat and/or a liberal first and then make decisions about which issues are worth supporting? Though an argument can surely be made for the former case, we will here assume the latter interpretation. We base our assumption on the political socialization literature that demonstrates that, for the most part, political ideology and party identification are the result of early socialization and are characteristics one carries into adulthood.**

The Political Predispositions of Congress

Political party is often cited as a very strong predictor of congressional voting behavior (MacRae 1958; Truman 1959; Mayhew 1966; Kingdon 1981; Page et al. 1984; West 1988). In fact, Bullock and Brady (1983) found party control to be stronger than any other variable tested. Although most research has addressed public voting behavior, the same party factors might likewise influence congressional attitudes. It is this relationship that the political predispositions explanation of support examines.

Although exactly how party platforms are determined and what strength they have is still debatable (Kirkpatrick 1971; Downs 1957; Page 1978; Clausen 1973), they no doubt play some role in the decision-making process. Some commentators have suggested that political party represents a shared ideology among a group of individuals (Page et al. 1984). Since everyone in the group does not necessarily hold an opinion about every issue, party affiliation helps to guide decisions. When it becomes necessary for legislators to vote on a relatively unknown topic, those without confirmed attitudes will depend on colleagues in the group who are considered "experts." This thesis is strengthened by the finding that Congress follows the party line most closely on issues with relatively less importance (Clausen 1973; Kingdon 1981).

Unlike the self-interest model, there are few electoral benefits to maintaining a party line (Parker 1986). Although political party offers cues on how to vote (Kingdon 1981), the public does not pay strict attention to party when voting for Congress (Ornstein et al. 1982; Kritzer and Eubank 1979; Ferejohn 1977), nor is congressional party affiliation particularly reflective of public opinion (Page

---

** A third possibility is reciprocal causation. As Page et al. (1984:754) point out, the estimation of such a model is quite difficult to test because of the lack of the necessary theoretically exogeneous variables.

et al. 1984). There are, however, other reasons for Congress members to remain close to the policies of their respective parties. Politicians gain access to higher offices through the party (for example, moving from the House to the Senate), and assignments on prestigious committees arise through party mechanisms (Davidson and Oleszek 1985).

If party identification is clearly more than a label for gaining electoral support, what then is it? Norpoth (1976) has suggested that party represents a compilation of shared attitudes. When party is used to predict voting behavior, it is acting as a proxy for underlying attitudes. Thus, that political party affiliation is predictive of an individual's support for social welfare programs may actually be a test of multiple attitudinal models simultaneously. That is, party affiliation may merely be a proxy for beliefs about who should be helped and how best to help them. Using roll call votes in the 95th Congress (1977–78), Page et al. (1984) found that political party explained 28 percent of the variance in social welfare votes (compared with 20 percent on racial issues, 28 percent on law and order, 8 percent on women's rights, and 8 percent on abortion). They suggested that shared ideology is a more plausible explanation of the relationship between party and social welfare voting than is party discipline, given the decentralized structure of Congress and the wave of "political individualism" that began to surge through Congress in the late 1960s.

Similar to the predictions for the public, a political predispositions model of congressional support for social welfare would be accepted if Democratic members of Congress are more supportive of social welfare programs in general than Republican Congress members.

The four preceding explanations are not mutually exclusive. We hope to demonstrate how each makes its own unique contribution to our understanding of support for social welfare and how attitudes and group affiliations interact with one another to influence support of policy. Furthermore, we remain open to the possibility that one rationale might prove more useful in understanding support for one type of program, while a different explanation might work better with other programs.

One goal of this book is to probe the legitimacy of the theories. Thus, we intend to make some estimate of the roles these explanatory theories of support play in accounting for the levels and patterns of support actually found among Congress and the public. Although each is distinct, it is altogether likely that no single theory can explain support and that the best explanation is comprised of several together.

3

Public and Congressional Support for the Social Welfare System: A Description

When social historians and social scientists write about the social welfare beliefs of the public and the U.S. Congress, they use sources that often provide only a narrow view of attitudes (e.g., Patterson 1981). For example, to gauge public support for existing social welfare programs, authors frequently rely upon responses to simple, undemanding questions about support for "welfare" in general. Likewise, for members of Congress, political commentators and social scientists reach conclusions about support based upon voting records for select pieces of legislation. Both these methods have problems.

As we discussed in chapter 1, the problem with questions about support for "welfare" is that the referent of this term is unclear; it has a multiplicity of meanings. To some it denotes AFDC, to others Medicaid, and to yet others the many programs of the welfare state as a whole. The fact is that there is no program called "welfare," and the meaning of the term varies with the individual respondent and with the context in which the question is asked. For many, the term *welfare* has come to have negative connotations, conjuring up images of cheaters, people who get "something for nothing" and abuse government largesse (Popkin 1985). Because of the lack of specificity, it is difficult to draw conclusions concerning support for the many programs within the social welfare system. To understand the extent to which members of the public support the American welfare state, we must ask them about their support for particular programs rather than relying on ambiguous terms intended to measure support for the system as a whole.

There are at least three different perspectives on public support in the scholarly literature. One holds that the public is not supportive of any tax-financed social welfare program (e.g., Katz 1986); the second contends that the public is supportive of social insurance programs but not public assistance programs (Skocpol 1990); and the third maintains that support exists for all types of programs that target the elderly, but not programs aimed toward other groups (Preston 1984). The nature of past research prevents us from concluding which of these three views is most correct because little prior research has been comparative, i.e., asking respondents about a range of programs in the context of one interview. The data presented in this chapter will address support for the welfare state by probing how members of the public differentiate among programs in their support decisions. If we find that they do differentiate, we can observe which programs are supported more than others and test which of the three perspectives on support seems to fit the data best. Such an examination is the first purpose of this chapter.

When political commentators discuss what members of Congress think about social welfare programs, they cannot turn to survey data because pollsters rarely attempt to quantify the personal views of Congress members. Instead, researchers gain their greatest understanding of Congress through analyses of voting decisions. Voting behavior offers at best a shaky guide to preferences for social welfare programs. Because most bills voted on by Congress contain numerous components and subcomponents, it is difficult to know exactly what a negative vote means with respect to any single potential welfare provision. Voting decisions cannot give the entire picture. To understand the supportiveness of legislators toward various social welfare programs requires asking about each directly; only then can we see highs and lows in support for major social welfare programs. A second purpose of this chapter, then, is to examine congressional support by summarizing what we discovered from our interviews with members of the U.S. House of Representatives.

As a group, members of the U.S. House of Representatives play a crucial role in shaping the direction of social welfare policy. Thus, their views are important to understand. Since they are elected as agents of the general public, it is also important to compare the views of members of Congress to those of the larger public. Research on the relationship between public opinion and congressional decision making presents mixed findings. Some studies observe public opinion affecting voting behavior (Burnstein and Freudenburg 1978), others show congruence between changes in the beliefs of the two groups (Rochefort 1986), and still others have suggested that the public has no consistent belief system (Converse 1964), thus implying that there is no need to look for a relationship with congressional beliefs. As a third goal, this chapter explores the similarities and differences in opinions between the general public and Congress. To this end—and unlike in other studies of Congress and the public—both samples were asked some identical questions about their support for social welfare groups and programs.

The analyses we present in this chapter will help clarify whether there is indeed a crisis in support of the current American welfare state. Do most members of the public and of Congress want cuts in programs? Is the public willing or unwilling to make behavioral commitments to support the programs by contacting their representatives in Congress or by expressing a commitment to pay higher taxes to prevents cuts? Do representatives consistently fail to vote for measures designed to maintain or increase the social welfare state? A crisis might be inferred if any of the preceding proves true and certainly if all of them prove true.

The Public's Views

We interviewed a random nationwide sample of 1,209 residents of the United States during the fall of 1986 (for details on the sample and sampling design, see appendix A). In a telephone interview averaging forty-five minutes, members of the public answered an in-depth series of questions on social welfare policies and programs. (For the questionnaire, see appendix B.)

We use several measures to assess respondents' levels of support. The first set of questions asks whether benefits for each of seven specific social welfare programs should be increased, decreased, or maintained at their current levels, keeping up with inflation. These questions are intended to measure general preferences. The second set of questions are designed to measure the depth of commitment behind these preferences; thus, these questions explore the individual's behavioral intentions. That is, they ask how willing respondents are to back up their preferences with actions such as paying higher taxes and writing letters to their congressional representatives. Although ideally we would prefer to observe actual behavior, we must settle for verbal commitments because of the difficulties in observing such behaviors. Fortunately, research suggests that questions demanding a behavioral commitment provide a reasonable prediction of future behavior (Kothandapani 1971; Fishbein and Ajzen 1975:373–374). The third series of support questions examines which target groups the public most prefers to help through a variety of tax-based social services. Thus, the first two sets of questions ask about social welfare programs, while the third focuses on targeting groups for social welfare services.

Public Preferences

Unlike previous studies that have asked only about spending for "welfare," we asked about support for seven of the major social welfare programs—Social Security, Medicare, Unemployment Insurance, Aid to Families with Dependent Children (AFDC), Supplemental Security Income (SSI), Food Stamps, and Medicaid. These programs are different in several ways. Three are social insurance programs that base distributive criteria on employment history and contributions (Social Security, Medicare, and Unemployment Insurance), and four are public assistance programs that base distributive criteria on a test of recipients needs and financial means (AFDC, Medicaid, SSI, and Food Stamps). Whereas some programs target mainly the elderly (Social Security, Medicare, and SSI), others target mainly nonelderly adults and their children (AFDC, Medicaid, and Food Stamps). Some provide cash benefits (Social Security, SSI, AFDC, and Unemployment Insurance), others in-kind services. The public's responses to questions about benefit levels in these seven programs can therefore provide general information about the extent to which differences in public preferences exist for the various major programs constituting the

American welfare state and whether these differences seem to be related to the nature of the progams themselves, i.e., social insurance versus public assistance and targeting the elderly versus younger age groups.

Table 3.1 presents the public's responses to the questions regarding whether benefits for each of the seven programs should be increased, decreased, or maintained at their current levels adjusted for inflation. The most striking result is how few respondents believe benefits should be decreased for any of the programs; in fact, for no program does a majority of respondents favor decreases. With the exception of Food Stamps, fewer than 20 percent ever prefer decreases and for some programs those favoring decreases do not even comprise 10 percent of the respondents.

Food Stamps, a program often depicted by the media as laden with fraud and abuse, is clearly the loser when considering public support. About one in every four respondents want to see Food Stamps cut back. AFDC and Unemployment Insurance run a distant second with roughly one in six favoring benefit reductions.

Table 3.1

Public Support for Increasing, Maintaining, or Decreasing Benefits
for Seven Social Welfare Programs

| | Percent of respondents saying programs should be: | | | |
	Increased	Maintained	Decreased	Mean Support Score[a]
Medicare (N = 1198)	67.6	29.9	2.5	2.65
Supplemental Security Income (N = 1167)	57.3	40.0	2.7	2.55
Social Security (N = 1200)[b]	56.7	40.0	3.3	2.53
Medicaid (N = 1170)	47.1	46.3	6.6	2.40
Unemployment Insurance (N = 1155)	31.5	55.5	13.0	2.18
Aid to Families with Dependent Children (N = 1170)	32.6	51.9	15.5	2.17
Food Stamps (N = 1132)	24.6	51.0	24.4	2.00

[a]The mean scores based on a 3-point scale ranging from 3 (increase) to 1 (decrease). Standard deviations range from 0.44 to 0.72.

[b]Mean support for Social Security is comparable to that for the Supplemental Security Income [Paired $T(1152) = -0.33$, n.s.] but significantly lower than the mean support for Medicare [Paired $T(1155) = 5.83$, $p < .001$], Unemployment Insurance [Paired $T(1137) = 16.08$, $p < .001$], AFDC [Paired $T(1150) = 15.94$, $p < .001$], and Food Stamps [Paired $T(1115) = 22.09$, $p < .001$].

Significantly smaller proportions of respondents favor cuts in the other programs: only about 3 percent support reductions in Social Security, SSI, and Medicare. For each of these, a majority favor increases.

The picture painted by these data is hardly what one would have expected given the so-called crisis rhetoric of the 1980s, when opponents of social welfare argued to the federal administration that social welfare programs had lost their legitimacy in the eyes of the public. Our respondents show little desire for cuts. Instead, we find small minorities wanting cuts, and, in most cases, majorities favoring increases. Indeed, table 3.1 shows that at least 75 percent of the public want benefits for each of the seven programs to be either maintained at their current levels or increased. For Social Security, Medicare, and SSI, the proportions expressing such support are even higher, at a level between 96 and 97 percent.

Program Support as Behavioral Commitments

That most of the public does not want decreases in the seven principal social welfare programs is important in and of itself, but knowing the strength of the commitment behind those preferences is even more important. Members of the public who say they want program benefits maintained or increased but are not willing to act on their preferences are not likely to have a significant impact upon policy-making. Ideally, according to democratic theory, congressional representatives should pay attention to everyone's preferences, but policymakers are not apt to act upon support unless it is committed and active, especially in times of fiscal constraint. Therefore, it is important to know the extent to which the public is willing to stand behind its preferences with active commitment. There are, of course, any number of ways that citizens can demonstrate their support. They can vote for those candidates promoting a pro-welfare platform and they can march in protest of cutbacks, but perhaps most significantly, they can write letters to their representatives and commit themselves to paying higher taxes to support programs financially.

To understand the degree of commitment behind statements of support, we asked a series of in-depth questions about actions that respondents would be willing to take to demonstrate support. Since the questions took a good deal of time to answer in our telephone interview, we could not ask in detail about all seven programs. Therefore, we chose to focus our attention on three: AFDC, Medicaid, and Social Security. We selected these three programs because they represent the diversity in types of social welfare programs. One is an in-cash public assistance program (AFDC), another is an in-cash social insurance program (Social Security), and the third is an in-kind public assistance program (Medicaid). Furthermore, although we did not know it when designing the survey, these programs represent different levels of support as defined by preferences of increases or decreases in benefit levels. Social Security enjoys high levels of support, Medicaid receives moderate support, and AFDC is one of the least preferred programs. Thus, using these three programs achieves a wide range of types of social welfare programs as well as the full scope of public preferences.

To assess behavioral support, we asked a series of questions, each demanding a greater commitment from the respondents. Respondents first answered a question about how satisfied they are that a portion of their tax dollars goes to support the given program. We asked those who are satisfied how opposed they would be to cuts in the program, and if they are opposed, whether they would sign a petition or write their representatives in Congress to express their opposition. Further, we asked them whether they would be willing to pay higher taxes to prevent such cuts. To those who state they are not satisfied that their tax dollars are going to finance a given program, we asked how opposed they would be to program expansion. If opposed, we asked whether they would be willing to write their representatives in Congress to express their opposition and by how much they would like the financing of the program to be cut. (See appendix B for exact wording of the questionnaire.)

Given all the discussion about the crisis of public support for the welfare state, we expected to find only a minority of respondents satisfied that a portion of their tax dollars funds social welfare programs, especially the public assistance programs, and even fewer willing to go beyond attitudinal support with actions. As our data show (table 3.2), however, we were wrong in our predictions. Over two-thirds of the respondents report satisfaction that taxes help fund these social programs. Social Security receives the largest proportion of supporters (81 percent), and Medicaid the next largest (78 percent). What was unforeseen are the 65 percent satisfied

Table 3.2

Percentage of Respondents Willing to Perform Actions as Proportion
of Total Sample and as Proportion of Satisfied and
Dissatisfied Respondents

Satisfied	AFDC		Medicaid		Social Security	
	% of total	% of satis.	% of total	% of satis.	% of total	% of satis.
Satisfied with paying taxes for program	64.5	100.0	78.4	100.0	81.4	100.0
Opposing spending cuts	50.8	77.6	63.4	80.8	73.1	89.8
Willing to write a letter or sign a petition against spending cuts	35.4	54.8	49.2	62.7	62.8	77.3
Willing to pay more taxes to avoid cuts	36.2	56.1	47.5	60.6	58.0	71.2
Dissatisfied	% of total	% of dissat.	% of total	% of dissat.	% of total	% of dissat.
Dissatisfied with paying taxes for program	33.6	100.0	21.6	100.0	18.6	100.0
Opposing spending increases	24.9	74.4	13.2	66.0	10.9	60.6
Willing to write a letter or sign a petition against spending increases	19.0	56.7	9.1	45.4	7.9	43.8
Willing to decrease taxes spent on program	15.0	44.7	9.3	46.4	4.8	26.9

with paying taxes for AFDC since this program has long been a
"punching bag" among welfare opponents. The results suggest
that a majority of the public believe their tax dollars should finance
AFDC.

When the questions require behavioral commitments, levels of
support decrease dramatically and especially among the programs
that originally receive lower support. While roughly two-thirds of
the respondents are willing to write a letter or sign a petition
protesting cuts in Social Security benefits, and about half are willing to take such action for Medicaid, only a third report being
willing to do so for AFDC. Similarly, three in five respondents say
they are willing to have their taxes raised to avoid cuts in Social

Security benefits, but only one in three say they would pay higher taxes to avoid cuts in AFDC.

There is another way that we can think about support using these data. We can ask: Are supporters equally committed behaviorally, regardless of the program in question? That is, given that respondents are satisfied to pay taxes to finance a given program, are those who are satisfied to finance one program, say, AFDC, just as committed to write letters and pay higher taxes as those who are satisfied to finance another program, say, Social Security? Examining the data in the second column under each program, we see that the answer is no. Among those satisfied with Social Security taxes, 77 percent report they would write letters opposing cuts and 71 percent report they would pay higher taxes. For Medicaid, these proportions are 63 percent and 61 percent, respectively. But for AFDC, the least supported program on earlier questions, the percentages expressing behavioral support are considerably lower; 55 percent would write letters and 56 percent would pay more taxes (roughly 75 percent as high as for Social Security). Despite the program differences, it is important to note that more than half of the supporters of AFDC say they are willing to back up their general beliefs with specific actions.

While the preceding focuses specifically on program supporters and their willingness to perform actions when faced with cutbacks, equally important to understand is the strength of opposition to programs. Are those dissatisfied with AFDC, Medicaid, or Social Security just as willing to act to prevent program growth as proponents are to stop cutbacks? Just as with program support, we find that opposition decreases if respondents are asked about their willingness to make active commitments that are more demanding. That is, fewer opponents are willing to demand tax decreases and write letters. The level of behaviorally committed dissatisfaction is greater for AFDC than for Social Security. Nearly 45 percent of those dissatisfied with AFDC would like taxes reduced and 57 percent would write letters, but only 27 percent of those against Social Security support tax decreases and 44 percent would write. The differences between AFDC and Medicaid are interesting. Although fewer opponents of Medicaid would write letters as compared with AFDC opponents (45 percent versus 57 percent), the percentages favoring tax cuts are equal between the two programs

(46 percent for Medicaid and 45 percent for AFDC). Thus, the level of dissatisfaction to the point of action is roughly similar between AFDC and Medicaid, but far lower for Social Security.

The picture that emerges is that Social Security supporters are not only more numerous but also more committed than supporters of the other two programs. Conversely, Social Security opponents are fewer and less committed than adversaries of AFDC and Medicaid. Thus, Social Security seems doubly blessed—it has both supporters who are more actively committed and opponents who are less active. AFDC, on the other hand, is doubly cursed with less active supporters and more active opponents. Support for Medicaid falls between that of Social Security and Medicaid.

Support for social welfare programs is not a simple construct. In policy debates it is often not the number of supporters that counts but the degree of commitment. The same is presumably true for opponents: a few active opponents can have a greater impact than many passive supporters. To delineate the differences in active commitment among supporters and opponents, we define active supporters and opponents as those who are willing to write letters and to pay higher taxes to protest cuts or expansions within the program. Partial supporters and opponents are those who are willing either to write letters or to pay higher taxes but not both. Passive supporters and opponents are those who are not willing to write letters or pay higher taxes.

Figure 3.1 shows the findings for each program. Since there are far more supporters than opponents for all three programs, the trend line for supporters is higher on each graph. Equally important, however, is the fact that supporters and opponents are dissimilar across the three programs. For AFDC, proponents are only slightly more likely to be active as to be passive or partial supporters. But for the other two programs, proponents are far more likely to be active than are opponents, especially for Social Security where two-thirds of the supporters are active. The supporters of Social Security are clearly more committed than those of Medicaid who are in turn more committed than the supporters of AFDC. While only 30 percent of respondents are active AFDC supporters, 43 percent are active Medicaid supporters, and 56 percent are active on behalf of Social Security . Only a minority of respondents are active or partial opponents, and opponents are much more

Figure 3.1
Differences in Behavioral Commitment between
Supporters and Opponents

Social Security

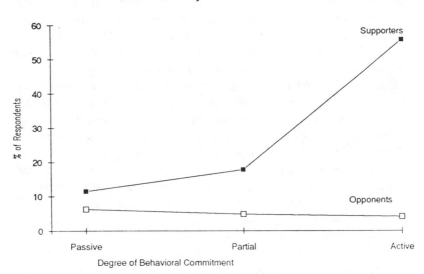

Degree of Behavioral Commitment

Medicaid

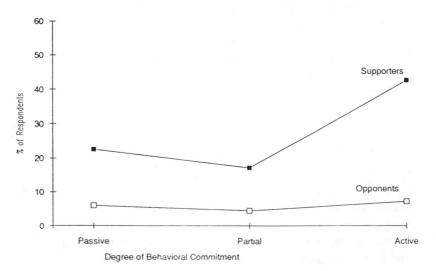

Degree of Behavioral Commitment

AFDC

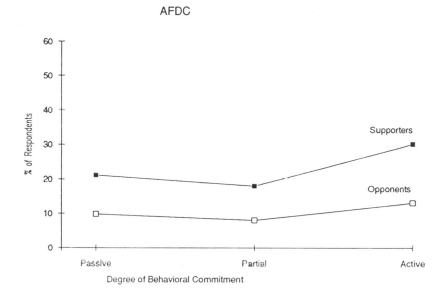

likely to be working actively against AFDC than against Social
Security or Medicaid. Less than one in ten respondents are active
or partial opponents of Social Security, while more than one in five
are active or partial opponents of AFDC.

Finally, there is one more point worth making with these data.
Some social researchers suggest that the opinions of the public are
inconsistent and incoherent, even to the extent that they vary
randomly within the context of a single questionnaire (Converse
1964). On the contrary, our data show that members of the public
are consistent in their support preferences and that their responses
in one part of the questionnaire quite accurately predict their responses in a later part. For example, there is a strong relationship
between respondents' answers to the question about increasing,
maintaining, or decreasing benefits for a particular program and
their willingness to perform actions to defend the program ($r = .45$
for AFDC, $r = .34$ for Medicaid, and $r = .26$ for Social Security).
More specifically, the majority of respondents who believe benefits
should be increased early in the interview say they are willing to
pay higher taxes to finance the program later in the interview (52
percent for AFDC, 63 percent for Medicaid, and 66 percent for
Social Security). Only a very tiny minority of respondents are so

inconsistent that they want increased benefits for a program but later say they want their taxes decreased (6 percent for AFDC, 3 percent for Medicaid, and 4 percent for Social Security).

In the beginning of this chapter we said that a crisis in support for social welfare might be said to exist 1) if most members of the public and Congress want cuts in programs, 2) if the public is not willing to make active commitments to support programs through either contacting their congressional representatives or paying higher taxes to prevent cuts, or 3) if representatives consistently fail to vote for measures designed to maintain or increase the social welfare state. We can now address the first two conditions. Clearly, we see that most members of the public do not want cuts in any of the major social welfare programs. The vast majority of the public believe programs should be maintained or expanded. In addition, roughly half the public is willing to make commitments to support Medicaid, and a majority is willing to make such commitments to support Social Security. AFDC, however, receives much less actively committed support.

Thus, if a crisis of support can be said to exist, it is specific to a reported willingness to take political action, and then only with respect to AFDC rather than the two other programs we examined in depth. This hardly suggests a lack of public support for the American welfare state in general. Almost two-thirds of the public appear inclined to support AFDC when the question posed has to do with their preferences and does not imply behavioral obligations, but only a third are willing to stand behind their beliefs with actions. Thus, citizens are not likely to communicate their displeasure to Congress if AFDC were to be threatened with cuts, nor are many people willing to pay higher taxes to prevent cutting the AFDC program. There is cause for concern on the part of program proponents to the extent that it is vigorous active commitment that captures the attention and responsiveness of the executive and legislative branches of government (Keefe 1984).

Support for Groups to Receive Services

So far our discussion has focused on public support for specific social welfare *programs*. Of equal importance is understanding which *groups* the public would most like to see helped with tax dollars.

Thus, rather than exploring support for individual programs, we turn now to examining support for potential recipients.

In the social welfare arena, decisions must be made not only about particular social welfare programs but also about who should be helped through a range of social services. An example of this can be seen in the history of Medicaid. Intended from its inception in the Great Society programs of the 1960s as a program to assist those unable to afford health care—including the working poor without employment-sponsored benefits—current program recipients are in fact largely nonworking families and the elderly, not the uninsured working poor (Levitan 1990). However, rising health care costs are forcing Congress to reconsider the merits of Medicaid for the working poor. Social welfare programs address various kinds of needs, including health, financial, nutritional, and educational needs, and knowing for whom the public wishes to address these needs is just as important as understanding support for major social welfare programs.

Given the preferences for social welfare programs that we have already seen in which Social Security, Medicare, and SSI enjoy higher rankings than other programs, one might speculate that the public prefers helping the elderly above other groups. On the other hand, support for these programs may have less to do with helping the elderly per se than with the particular match of the perceived needs of the elderly to services in question. We address the linkage between groups to be helped and the preferred means of assistance by presenting respondents with service areas and beneficiary groups. Are members of the public more supportive of one particular group— for example, the elderly—regardless of the service in question? Or do they differentiate in their priorities of who to help through specific services? Specifically, we asked respondents which groups they would help with additional financial assistance, food assistance, educational programs, and catastrophic health insurance. For each of these four service areas, respondents assigned priority rankings to particular target groups.

First, we will explore the public's preferences for which groups should receive additional financial assistance. Because money is the resource to be distributed, all the possible recipient groups were defined as being poor, but they differed as to whether they were children, elderly, or nonelderly adults. Thus, respondents were asked to evaluate six groups for financial assistance: poor elderly

who are either disabled or not, poor adults who are either disabled
or not (included in the nondisabled group are unemployed men
and female heads of household), and poor children.

Table 3.3 presents the mean rankings and the rank ordering of
public preferences for helping these groups through monetary assistance. Of the six recipient groups, respondents give physically
disabled elderly who are poor the highest average ranking. Over
half of the respondents (53.1 percent) choose poor physically disabled elderly as the most important group to help. The poor elderly
achieve the second highest mean ranking, and it is also the group
receiving the highest percentage of second place priority scores
(29.8 percent). Close behind poor elderly in preferences are poor
children. Although 22.3 percent of the respondents give this group
highest priority, it is chosen less often as a second or third priority,
thus attaining its third place rank. The remaining three target
groups—poor disabled adults, poor female-headed households, and
poor unemployed men—are less likely to be favored for monetary
assistance. The public expresses very little interest in helping poor
able-bodied men of working age who are unemployed, and in fact

Table 3.3

The Public's Mean Ranking of Targeted Groups for
Specific Services

	Financial assistance[a]		Food programs[a]		Education-type programs[a]		Catastrophic health ins.[b]
	Rank	Mean	Rank	Mean	Rank	Mean	% first choice
Disabled elderly[c]	1	1.84	1	2.44	4	3.75	—
Poor elderly	2	2.86	2	3.33	6	3.97	—
Elderly in general	–	—	–	—	–	—	36.6
Disabled children	–	—	4	3.89	1	2.81	—
Poor children	3	3.11	3	3.53	5	3.79	—
Children in general	–	—	7	5.82	–	—	46.4
Disabled adults	4	3.41	5	3.93	2	3.25	—
Poor adults	–	—	6	5.03	3	3.41	—
Poor fem. heads	5	4.15	–	—	–	—	—
Poor unempl. men	6	5.52	–	—	–	—	—
Adults in general	–	—	–	—	–	—	13.9

NOTE: Blanks indicate that the group was not given as an option.
[a] Dependent t-tests show that the mean ranks are each different from the others at the $p < .05$
level.
[b] Rankings are not provided because the categories are not mutually exclusive. Instead, numbers
given represent the percent of respondents giving the group first choice.
[c] For financial assistance programs all groups, including the disabled, were given as poor.

less than 6 percent of the respondents place this group within their top three priorities.

Thus, the first picture we see from the ranking of groups for services shows the public targeting the elderly (both the poor and the disabled) for governmental assistance. The public also appears to be expressing a low priority for helping able-bodied individuals (both men and women) through the provision of financial resources.

Although people can survive without adequate financial resources, no one can live long without food. Although there is much controversy surrounding government provision of general financial assistance through monthly checks, far fewer debates arise in the United States about food relief, as long as it is given as actual food rather than as coupons to buy food. We asked respondents whom they would like to see helped through various food and nutrition programs. Each program presented to respondents was tailored to the particular needs of the group under consideration. Thus, assistance for children (poor and disabled children as well as children in general) was linked to the school lunch program; aid for disabled elderly and disabled adults was linked to Meals on Wheels; and relief for the poor elderly and poor adults was linked to the distribution of basic food staples.

Two pieces of information about current food services may be relevant here. The school lunch program, as it is currently constituted, allows schools to offer low-cost meals to all children. Further, it allows even greater price reductions for low-income children and free meals for the very poor. Although its intention is to help the poor, in order to be financially viable it must subsidize all school cafeteria food. Were nonpoor children required to pay the much higher true price of a hot meal, few would do so, and many schools would not be able to support a kitchen and staff. Thus, only by cooking in large quantities is the school lunch program economically feasible. Second, the Meals on Wheels program is designed to bring warm meals to homebound adults who are either temporarily or permanently disabled and have no one else to cook for them. Funding for the program covers the food supplies and kitchen staff, but much of the delivery is performed by volunteers whose labor allows the benefits to continue with limited public expenditures. However, it is unlikely that the majority of the general population knows either that the school lunch program subsidizes meals for middle-income children as well or that Meals on Wheels depends upon volunteer assistance.

Returning to the question of support for recipients of food assistance programs, we see once again that the elderly receive top priority (table 3.3). We also find that, as with additional financial assistance, the disabled elderly enjoy the highest favor of all with 40 percent of the respondents giving this group first priority. Similarly, the poor elderly are ranked second overall and poor children third. Despite the fact that school lunch programs do indeed help all children, few members of the public suggest that the program should target every child: only 14 percent rank this within the top three categories. Once again nonelderly adults remain at the bottom of the list. The public appears adamant about not helping able-bodied working-age adults, with only 1.9 percent suggesting the group should be targeted first.

A shift occurs in priorities for education programs. Each of the education programs presented to the respondents addressed seemingly immediate needs of the target group. The programs for the elderly (both the poor and the disabled) focused on their need for increased information about the services available to them and for referral services to assist them in applying for other social welfare benefits. For working-age adults, the education question referred to job training programs, including rehabilitation services for the physically disabled. Because poor children often come from academically deprived backgrounds, special preschool programs, such as Head Start, are seen as ways of helping them perform similarly to their more advantaged peers. Thus, the assistance for poor children took the form of preschool educational programs. For physically disabled children it took the form of special education programs. These six education-type programs describe what is currently available in our social welfare system for the groups under consideration.

Unlike their responses to questions about financial and food assistance, members of the public are much more willing to support working-age adults and disabled (rather than poor) children when they rank who should be helped through education-type programs. They give top priority to helping physically disabled children, and second and third priority to physically disabled and poor adults (see table 3.3). The poor elderly, who had enjoyed second place for monetary and nutritional services, drop to sixth when educational benefits are the service in question. Clearly, members of the public do not see the elderly as appropriate recipients of education services. Instead, they believe that nonelderly adults should be helped through improved educational opportunities, bringing them closer to employment.

What we see from these three examples is that the public does not have a stereotypical mindset that leads to the same target groups consistently deserving more help or less. The fourth scenario we presented to respondents, touching upon health issues, was a bit more complicated than the others. We asked questions about coverage against catastrophic illness in a slightly different way: respondents had only to give their top three priority groups rather than rank order all of them, and we gave respondents the option to be specific about a target group (e.g., poor elderly, disabled elderly) or to choose an entire age group (e.g., the elderly in general). This way of posing the question made it similar to what policymakers were actually considering at the time but created difficulties when we tried to compare the results with those from previous scenarios. For example, if a respondent chooses "children in general" as top priority, it is unlikely that a second or third choice would be "poor children" or "disabled children" since that would already be assumed. For this reason, we cannot make one-to-one comparisons between the preferences for catastrophic health insurance and financial, nutritional, and educational assistance.

Although the interview allowed respondents to be specific in their target group preferences, they actually tend to prefer targeting general rather than specific groups for catastrophic health insurance. They favor the elderly and children, regardless of the physical or financial situation, as principal targets for the insurance program. Thus, table 3.3 combines all responses concerning children, whether poor or physically disabled, into the "children in general" category. When we do this, we find that children receive top priority more often than the elderly. The highest percentage of respondents rank children first (46.4 percent), and fewer give the elderly top billing (36.6 percent). Only 13.9 percent select nonelderly adults as the most important target group. Furthermore, although not asked directly, 2.5 percent of the respondents volunteer that the new program should be universal. It appears, therefore, that when forced to rank groups to receive catastrophic health insurance, the public prefers helping children slightly more than assisting the elderly. As with the other services discussed thus far, we will address reasons for the prioritizations in chapters 4 and 5.

So far we have focused on public preferences for helping different age groups, and we have seen that the age of group members does not appear to determine its priority. That is, the public does not seem to automatically favor one age group over another, but instead it differentiates by the kind of service in question. Looking at the rankings across all services, we also note differences in preferences relating to poverty or physical disability. In general, respondents tend to favor helping the physically disabled more than the poor, regardless of the age of the potential recipients. Thus, the disabled elderly receive greater support than the poor elderly, and disabled adults achieve greater favor than poor adults. The trend is the same for children with one exception: poor children are seen as more in need of food assistance than physically disabled children.

Though respondents hold general preferences for some welfare groups over others across the services we sampled, they are discriminating in their preferences. A group that they rank high for one service—for instance, food assistance—may not be the same group receiving priority for another service—for example, education. Indeed, while respondents prefer the elderly for food services, they rank nonelderly adults higher for education assistance. The American public appears, therefore, not only to be supportive of social welfare programs and to be willing, for the most part, to back its beliefs with actions, but also to hold clear yet complex beliefs about who should be helped and which types of services are best suited to help that group.

Congressional Views

Fifty-eight members of the U.S. House of Representatives answered in-depth questions about social welfare policies and programs in personal interviews conducted in Washington, D.C. during the spring and summer of 1986 (see appendix A for the sampling design). As with the general public, we asked members of the House their views about the seven major social welfare programs—the social insurance programs of Social Security, Unemployment Insurance, and Medicare, and the public assistance programs of Medicaid, SSI, AFDC, and Food Stamps. The first series of questions posed to representatives were exactly the same as those given members of the public; for each of the seven programs, we asked whether benefits should be increased, decreased, or maintained with adjustments for inflation. We also asked the exact same questions concerning which groups should be helped through additional financial assistance, food assistance, education-type programs, and catastrophic health insurance. We did not ask representatives the same action-oriented support questions as to their willingness to pay higher taxes and sign petitions or write to their respresentatives. Instead, to gauge the extent of representatives' commitment, we examined their voting record in the social welfare domain. (A copy of the congressional questionnaire is included in appendix C.)

The first column of table 3.4 reports the responses to the set of questions about benefit levels for each of the seven programs. If we define support as wanting to maintain or increase benefits for the major programs, a tremendous amount of support exists among members of Congress. At least three-fourths say they believe benefits should be maintained or increased for each program.

Separating supportive representatives into those who want to maintain and those who want to increase benefits, we see that for no program does a majority favor increasing benefits. Medicaid—a means-tested health program for the poor—receives the highest percentage of advocates for increases (42 percent). Medicare, a program primarily helping the elderly meet health care costs, follows close behind with 32 percent favoring increases. A startling 33 percent of the representatives want to increase existing benefits for AFDC. Thus, while most representatives prefer the status quo (i.e., "maintain benefits"), a sizable minority of members of the House of Representatives would like to see Medicaid, AFDC, and Medicare benefits increased beyond their current levels.

Although no representative favors decreasing Social Security, neither do many elect to increase benefits. The overwhelming feeling appears to be that Social Security benefits are adequate at their current level and need not be changed. A similar belief holds with regard to Unemployment Insurance except that, although the large majority prefer maintaining present levels (76.5 percent), just as many desire cuts as increases (11.2 percent versus 12.3 percent, respectively). By far the least preferred among the seven programs is Food Stamps, an in-kind service providing coupons for the purchase of foodstuffs. One quarter of the representatives suggest that benefits should be reduced and only 15.7 percent want increases.

Thus, among members of the U.S. House of Representatives

Table 3.4

Congressional Support for Increasing, Maintaining, or Decreasing
Benefits for Seven Social Welfare Programs

	All Congress[a] percent	Non-leaders percent	Leaders percent
Medicaid			
Increase	41.8	41.2	54.5
Maintain	52.8	52.9	45.5
Decrease	5.4	5.9	—
AFDC			
Increase	32.7	32.4	40.9
Maintain	58.7	58.8	54.5
Decrease	8.2	8.8	—
Means-tested	0.4	—	4.5
Medicare			
Increase	32.4	32.4	36.4
Maintain	55.6	55.9	50.0
Decrease	10.9	11.8	—
Means-tested	1.2	—	13.6
SSI			
Increase	23.8	23.5	31.8
Maintain	68.0	67.6	68.2
Decrease	8.2	8.8	—
Social Security			
Increase	11.7	11.8	13.6
Maintain	85.5	85.3	86.4
Decrease	—	—	—
Means-tested	2.7	2.9	—
Unemploy. Comp.			
Increase	12.3	11.8	22.7
Maintain	76.5	76.5	72.7
Decrease	11.2	11.8	4.5
Food Stamps			
Increase	15.7	14.7	31.8
Maintain	59.4	58.8	63.6
Decrease	24.9	26.5	4.5

[a]Weighted sample (see Appendix A).

we see far greater support for Medicare, Medicaid, and AFDC than
for Food Stamps and Unemployment Insurance, and we see a
desire for the status quo with respect to Social Security.

Votes and Support for Social Welfare

An important measure of representatives' support for the welfare
state is their votes on legislation pertaining to social welfare. In this

regard, we ask two questions: What do the votes of representatives reveal about their support for the welfare state? Are members of Congress who say they support social welfare programs in our interviews also more likely to vote in favor of social welfare legislation?

Our measures of representatives' voting behavior use ratings computed by two organizations—the Children's Defense Fund and the National Council of Senior Citizens. Each year the Children's Defense Fund (CDF) compiles records on ten key votes affecting low-income children, adolescents, and families cast by representatives and senators. Similarly, the National Council of Senior Citizens (NCSC) compiles records of ten votes most important to the lives and well-being of the elderly. In 1986 the Children's Defense Fund recorded ten votes on legislation related directly to the welfare of low-income children and families, such as Head Start reauthorization, as well as related indirectly, such as the Gramm-Rudman spending provisions and the Tax Reform Act. The National Council on Senior Citizens (NCSC) recorded ten votes on legislation that affected low-income elderly directly, such as catastrophic health insurance, and indirectly, such as an act to cut the budget for the Legal Services Corporation, which funds legal assistance programs for senior citizens. These two measures of voting behavior each range from 0 (voting against every issue important to the group) to 10 (voting for every issue critical to the social welfare of the group).

At one extreme, 5 percent of the representatives in our sample voted for none of the legislation to benefit children and families and 11 percent voted for none of the legislation to benefit the elderly. At the other extreme, 9 percent of the representatives voted for every issue critical to children and families, and 12 percent voted for every issue critical to the elderly. The mean number of pro-welfare votes is 6.1 for children and families and 6.2 for the elderly (the median numbers are 8 and 7.8, respectively). Only one-third of the representatives we interviewed did not support at least half of the votes on either measure. We interpret these findings as meaning that, over all, representatives are more likely than not to vote in favor of the welfare of children, families, and the elderly, at least as defined by CDF and NCSC. Yet clearly there are a range of voting patterns, and some representatives are very supportive while others are not.

We now turn to address the second question posed above—

whether those who self-report support for the seven major programs of the welfare state are also those who are more likely to vote on issues critical to the welfare of children, families, and the elderly. To answer this question, we developed two scales of program support from representatives' answers to the questions about whether they favored increasing, maintaining, or decreasing benefits for the seven social welfare programs. One measure pertains to support for low-income children and families and combines support scores for AFDC, Medicaid, and Food Stamps. The second deals with support for the elderly and combines support scores for Medicare, Social Security, and SSI. We correlate the first to voting records compiled by CDF and the second to voting records compiled by NCSC in order to examine the strength of the relationship between the support that representatives self-reported and the support that they demonstrate through their votes.

There is a strong relationship between the level of support that representatives express for programs targeted at children and families and the votes they actually cast for legislation affecting low-income children and families (r = .47). For example, looking specifically at AFDC, we find that those representative who favor increases in benefits have a CDF voting rating of 6.7, while those who favor decreases have a voting rating of 3.7.

A similarly strong relationship exists between the level of support that representatives express for programs targeted mainly at elderly persons and the votes they cast for legislation affecting the elderly (r = .52). For example, those representatives who favor increases in benefits for Medicare have a NCSC voting rating of 8.2, whereas those who favor decreases have a voting rating of 3.1. Thus, members of Congress are relatively supportive of social welfare in their attitudes as well as in their voting behavior, and these results show that their reported beliefs about social welfare programs are consistent with their actions.

Support for Groups to Receive Services

Policy-making is, at its core, a matter of making difficult decisions. In the social welfare domain, policymakers are often faced with tough choices about who to help and how best to help them. In American social policy, this process often entails categorizing and setting priorities among needy groups. Just as discovering Congress

Table 3.5

Congressional Rankings of Targeted Groups for Specific Services[a]

	Financial assistance		Food programs		Education-type programs		Catastrophic health ins.[b]
	Rank	Mean	Rank	Mean	Rank	Mean	% First
Poor children[c]	1	2.73	1	1.82	1	2.66	—
Disabled children	–	—	5	$4.31_{1,2}$	2	2.89	—
Children in general	–	—	7	$5.98_{1,2,3,4,5,6}$	–	—	25.9
Poor elderly	4	$4.39_{1,2}$	4	$4.26_{1,2}$	5	$4.68_{1,2,3,4}$	—
Disabled elderly	2	3.57_1	2	2.73_1	6	$4.71_{1,2,3,4}$	—
Elderly in general	–	—	–	—	–	—	35.4
Poor adults	–	—	6	$5.18_{1,2,3,4,5}$	3	2.92	—
Poor fem. heads	3	4.07_1	–	—	–	—	—
Poor unempl. men	6	$5.61_{1,2,3,4,5}$	–	—	–	—	—
Disabled adults	5	$4.60_{1,2}$	3	$3.85_{1,2}$	4	3.14	—
Adults in general	–	—	–	—	–	—	0.6
All groups equally	–	—	–	—	–	—	31.8

NOTE: Blanks indicate that the group was not given as an option.

[a] Dependent t-tests show whether there are differences between the means. The subscripts indicate the groups with whom comparisons were significant at the $p<.05$ level.

[b] Rankings are not provided because the categories are not mutually exclusive. Instead, numbers given represent the percent of respondents giving the group first choice.

[c] For financial assistance programs all groups, including the disabled, were given as poor.

members' views about specific programs is useful for discerning legislative support, it is also important to understand beliefs about who should be helped through governmental assistance.

Similar to the questions posed to members of the general public, we asked congressional respondents to prioritize target groups for specific services. The mean rankings for the four services are presented in table 3.5. The first type was additional financial assistance for poor children, poor elderly, poor physically disabled elderly, poor female-headed households, poor physically disabled adults under sixty-five, and poor able-bodied men of working age who are unemployed. We also included the categories of poor people in small towns and rural areas, and members of the so-called urban underclass, but Congress members chose not to make such geographic distinctions. In fact, so few Congress members give priority to either group that we had to omit them from further analyses.

By far, the recipient group chosen most often to receive additional financial services is poor children; 55 percent of Congress members elect to help poor children first. The second most favored group is the physically disabled elderly, who receive far fewer first choice rankings (17 percent) than do children, but many second choice rankings. Despite expectations, a slightly larger proportion of respondents want to help female-headed households than poor elderly (11 percent versus 7 percent for first choice). Finally, Congress members are not inclined to offer additional financial assistance to poor physically disabled adults and unemployed men. Only 3 percent suggest disabled adults for top priority and none values helping the unemployed through additional financial assistance. Pinpointing an age- or disability-based trend with regard to financial assistance is difficult. The first choice seems to be poor children, second poor disabled elderly, but poor single mothers rank above the poor elderly.

We next asked Congress members about their recommendations for targeting groups for food services. Here the rank orderings are similar to those for additional monetary help. Highest priority is granted to poor children, and then to the disabled elderly (in this case, however, not necessarily the poor disabled elderly). Disabled adults achieve higher standing than poor elderly, but once again poor adults are near the bottom of the choices. Neither additional monies nor nutritional services appear to be preferred services for able-bodied adults. Instead, Congress members recommend aiding children in both cases.

Poor children remain representatives' preferred beneficiaries when we turn to education-type services. Nearly half (46 percent) of the respondents believe that, if forced to prioritize, they would aid poor children through preschool programs, and an additional 20 percent would target physically disabled children for special education services. Working-age adults are also favored to receive job training services. About 22 percent of the Congress members want to help first and foremost poor adults who otherwise could be working, and 8 percent would target disabled working age individuals. The elderly, whether poor or disabled, are rejected for education-type services.

Finally, when we look at priorities for catastrophic health we see a different pattern of support. A sizable number of Congress members choose not to position any recipient group above another for catastrophic health insurance. Instead, these respondents (31.8 percent) want to see the program initiated as universal and available for all citizens, regardless of age, financial well-being, or disabilities. Those who opt to prioritize, lean toward targeting the elderly (35.4 percent). The survey was conducted during a time when Congress was considering the implementation of a catastrophic health insurance bill. Although the bill had been originally introduced as a universal program, by the time of this survey, it was being spoken of as a program restricted to the elderly. Thus, the congressional respondents may have been responding to their perceptions of the political feasibility of passing the bill. In other words, they saw that the easiest means to winning general congressional acceptance of the program was to target the elderly. In the end the bill failed, but not before the targeted beneficiaries were reduced from all citizens, to all elderly, to only the very poorest among the elderly. (A different version of a catastrophic insurance bill for the elderly passed in 1988 only to be repealed a year later.)

Despite the discussions that were under way at the time in Congress, a substantial proportion of representatives think catastrophic health benefits should be given to children (25.9 percent). When children are not selected as a first choice, they are often selected as the second (30.5 percent). Nonelderly adults receive neither first choice support (0.6 percent) nor second place ranking (1.0 percent). Clearly, those Congress members who think the program should be targeted do not have adults under age sixty-five in mind as the recipients. Finally, it should be mentioned that 6.2 percent of the congressional respondents do not favor any form of government-sponsored catastrophic health insurance and thus refuse to prioritize any target recipient group.

In summary, these data present a Congress that wants to place a high priority on help to America's children. For nearly every social service in question, Congress members give a high position to children when forced to rank the most important recipient group. Furthermore, the poorest children remain the primary targets. The only exception to this relatively consistent finding centers on the controversial catastrophic health insurance package. Congress members are divided in their beliefs: about one-third favor a universal program and one-third would focus on helping the elderly. Only one-quarter advocate using catastrophic health coverage to help children. As we shall demonstrate in the next section, these beliefs are also fairly representative of the beliefs of select congressional leaders.

The Support of Committee Leaders

The experiences of representatives are not all alike, nor are all their responsibilities within the House the same. Every representative serves on a number of committees, subcommittees, and task forces, and each of these groups has specific goals. Some of the 435 members who serve in the U.S. House of Representatives are closely involved with social welfare issues through their committee assignments while others perform their primary legislative duties in other policy arenas. We interviewed twenty-four leaders (chairs and ranking minority members) of the committees and subcommittees that have jurisdiction over social welfare policy issues, including Appropriations, Budget, Ways and Means, Education and Labor, Energy and Commerce, Select Committee on Aging, and Select Committee on Children, Family, and Youth (for the specific subcommittees within these, see appendix A). We also interviewed thirty-four Congress members randomly selected from among the remaining nonleaders. (For greater detail on the sampling scheme, see appendix A.) These two separate samples allow us to compare the opinions of representatives with and without special legislative expertise in the social welfare area.

Congressional committees have traditionally held great power over the shape of legislation (Smith 1989). The charge of each committee is to write and modify legislation through compromise so that any proposals it makes are acceptable, not only to a majority within the committee, but also to the House as a whole. Members of committees relevant to social welfare issues attend hearings, read reports, and spend a greater amount of time with a particular piece of welfare legislation than do their colleagues on different committees. And within the standing committees, the chairs and ranking minority members have the greatest degree of authority over the committee agenda, although much of this power has been curtailed by legislative reforms in the 1970s (Smith 1989; Smith and Deering 1984). The direction a committee takes is in large part determined by the wishes of its leaders, and it is therefore useful to understand the opinions of leaders separate from those of Congress as a whole. Furthermore, among all committee members, leaders tend to be those involved for the longest period of time, and thus those most knowledgeable about the issues. By examining differences in views between leaders and nonleaders on social welfare issues, we can perhaps acquire a clearer understanding of whether leaders' opinions reflect a stronger sense of a welfare crisis.

Leaders' support for social programs. Returning to the results displayed on table 3.4, the two right columns depict the separate beliefs of leaders and nonleaders. Because the majority of representatives are not leaders of committees with social welfare relevance, the responses of the nonleader sample are basically identical to the weighted sample of Congress as a whole, which we have already discussed. However, the support for social welfare given by leaders of relevant committees and subcommittees (i.e., the chairs and ranking minority members) is indeed different from the support found in the House as a whole. The data show a small but clear trend that congressional leaders are more likely to want to increase or maintain benefits when compared with representatives who do not play leading roles on relevant committees. These differences hold for six of the seven programs but not for Social Security. Both groups of representatives seem equally committed to Social Security; approximately the same proportion of leaders as nonleaders support maintaining benefits (86.4 and 85.3 percent, respectively) and increasing them (13.6 percent and 11.8 percent, respectively).

Although leaders tend to be stronger than nonleaders in their levels of support, the pattern of their support is similar. That is, both leaders and nonleaders tend to favor Medicaid, AFDC, and Medicare more highly than the other programs. Some differences exist between their least preferred programs, though. Roughly a quarter of the nonleaders believe that Food Stamps should be reduced, making it by far their least favored program. Leaders, on the other hand, are not nearly as anti Food Stamps and, in fact, more support increases in benefits for Food Stamps than for either Social Security or Unemployment Insurance. Thus, we see that leaders and nonleaders differ in their overall levels of support and in their specific preferences about the food stamp program, but as far as their general pattern of program, the two groups are similar.

Leaders' votes in support of social welfare. We have seen that leaders of committees with jurisdiction over social welfare issues are more supportive than nonleaders in their beliefs about what the levels of benefits should be for the seven programs. Do their voting patterns on legislation in the social welfare domain also differ? Earlier, we reported the votes for all representatives in our sample on issues related both to low-income children and their families (using the ratings developed by the CDF) and to elderly persons (using the ratings developed by the NCSC). Now we will examine the votes of committee leaders using these same ratings.

Committee leaders vote in favor of the interests of children and their families on 7.2 out of the 10 possible votes. When we compare this record to non-committee leaders' voting record of 6.2, we see that in fact committee leaders' behavior mirrors their verbal expressions of support. The correlation between leaders' verbal support for AFDC, Food Stamps, and Medicaid and their votes is .51. Looking next at votes for issues related to the elderly, we find that committee leaders vote in favor of the interests of senior citizens an average of 6.8 times out of 10. Again, this is higher—though not significantly higher—than for non-committee leaders, whose NCSC vote score is 6.2. The correlation between their verbal expressions of support for Social Security, Medicare, and SSI and their votes is .51.

The conclusion is clear: just as committee leaders tend to be more supportive in the beliefs they express about benefit levels, they demonstrate this support in terms of their voting. Is this because members of Congress who are more supportive of social welfare programs rise to leadership roles in committees, or is it because something occurs in the work of the committee that causes one to change his or her views? We will speculate further on this in following chapters.

Leaders and targeted services.   Whom do leaders think should be helped with targeted services? Earlier we discussed congressional preferences in helping particular recipient groups through specific services. For most services, Congress as a whole leans toward giving high priority to poor children, with catastrophic health benefits being the only notable exception (the elderly take precedence over children). Looking at table 3.6, we can see the strong similarities between congressional leaders and nonleaders. For additional financial assistance, food and nutrition programs, and education-type services, both social welfare leaders and nonleaders give highest priority to children living in poverty. The rank ordering throughout these three types of services is nearly identical for both groups. There are several exceptions, yet no clear pattern to them. In one instance, for additional monetary assistance, nonleaders give

Table 3.6

Preferences of Congressional Leaders and Non-Leaders for Targeted Groups for Services

	Financial assistance		Food programs		Education-type programs		Catastrophic health ins.[a]	
	Non-lead.	Leaders	Non-lead.	Leaders	Non-lead.	Leaders	Non-lead.	Leaders
Poor children[b]	1	1	1	1	1	1	–	–
Disabled children	–	–	5	3	2	3	–	–
Children in general	–	–	7	7	–	–	30.0	18.5
Poor elderly	4	4	4	4	5	5	–	–
Disabled elderly	2	3	2	2	6	6	–	–
Elderly in general	–	–	–	–	–	–	30.3	51.8
Poor adults	–	–	6	6	3	2	–	–
Poor fem. heads	3	2	–	–	–	–	–	–
Poor unempl. men	6	6	–	–	–	–	–	–
Disabled adults	5	5	3	5	4	4	–	–
Adults in general	–	–	–	–	–	–	0.0	11.1
All groups equally	–	–	–	–	–	–	33.3	14.8

NOTE: Blanks indicate that the group was not given as an option.

[a]Rankings are not provided because the categories are not mutually exclusive. Instead, numbers given represent the percent of respondents giving the group first choice.

[b]For financial assistance programs all groups, including the disabled, were given as poor.

priority to the disabled elderly above female-headed households, while leaders of social welfare committees believed the latter group should be given assistance first. For education-type programs, leaders once again gave higher priority to adults than did nonleaders, but in this instance the group to receive lower standing was disabled children. In the third case (food services), social welfare leaders gave precedence to disabled children while nonleaders ranked disabled adults higher. Thus, we see the two groups within Congress agreeing that poor children should be helped first, but trading off in the importance of helping disabled children, poor adults, and disabled adults.

The similarities we have noted so far among congressional members begin to fade when we turn our attention to catastrophic health insurance. Earlier we explained that the House of Representatives as a whole (that is, leaders and nonleaders combined according to their representation within the House) is split in the decision to introduce catastrophic health insurance either as a universal program or one favoring only the elderly. From the data in table 3.6 it becomes evident that the division in Congress is due in large part to the differences between general members and leaders of social welfare-relevant committees. The nonleaders fall nearly equally into three groups: those favoring a universal program (33.3 percent), those preferring to target the elderly (30.0 percent), and supporters of a child-oriented program (30.0 percent). The opinions among leaders are quite different because the majority (51.8 percent) believes that catastrophic health insurance should be provided first for the elderly. The beliefs of the remainder of the leaders are split across the three other options.

That leaders are far more likely than nonleaders to support catastrophic health insurance as a program for the elderly may be a reflection of political reality. These individuals are the leaders of committees working daily on the issue, and they undoubtedly think that the best way to introduce a program is to start simply, with a single targeted recipient group. They perceive the elderly to be such a group, and a politically favorable one given its general preference ranking among the public. Nonleaders, on the other hand, not necessarily well-versed in the recently proposed catastrophic health insurance program, may well base their responses upon idealistic beliefs about universality rather than what some consider political reality. Thus, we see leaders recommending a more limited program than nonleaders.

The results from members of Congress demonstrate several interesting aspects of congressional opinion. First, the majority within the House of Representatives supports current social welfare programs. Although only a minority favors expansions, a much smaller minority favors reductions. The general feeling seems to be that current funding levels are appropriate and programs should be kept alive, including adjustments for the cost of living increases. Second, some programs receive more support than others. Congress members are more likely to prefer increases for Medicaid, AFDC, and Medicare than for Social Security, Unemployment Insurance, or Food Stamps. Third, leaders of committees relevant to social welfare tend to be more supportive of programs than nonleaders, but their priorities on welfare issues are generally similar to those of the nonleaders. Fourth, when ranking the importance of certain recipient groups for specific programs, Congress members tend to favor helping poor children above others. This is true for both leaders and nonleaders, with the only exception being the newly introduced catastrophic insurance program. In this case, while non-leaders are split between preferring the universal distribution of benefits and benefits limited only to the elderly for catastrophic health coverage, leaders largely favor helping the elderly. It seems, then, that representatives are particularly interested in helping children in poverty but are willing to favor other recipient groups when they deem a program especially likely to benefit that group.

Congress and the American Public

The final question addressed in this chapter is perhaps the most important one for understanding the workings of a representative democracy. We have seen the views of the general public in their support for social welfare, and we have discussed separately the views of members of the U.S. House of Representatives. In this section we look at the similarities and differences between the beliefs of the public and their representatives. One important factor must be kept in mind when reviewing these comparative findings. Every member of the House of Representatives is elected by the citizens of his or her particular district to represent their interests as well as the interests of the nation as a whole. We have no way of linking our public respondents specifically with their district representative. Furthermore, because we interviewed only fifty-eight members of Congress, we missed many of the representatives who serve the individuals sampled in our survey of the general public. For this reason, we cannot conclude whether or not individual representatives are projecting the opinions of their constituency. Rather, we discuss what political scientists refer to as "collective representation"—the extent to which representatives as a group represent the American people (Weissberg 1978).

In our exploration of public and congressional similarities and differences let us start with support for existing social welfare programs. Table 3.7 summarizes previous tables so that we can more easily examine the relationship between the preferences of the general public and members of Congress. The first and most important conclusion is that support for the social welfare system is high when we conceptualize support as wanting either to maintain or increase benefits. An overwhelming majority among both the

Table 3.7

Comparison between Public and Congressional Support for
Increasing, Maintaining, or Decreasing Benefits in Seven Social
Welfare Programs

	Public percent	All Congress[a] percent
Medicare		
Increase	67.6	32.4
Maintain	29.9	55.6
Decrease	2.5	10.9
Mean	(1) 2.65	(3) 2.22
SSI		
Increase	57.3	23.8
Maintain	40.0	68.0
Decrease	2.7	8.2
Mean	(2) 2.55	(4) 2.16
Social Security		
Increase	56.7	11.7
Maintain	40.0	85.5
Decrease	3.3	—
Mean	(3) 2.53	(5) 2.12
Medicaid		
Increase	47.1	41.8
Maintain	46.3	52.8
Decrease	6.6	5.4
Mean[b]	(4) 2.40	(1) 2.36
Unemploy. Comp.		
Increase	31.5	12.3
Maintain	55.5	76.5
Decrease	13.0	11.2
Mean	(5) 2.18	(6) 2.01
AFDC		
Increase	32.6	32.7
Maintain	51.9	58.7
Decrease	15.5	8.2
Mean	(6) 2.17	(2) 2.25
Food Stamps		
Increase	24.6	15.7
Maintain	51.0	59.4
Decrease	24.4	24.9
Mean	(7) 2.00	(7) 1.91

[a]Weighted sample.

public and Congress favor maintaining or increasing benefits for all seven of the programs under consideration; only a small minority favor cuts.

The second similarity between members of Congress and the public is that both display comparable levels of support for Medicaid and AFDC. However, whereas these are two of the programs that members of Congress are most likely to support vis-à-vis increases in benefits, they are not among the public's most favored programs. Third, the public and representatives are similar in that their least favored program is Food Stamps. One-quarter of the respondents in each group favor cuts.

As clearly as we can see these similarities between Congress and the public we can also see the differences. The most noticeable difference is that members of the public are more likely than representatives to favor increases in program benefits. Were we to define support for social welfare based solely upon a willingness to increase benefits, we would see representatives holding less favorable views toward programs than the general public. However, the representatives interviewed explain quite clearly why they are hesitant to say "increase." They are concerned about the cost of adding more benefits to an already financially overburdened system. Two representatives express this view succinctly:

> I'm going to sound like I'm just for the status quo, but the reason I favor maintaining the current levels . . . is not that I don't think we should do more, but just taking into account the economic realities, I think that's about all we can do. [#8]*

> Everything that you ask me is going to be colored by the fact that we have a budget deficit and that we are struggling to try and get a handle on that. And I envision some very hard economic times over the next few years to the point that I don't anticipate that very many of the programs are going to be able to receive any heavy additional benefits just because of the nature of the problem we are facing. [#38]

A second difference between representatives and the general public can be seen in the choice of program favored most by the two groups. Both members of Congress and the general public are interested in supporting the Medicare program, but while this is

---

* Numbers in brackets after excerpts from our interviews refer to the identification number of the representative.

the most favored program among the public, two other programs are seen as more needy by Congress members. One is Medicaid, where 42 percent of Congress members would like to see benefit increases. The other is AFDC, where 33 percent of Congress members would like to see benefit increases. Members of the public value three other programs more than either Medicaid or AFDC—Medicare, SSI, and Social Security. The three programs favored most by the public generally target the elderly, but among Congress higher support is given to programs principally seen to help poor children and their parents—AFDC and Medicaid (in fact, of course, Medicaid also helps the poor elderly). We will explore reasons for these differences in later chapters.

The rankings of recipient groups for social services also differ between Congress and the general public. Given the findings for program support, the primary dissimilarity should not be surprising. In three out of the four services, members of Congress rank poor children first while the public gives them the highest ranking only once (for education-type programs). In other cases (additional financial assistance and nutrition programs), the general public leans toward helping the disabled elderly rather than children. For catastrophic health insurance coverage, more respondents within the public favor helping children, while the most often preferred group among Congress is the elderly. Despite disagreement between the public and Congress over the relative priority of children versus the elderly, both groups agree that the needs of children and the needs of the elderly should come before the needs of nonelderly adults. The latter group is favored only for job training programs.

The views of Congress may reflect Congress members' more up-to-date knowledge of the needs of potential recipient groups as well as the political context in which programs operate. Given fiscal constraints, Congress members are less enthusiastic about expanding the welfare state, though they generally support maintaining what is already in place quite strongly. Leaders of committees relevant to issues of social welfare tend to be more supportive of the major programs of the welfare state than their nonleader colleagues, and this is especially true with regard to programs aimed at poor families with children—AFDC, Food Stamps, and Medicaid. Indeed, leaders' support for these programs exceeds even that of the general public, while for the social insurance programs—Social Security, Medicare, Unemployment Insurance—the congressional welfare leaders are less supportive than the general public.

We can now answer a question posed earlier in the chapter. Does the American welfare state suffer from a crisis of legitimacy? We said that a crisis might be inferred if most members of the public and Congress want cuts in programs, if the public is not willing to make active commitments to support the programs, or if representatives fail to vote for measures designed to maintain or expand the social welfare state.

Our data lead us to conclude that the American welfare state suffers from no generalized crisis of legitimacy. Support from the public and Congress is strong in that the overwhelming majority favor maintaining or increasing benefits and only a small minority want cuts. Moreover, the majority of the public is satisfied that their tax dollars go to support Social Security and Medicaid, and half or more are willing to make commitments to action on behalf of Social Security and Medicaid through contacting their representatives to Congress or by willingness to pay higher taxes. In regard to voting in Congress, more than half of the representatives vote on legislation deemed important to the lives and well-being of children, families, and the elderly.

Although a majority of the public are satisfied that their tax dollars go to finance AFDC, only a third report being willing to make behavioral commitments to support AFDC in the way of writing letters to congressional representatives and paying higher taxes. It is here, in support for AFDC, that we find the greatest weakness in public support for the welfare state. Yet this hardly constitutes a "crisis" of legitimacy.

4

Beliefs About Recipient Deservingness and Program Effectiveness as Explanations of Support

In the preceding chapter we found higher overall levels of support than we expected given the widely discussed crisis. But we also found that some members of Congress and the public are more supportive than others of social welfare programs in general and that all respondents tend to prefer certain programs over others. In chapter 2 we introduced four possible reasons for differences in support. In the next two chapters we will test the usefulness of each of these explanations. This chapter probes two of them. The first suggests that individuals are more likely to support programs and services if they believe that recipients are deserving, whereas the second proposes that individuals are more likely to support programs if they believe the programs are effective in meeting important social welfare goals. These are both program-based explanations in that they relate either to the recipients of program benefits or to attributes of the program's design. In chapter 5, we will test the two remaining explanations (self-interest and political predispositions) that focus on characteristics of individuals evaluating a program rather than on program specifics.

Recipient Deservingness and Support

In social welfare literature, the deservingness of recipients is frequently invoked to explain support preferences. Rose (1989) argues that the present welfare system makes a clear distinction between the deserving poor, who she claims are assisted through social insurance-type programs, and the undeserving poor, who must rely on public assistance. More often, though, commentators are less open about explicitly using recipient deservingness to justify their support or lack of it. For example, Butler and Kondratas (1987) suggest that "society should not condone such irresponsible behavior [teenage pregnancy] on the part of some individuals when it imposes enormous burdens on the rest of us. Welfare programs should not be 'value-neutral' when it comes to self-destructive actions" (p. 57). No explicit mention is made of the worthiness of teenage parents, but the choice of value-laden words such as "irresponsible" and "self-destructive" clearly implies that adolescent mothers are less deserving of governmental assistance because their situation is perceived as self-inflicted. Financial aid for teenage parents is only one public policy scenario in which issues of deservingness appear to be important.

The theme of recipient deservingness occurs often in the history of social welfare (e.g., Ryan 1971; Macarov 1978; Stein 1971; Katz 1986). Despite arguments against helping the "undeserving poor," we do not know how beliefs about deservingness are related to support for programs. On an individual level, it would seem reasonable to assume that few people will want to support a particular individual they consider to be undeserving. But can we generalize from such feelings about an individual to an entire class of potential recipients? As discussed in chapter 2, Carter, Fifield, and Shields (1973) found that their respondents were more willing to help a recently divorced mother than a never-married mother because the never-married mother seemed less deserving. In this case, the respondents have used general values about marriage, divorce, and motherhood to influence their desire to help certain individuals. "Deservingness" was not determined by particular needs, therefore, but by a societal value, in this case marital status.

Carter, Fifield, and Shields provide a specific example in which recipient attributes influenced the desire to provide help. Their focus was on recipients and not the specific type of program. An as yet unanswered question is whether Americans are less supportive of governmental programs when they believe that the recipients do not deserve assistance. We will test a recipient deservingness theory of support by linking respondents' beliefs about program recipients with their level of supportiveness of existing programs. We address four specific questions: 1) Do members of the public and Congress believe social welfare program recipients are deserving? 2) Do beliefs about recipient deservingness influence willingness to support programs? 3) Do beliefs about deservingness affect choices in targeting groups for services? 4) Do beliefs about deservingness influence support among members of the public differently than they affect congressional support?

The Public

Beliefs about recipients.   Before examining the relationship between deservingness and support, we will examine to what extent the public perceives welfare recipients to be deserving or undeserving. In the questionnaire administered to the general public (see appendix B), we included several items designed to measure public beliefs about recipients of three existing representative programs: AFDC, Medicaid, and Social Security. We selected AFDC because it is a program that provides cash assistance to the poor; Medicaid because it also targets the poor but through in-kind services rather than direct cash payments; and Social Security because it provides cash benefits but assists only those who have contributed to it. All respondents answered the AFDC questions, but because of time constraints, a randomly selected half of the respondents was queried about Medicaid while the other half was asked about Social Security.

Five statements tapped public beliefs about deservingness. Whenever possible, the identical wording was used for each program, but sometimes the wording had to be changed at the margin to match the specifics of a program (for example, AFDC recipients "really need the money provided" while Medicaid recipients "really need the assistance provided"). To qualify as deserving, recipients must first be perceived as in need and having no other resources on which to depend for help, such as family earnings, savings, pensions, and other private funds. How a survey respondent defines "need" is subjective, but these differences are not important for our purposes since the criterion states only that there must be a perception of need and a perception that recipients have no other resources. Hence, respondents were asked whether they agreed, somewhat agreed, somewhat disagreed, or disagreed with the statement: "Most people now receiving [benefits] really need the [benefit] provided"; and "Most people who get [the benefit] have no sources of income other than government benefits."

Figure 4.1 shows the proportion of respondents who agree or disagree with each of the statements. For all three programs, well over half the respondents agree that recipients need the benefits provided. However, more respondents think Social Security and Medicaid recipients need the benefits than think AFDC recipients need them (69 percent for AFDC, 85 percent for Medicaid, and 89 percent for Social Security).

Respondents might think recipients need assistance but that they have alternative sources of meeting their needs. Thus, a second characteristic of deservingness is whether respondents believe recipients have no sources of income (or, in the case of Medicaid, health care) other than government benefits. Seventy-four percent of recipients think Medicaid recipients would have no access to doctors and hospitals without Medicaid, 63 percent think Social Security recipients have no other sources of income without Social Security, and 51 percent think AFDC recipients are without other sources of assistance.

According to our conceptualization, a third criterion that must be met for recipients to be deserving is that they should not be perceived as responsible for their unmet need. The statement "It's their own fault that most [program] recipients [are on AFDC] [have Medicaid rather than private health insurance] [receive Social Security]" was designed to measure this aspect of perceived deservingness. To illustrate this, consider the example of programs for pregnant adolescents. The potential causes of adolescent pregnancy are many—for instance, a desire to be loved and to have someone to love, a means to get AFDC payments, a lack of birth control information or devices. Any one of these factors can be seen as individual-driven (e.g., the girl willfully decides to become pregnant to have someone to love) or externally driven (e.g., the girl's domestic situation fails to give her the needed love and attention). Whether one sees the pregnant teen as causing her own situation has important consequences for support. There are similar choices for other socioeconomic groups. For instance, the poor can be seen as failing to help themselves and thus falling into poverty, or their plight can be interpreted as a failure of society to reduce external barriers to success.

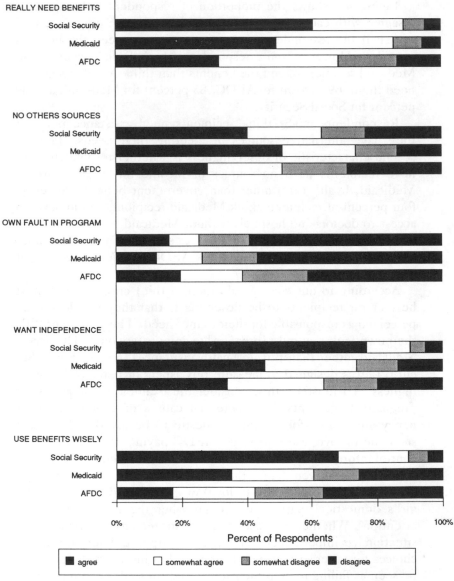

Figure 4.1
Public Responses to Questions of Recipient Deservingness

REALLY NEED BENEFITS
Social Security
Medicaid
AFDC

NO OTHERS SOURCES
Social Security
Medicaid
AFDC

OWN FAULT IN PROGRAM
Social Security
Medicaid
AFDC

WANT INDEPENDENCE
Social Security
Medicaid
AFDC

USE BENEFITS WISELY
Social Security
Medicaid
AFDC

0%   20%   40%   60%   80%   100%

Percent of Respondents

■ agree   □ somewhat agree   ▨ somewhat disagree   ■ disagree

Despite common stereotypes, the majority of the respondents disagree that recipients are responsible for their own dependence. Perceptions of blamelessness are greatest for Medicaid (75 percent) and Social Security (75 percent), and over half the respondents disagreed with the statement that AFDC recipients cause their own state of need (61 percent). Even when we examine only those respondents who feel strongly that recipients are not to blame (the ones listed in figure 4.1 as disagreeing completely) and omit those respondents who only somewhat disagree, the picture is still not as negative toward recipients as might be surmised from media and other portrayals of welfare recipients (Coughlin 1989; Sheehan 1977).* A relatively large 41 percent still completely disagree that AFDC recipients are responsible for their own state of poverty, and nearly 60 percent feel the same way about Medicaid and Social Security recipients. Again, the differences between perceptions of AFDC recipients and recipients of Medicaid and Social Security are worth noting. Respondents are considerably more likely to hold AFDC recipients at fault than other recipients.

The fourth criterion in our definition of deservingness concerns assumptions about the extent to which welfare recipients want to be self-sufficient. The media abound with examples of welfare dependency and the lack of initiative to be independent. In a 1981 *New York Times* article discussing the effects of President Reagan's budget cuts on the poor (Pear 1981), a working AFDC recipient was bothered because her welfare checks were being terminated while the benefits received by "recipients who stayed home watching soap operas on television" were to continue. The author of the article stressed how the working poor were to lose the most through cuts and made the implicit argument that those trying to make it through work were especially deserving. Although the word "deservingness" itself was never mentioned, underneath the rhetoric the message is clear: those social welfare recipients who work but still can't make it deserve more help than those who don't even try. In another *New York Times* piece, the journalist portrays public assistance recipients as irresponsible and lazy, refusing to work for

* Coughlin (1989) discusses newspaper headlines such as "Welfare Mother Begets 3 Welfare Daughters, Perpetuating Life Style" (*Wall Street Journal,* August 10, 1982); "Controversial Mother of 14 Won't Stop" (*Los Angeles Times-Washington Post Service,* April 18, 1987); and "Suspect May Dethrone Current 'Welfare Queen' " (*Albuquerque Journal,* December 20, 1980).

their benefits even if the costs of this refusal to work mean being dropped from the benefit rolls (Wald 1981).

Despite negative portrayals such as these, most of those interviewed believe that recipients want to be self-sufficient and independent (63 percent for AFDC, 74 percent for Medicaid, and 90 percent for Social Security). Specifically, the survey respondents were asked whether they agree with: "Most people who get [the program] want to be independent and self-reliant." Across all three programs, the overwhelming majority of Americans believe that social welfare recipients want to be independent.

The final dimension of deservingness concerns the fiscal responsibility, or "prudence," of recipients. We have all read and heard about welfare mothers buying cigarettes instead of food, or buying junk food and luxury items instead of nutritious staples. But does the public believe that this portrayal adequately represents the majority of welfare recipients? To determine this, respondents were asked whether or not they agree with the statement: "Most people who get [benefits] spend their [benefits] wisely." (To probe the same concept in the case of Medicaid, we asked "Most people who get Medicaid only use it when they really need to.") In contrast with the other four measures of deservingness, this item resulted in the greatest divergence across the three programs. Only 42 percent of the respondents believe that AFDC recipients are prudent with their benefits, 61 percent believe the same about Medicaid recipients, while an even larger percentage think Social Security recipients are prudent (89 percent). As many as 36 percent of the respondents for AFDC and 25 percent for Medicaid believe that recipients actually waste their benefits or otherwise spend them unwisely.

Although the majority of respondents express generally positive views toward the deservingness of program recipients, there is no unanimity. Furthermore, differences between perceptions of programs emerge. In general, fewer members of the public held positive views about the deservingness of AFDC recipients than of Social Security or Medicaid recipients. Even so, on some dimensions of deservingness the program differences are slight—for example, only a minority of respondents believe any of the program recipients are to blame for their dependence. In other cases, differences between programs are larger. For example, respondents were far more likely to believe that AFDC recipients waste their benefits than to think Social Security recipients do so, and only 10 percent of respondents state that Social Security recipients do not want to be self-sufficient, whereas 36 percent believe this about AFDC recipients. The most striking difference in program perception is between AFDC and Social Security recipients. Attitudes toward Medicaid recipients tend to fall in the middle of these two extremes. The one exception to this is that more respondents believe Social Security and AFDC recipients could meet their needs through other means than is the case with Medicaid recipients. This is not surprising since Medicaid recipients need professional medical assistance of a type that can rarely be supplied by family members or friends, some of whom may be able to supply the types of benefits offered by Social Security and AFDC.

From the responses on these items, we can construct a picture of the public's attitudes toward program recipients. Social Security recipients are almost universally seen as strongly deserving. The image held by the majority of the public is one of prudent people who need the money and have few alternative sources of income. Moreover, the public believes that Social Security recipients want to be independent and self-sufficient and are not at fault for needing benefits.

The picture of Medicaid recipients is similar, though not quite as consistently positive. Members of the public agree that Medicaid recipients have legitimate needs, no other ways to meet these needs, and have not caused their own dependence. Unlike Social Security, however, the public is not as much in agreement that Medicaid recipients prefer to be independent (74 percent versus 90 percent for Social Security), and about 40 percent of respondents believe that recipients use their limited medical resources unnecessarily, perhaps visiting physicians for minor illness or feigning sickness. Thus, although the view of Medicaid recipients is for the most part positive, there is somewhat less consensus on the deservingness criteria than is found with Social Security.

The picture of AFDC recipients is least clear-cut, though not as negative as they are depicted in popular portrayals. While most of the public agrees that AFDC recipients have a legitimate need (69 percent), the proportion who agree completely is less than for the other programs examined. One-half of the respondents (58 percent) believe that AFDC mothers do not use their benefits wisely, perhaps squandering money intended for their children's school clothes or next week's heating bill, and almost half think AFDC recipients have alternative sources of income. Even so, respondents perceive more positive than negative characteristics in AFDC recipients, with 60 percent attributing at least three of the five deservingness characteristics to AFDC recipients. While few members of the public believe that all AFDC recipients have all five deservingness characteristics (17 percent), even fewer believe that they have none of the characteristics (10 percent). Thus, the public's portrait of AFDC recipients is more mixed than for Social Security and Medicaid recipients. But there is no universal belief that AFDC recipients are undeserving.

Thus far, we have outlined the public's perception of program recipients. Yet the question that concerns us more is the extent to which these perceptions influence an individual's support for social welfare programs. We now turn to address this question.

Recipient deservingness and support for programs.   To test the effect deservingness beliefs have on program support we have constructed three multiple regression models—one for each of the three programs about which we asked respondents in detail. The full model seeks to determine how beliefs about recipient deservingness influence respondents' general support for each social welfare program. Thus, the independent variables are the five measures of deservingness outlined above—need, no other sources of assistance, no personal fault, desire for independence, and prudence in financial and lifestyle matters. The dependent variable is program support.

Together the five measures of recipient deservingness are able to explain 40 percent of the variance in support for AFDC, 35 percent of the variance in support for Medicaid, and 9 percent of the differences in support for Social Security. This fit is quite good for the two public assistance programs but relatively weak for Social Security. The results show, therefore, that deservingness issues play an important role in predicting public support for AFDC and Medicaid but not for Social Security.

More specifically, the analyses show that all five deservingness attributes help determine support for public assistance programs (AFDC and Medicaid) but that only three of the attributes help shape support for Social Security. Table 4.1 presents the standardized and unstandardized regression coefficients for the models of

Table 4.1

Regression Coefficients for Models Predicting Public Support of Programs through a Model of Recipient Deservingness

	AFDC[a]		Medicaid		Social Security	
	Deserve	w/Demo	Deserve	w/Demo	Deserve	w/Demo
Really need money	.252***	.326***	.237***	.235***	.163***	.179***
	(1.35)[b]	(1.79)	(1.31)	(1.29)	(0.94)	(1.04)
Want to be independent	.223***	.190***	.181***	.179***	.112**	.118**
	(1.08)	(0.99)	(0.81)	(0.79)	(0.64)	(0.68)
Spend benefits wisely	.165**	.078	.166***	.157***	.116**	.110*
	(0.82)	(0.42)	(0.66)	(0.63)	(0.68)	(0.66)
Own fault on program	-.151***	-.193***	-.145***	-.147***	-.038	-.023
	(-.70)	(-.92)	(-.64)	(-.64)	(-.16)	(-.10)
No other sources	.128**	.081	.101*	.095*	.076	.078
	(0.59)	(0.39)	(0.45)	(0.42)	(0.30)	(0.31)
Demographic Characteristics						
Race (1 = black; 0 = white)		.002		.082*		.004
		(0.04)		(1.38)		(0.06)
Age		-.121**		-.014		.020
		(-.04)		(-.00)		(0.01)
Income		-.027		-.076		-.062
		(-.00)		(-.00)		(-.00)
Gender (1 = female; 0 = male)		.027		-.019		.019
		(0.32)		(-.18)		(0.18)
Education		-.005		.019		.008
		(-.01)		(.04)		(.015)
Constant	-7.23	(-4.20)	(-5.46)	(-5.23)	(-.387)	(-4.55)
Adjusted R²	.401	.428	.354	.352	.089	.103

[a]To make the number of respondents comparable across the three programs, the AFDC analysis is based on a random sample of 430 cases.
[b]Numbers in parentheses represent the unstandardized regression coefficients.
* p<.05; ** p<.01; *** p<.001.

the three programs. It shows that, regardless of the program, support by the public is most influenced by the belief that the targeted recipients truly need the program resources being offered. Those who believe that AFDC and Social Security recipients need money or that Medicaid recipients need medical assistance are more likely to support the program than those who do not recognize a legitimate need.

The second most important attribute of deservingness is that individual recipients want to be independent of the program. Public respondents who believe that recipients have a personal desire to live free from the constraints of public welfare tend to be the most supportive. This second aspect of deservingness is especially important for AFDC. The picture sometimes shown in the media is of AFDC recipients who prefer dependence to self-sufficiency and who intentionally have multiple children in order to collect benefits. Believing that recipients do not want to be independent appears to influence support. Those respondents who see AFDC recipients as preferring dependence to self-sufficiency support the program less than those who believe otherwise.

A third attribute of deservingness that shapes support for all three programs is the perception that recipients use their benefits wisely. The other two deservingness attributes—whether recipients are at fault for their condition and whether they have alternative sources of help—influence support for AFDC and Medicaid, but not for Social Security. These latter attributes probably have little effect on support for Social Security because most respondents think Social Security benefits should be given regardless of whether recipients have other sources of income at hand or whether they are somehow at fault for their condition.

Before concluding that deservingness has a direct influence on program support, however, we need to rule out the possibility that the relationship between support and deservingness is confounded with personal characteristics of respondents. In this analysis, we consider five such characteristics: the respondent's race, income, age, gender, and education. Alone, these respondent characteristics have only a mild influence on an individual's level of support for social welfare programs. Taken together, however, they still account for only 3.2 percent of the variance in Social Security support scores, 3 percent in Medicaid support, and 2.2 percent in support for AFDC. In other words, knowing a person's demographic characteristics hardly helps us predict his/her supportiveness for social welfare. Though these demographic characteristics alone are not particularly helpful in predicting support for social welfare programs, there are some significant relationships among them that are worth mentioning. In general, younger respondents are more supportive of AFDC than older respondents, females are more supportive than males of both AFDC and Social Security, black respondents are more supportive than whites of both public assistance programs, and for all these programs the poor are more supportive than the more affluent.

When the deservingness predictors are added to the demography of the respondents, there is little effect above what is achieved with deservingness alone. Columns two, four, and six of table 4.1 provide the relevant data showing that respondent characteristics have little effect, creating a difference in adjusted R^2 between the AFDC models of .03 and for Social Security a difference of .01. The adjusted R^2 values do not differ for Medicaid.

Why does this model explain so little of the variance in support for Social Security? Two statistical issues may be important. First, very few of the respondents oppose Social Security. With so little variation in support, it is not surprising that recipient deservingness has only weak predictability for support for Social Security. Second, nearly all the respondents agree at least somewhat that Social Security respondents are deserving. Thus, the model of support for Social Security must contend with limited variability in both support and beliefs about recipients. This may be one explanation why the proportion of variance accounted for in the Social Security model is so low (9 percent). However, we will later see that the adjusted R^2 can be raised to .40 using a more elaborate model, thus suggesting that the restriction in the range of the support variable is not the major cause of the poor prediction of support for Social Security.

The results of the deservingness model are important. For years, political commentators have written of the foibles and faults of recipients and of how the state has little business supporting lazy citizens who don't even try to fit into mainstream American society (e.g., Murray 1984). Others have taken critics of social welfare to task for failing to understand that public assistance recipients are victims of circumstance and need temporary assistance before they resume their economically independent lives (e.g., Duncan 1984).

Both camps use the deservingness concept to demonstrate why images of worthiness should drive support for programs. Beliefs about recipient deservingness often enter into political and scholarly debates, and now we know something more about these beliefs. We have learned that, in general, the public's image of recipients' deservingness is less negative than many would lead us to believe, and that perceptions of recipients' deservingness are an important influence on support for AFDC and Medicaid but a relatively minor influence on support for Social Security.

Recipient deservingness and targeting groups for services. So far, we have seen that perceptions of recipient deservingness are related to levels of support for social welfare programs, especially public assistance programs. But when given the opportunity to choose both whom they would like to help and what programs to provide for that group, are support decisions still related to perceptions of a group's deservingness? To test this, we turn to data on preferences for groups and general services, rather than particular programs.

Members of the public were asked to consider whom they would most like to see helped through government funding for 1) food and nutrition, 2) education-type services, 3) catastrophic health insurance, and 4) additional financial assistance. Respondents were given the option to choose between a number of different target groups—the poor or physically disabled elderly, poor or physically disabled adults, and poor or physically disabled children. Respondents were asked to rank which recipient group they would most and least like to see helped for each service. In chapter 3 we discussed the public's preferences; here we explore *why* people report making the choices they do.

Respondents indicated whether they choose to assist a particular group because of attributes having to do with deservingness or with program effectiveness. For this section, we conceptualize recipient deservingness in terms of having no other sources of assistance, being entitled to help, and having many unmet needs. Other options to be explored later relate to program effectiveness—whether the services could help the members of a group to help themselves or be an investment in the future of the country. Respondents were allowed to select only one justification for their ranking. Table 4.2 shows the percentage of respondents selecting the var-

Table 4.2
Percentage of Public Respondents Choosing Recipient Deservingness Reasons to Justify First Choice for Services

	No other sources	Entitled to help	Greatest need	Total	N
Poor elderly					
Nutrition	54.2	32.1	3.6	89.9	168
Catastrophic ins.	33.3	30.3	22.7	86.3	66
Additional help	31.9	49.6	1.7	83.2	119
Education	47.8	16.4	6.0	70.2	67
Disabled elderly					
Nutrition	57.9	29.6	3.7	91.2	378
Catastrophic ins.	37.9	24.1	21.6	83.6	116
Additional help	43.0	47.5	0	90.5	518
Education	43.7	25.9	2.2	71.8	135
Poor children					
Nutrition	48.3	14.3	4.4	67.0	203
Catastrophic ins.	20.0	15.2	20.0	55.2	105
Additional help[a]	19.7	26.0	0	45.7	254
Education	19.5	7.3	1.2	28.0	164
Disabled children					
Nutrition	34.2	29.7	4.5	68.4	111
Catastrophic ins.	18.5	21.0	16.0	55.5	162
Additional help	*	*	*	*	*
Education	20.0	9.4	6.4	35.8	265
Poor adults					
Nutrition	**	**	**	**	18
Catastrophic ins.	**	**	**	**	15
Additional help	**	**	**	**	16
Education	12.1	3.4	1.3	16.8	149
Disabled adults					
Nutrition	54.2	20.8	8.3	83.3	24
Catastrophic ins.	29.2	8.3	12.5	50.0	24
Additional help	33.9	40.7	0	74.6	59
Education	24.4	6.8	2.8	34.0	176

[a]Category includes female headed households.
*Respondents were not given an option of disabled children for additional help.
**Too few respondents selected the recipient group as their top priority for the type of service.

ious deservingness-oriented reasons for their top choice for services.

One of the most obvious findings is that the public tends to use deservingness more often when supporting the elderly as compared to children or nonelderly adults. This finding holds true for all types of service under consideration, except one.

A second interesting discovery is that respondents appear to relate the deservingness of the potential recipient group with specific services. That is, deservingness is cited most often as the reason for helping with food and nutrition programs and is cited least often when choosing groups for education-type benefits. This finding is consistent across all target groups, including children, adults, and the elderly.

Deservingness appears to be an important consideration when members of the public decide whom to help through public services. This is especially the case for respondents choosing to target the elderly for services. The most important aspect of deservingness to respondents appears to be recipients' inability to find alternative sources of help. In other words, members of the public often choose to rank groups high for assistance because they perceive that the group has no other option except government assistance.

Summary.   We can now answer three of the questions we posed at the beginning of this section on recipient deservingness. First, we find that the majority of the public believe recipients of Social Security, Medicaid, and AFDC are deserving. However, not surprisingly, members of the public make distinctions between recipients of the three programs and are much more likely to describe Social Security recipients as deserving than AFDC recipients. They are most critical of AFDC recipients insofar as the issues of "prudence" and alternative sources of income are concerned. That is, a majority think AFDC recipients do not "spend their benefits wisely," and almost half (49 percent) think AFDC recipients have alternative sources of income.

Second, these beliefs about recipient deservingness clearly influence the public's willingness to support programs. Again, however, we find differences by program. Perceptions of recipient deservingness have a stronger impact on support for AFDC and Medicaid (explaining 40 percent of the variance in support and 35 percent, respectively) than on support for Social Security (9 percent). Third, beliefs about deservingness also affect choices in targeting groups for services. In targeting, the elderly are seen as a particularly deserving recipient group.

Does deservingness figure in the belief structure of Congress members in the same way as it does for the general public? Or does their "insider knowledge" lend to a different cognitive structure altogether? These are the questions to which we now turn.

The Congress

Understanding the relationship between Congressional beliefs about recipient deservingness and support for social welfare programs is especially important because Congress has the legislative ability to authorize new programs and to expand or contract existing ones. If beliefs about recipient deservingness influence Congress members' support for social welfare programs, then Congress might be expected to change existing programs or add new ones if they come to realize that certain recipients are more or less deserving than they had originally thought. In other words, altering beliefs about aspects of deservingness might be one way to change congressional support for social welfare programs. The first step is to learn whether Congress members are indeed influenced by beliefs about deservingness.

As with the general public, there are two primary sources in our data from which to address the question for Congress members. We can examine why Congress members choose to increase, decrease, or maintain benefits for existing programs, and we can consider the reasons they give for choosing a particular group for a particular service. In addition, we can examine their votes on social welfare legislation. Our congressional questionnaire was somewhat different from the one used with the public primarily because we allowed Congress members to respond in their own words about their reasons for support decisions. They were not forced to choose among several predesigned options, as was the case with the public. Thus, the responses of Congress members and the general public are not exactly comparable. However, we will try to make the discussion as analogous as possible, using our coding of the Congress members' open-ended responses. We coded whether or not they discuss the deservingness of the recipients when they explain their support for a particular program. If they discuss recipient deservingness, we coded those aspects of deservingness cited, using the five deservingness criteria.

Recipient deservingness as an evaluative criterion. Each Congress member was asked whether he/she would like benefits for seven major social welfare programs to be increased, decreased, or maintained. As described in chapter 3, the results show that representatives are generally supportive of social welfare programs but are less willing to increase benefits than the general public. In our questionnaire to the public, we asked respondents in detail about AFDC, Medicaid, and Social Security. Congress members, on the other hand, were allowed to elaborate on any or all programs within the system. In order to make better comparisons between Congress and the public, we have limited our detailed analyses to four programs: two social insurance programs (Social Security and Medicare) and two public assistance programs (AFDC and Medicaid). Unemployment Insurance is also a social insurance program, but it differs in several ways from the other two, most notably in its target group (working adults instead of retired elderly) and level of administration (state rather than federal). The second scale of support, comparable to AFDC and Medicaid results from the public, looks at support for public assistance programs. We have not included either Food Stamps or Supplemental Security Income, even though they are also needs-based programs. SSI is omitted from the scale because its unique target audience (it helps only the elderly and disabled) does not make it comparable to our measures of AFDC and Medicaid for the general public. Similarly, we chose not to include Food Stamps in order to keep the public assistance support measure similar to that of the public.

The two attitudinal support scales range from 5 (decrease all benefits) to 15 (increase all benefits). The weighted mean across Congress members for the social insurance scale is 10.8, and for the public assistance scale it is 11.5. (As we showed in the previous chapter, Congress members are more supportive of public assistance programs than social insurance programs, $t(57) = 3.18$, $p < .01$, because they are more likely to want to increase public assistance benefits but maintain social insurance benefits.)

A second measure of supportiveness is Congress members' voting records on issues pertaining to social welfare. This provides a behavioral measure, just as willingness to write letters to their representatives and to pay higher taxes provided behavior measures for the general public. The two gauges of voting behavior are developed from ratings computed by the Children's Defense Fund (CDF) and the National Council of Senior Citizens (NCSC). These two organizations monitor congressional voting on issues key to the groups' particular concerns. The Children's Defense Fund records those votes that have an important impact on the welfare of America's children, adolescents, and families. In 1986, the votes included legislation targeted directly at low-income children and families, as well as issues indirectly related. Likewise, votes recorded by the National Council of Senior Citizens also tended to affect the elderly directly and indirectly. The NCSC scale can provide insight into congressional voting on social insurance programs and policies, and the CDF scale is useful for understanding support for programs and policies targeted at low-income children and families. Each instrument ranges from 0 (no votes for policies) to 10 (all policies supported). As described in chapter 3, the 58 Congress members in the sample range in their voting from favoring none of the policy issues to voting for all ten of them. The mean number of policies favored is 6.1 for children and 6.2 for elderly.

After asking members of Congress whether they favor increases or decreases in specific program benefits, we asked them to elaborate on why they make the particular decision. Justifications centering around the deservingness of the recipients occurs quite frequently with regard to the public assistance programs but less often in reference to social insurance programs. Approximately half of the representatives (54 percent, N = 31) use deservingness to justify their support for public assistance programs, whereas only a third (N = 20) use deservingness to justify their support for social insurance programs.

The first finding worth noting is that nearly all the comments are positive. Only three representatives discuss the undeserving qualities of recipients and one discusses both deserving and undeserving recipient characteristics.

When representatives evoke explanations of recipient deservingness, what characteristics of deservingness do they use? By far the most often-cited characteristic is need. About two-thirds of those representatives who use the recipient deservingness rationale mention the needs of recipients when they explain their level of support for public assistance programs, and all maintain that recipients have legitimate needs. Congress members offer need-based justifications such as the following:

It seems to me [AFDC] is a program where . . . when I look at the situation of the people involved I really think there is a need for assistance. In my state now a woman with two children would get maybe $400 a month . . . no way you can make a go on that! [#44]

Although many representatives think about needs in connection to deservingness, few also express a judgment about recipients' responsibility for their situation (9.2 percent, N = 6). Most of these maintain that the recipients' situation is due to unfortunate circumstances, as this representative says about AFDC recipients:

They're women who have been widowed or deserted. And most often, if they never had work experience, they have the added trauma in trying to face the world . . . without experience. [#41]

Of those representatives who mention recipient responsibility, only one maintains that recipients are at fault for their destitute situation. Believing that recipients do not take advantage of opportunities to help themselves, this representative explains:

I'm blaming [the AFDC recipient] for not taking her own initiative and going out and getting something to supplement her income. We've got too many cases like that. [#51]

The only other dimension of recipient deservingness that Congress members explicitly use in regard to public assistance programs is the recipients' desire to become independent and self-sufficient. But only three (4.6 percent) cite this to justify preferences for public assistance programs, with two believing recipients want independence and the other maintaining that recipients prefer dependence. Two western Democrats argue:

My contention is that 99 percent of the people on welfare would take the job [if it was offered]. They don't sit home out of choice and watch the rats run around the room. They would love to go to work. [#37]

The AFDC recipient would love to go to work and make her own living. . . . [When I was in the state legislature I visited a typical recipient:] She hates begging—and to her it's begging to get AFDC. Where she once had somebody who was providing for her, now she has to be the sole source of providing for her family, for the five children with no one to assist her, because her husband deserted her and her parents disowned her. She [felt she] was a disgrace—

asking for welfare and being on welfare. She didn't want to be dependent that way. She thought when she went to [the welfare] office they made her feel like she was the lowest thing in life to be asking for help and not willing to do anything for herself. Tell me, how does a woman of that age with five children do anything for herself. . . . You find the majority of those people that are on that really would rather not. [#41]

What is the relationship between beliefs about deservingness and support for public assistance programs? Congress members who explain their support for public assistance with a positive portrayal of recipient deservingness are considerably more supportive (mean = 12.2) than those presenting negative views of deservingness (mean = 7.7, $t(27) = 3.39$, $p < .01$). In addition, representatives using positive deservingness justifications vote more often on behalf of children and family issues than those using negative reasons (mean = 6.4 versus 2.1, $t(27) = 2.40$, $p < .01$). However, representatives who present a positive view of recipient deservingness are not significantly more supportive than those who do not spontaneously mention deservingness as an explanation for their level of support, although they tend to be slightly more supportive (mean = 12.2 versus 11.4). Moreover, they are no more likely to vote on behalf of children and families than representatives not mentioning deservingness (mean = 6.4 versus 6.5).

Thus, when representatives spontaneously mention deservingness with respect to public assistance recipients, their opinions can be useful for our understanding of their attitudinal and behavioral support for programs. We cannot predict, however, whether a representative will be more or less supportive if he or she does not indicate opinions about deservingness.

Let us now look at the relationship between respondents' beliefs about recipient deservingness and their support for social insurance programs. As already noted, members of Congress are less likely to invoke recipient deservingness for social insurance programs than for public assistance programs. Approximately a third of the representatives cite deservingness as a reason for their decisions about the level of support they assign social insurance programs, and all but one of these respondents focuses specifically on the needs of recipients. About half of these comments suggest that all Social Security and Medicare recipients really need the help. For example:

Most of the people who are on Social Security today are not getting benefits well above and beyond their need. If anything they are at or below their needs. [#58]

Medical costs are astronomical. I think if we increase somewhere, it should be with Medicare. I think that is where people are really hurting. [#54]

The other half of the respondents mentioning recipient deservingness contend that whereas some recipients really need the help, others really do not. For example, to illustrate this point, one member quotes his father as saying, "I don't understand why I'm getting $1,100 a month in Social Security benefits that I really don't need, and I can see neighbors who are struggling"[44]. Another says, "We have too many Americans living at or below the poverty level and not getting enough [benefits], and many who are practically wealthy and still receive Social Security. What I support is a means test. Our country is not ready for it at this time, but over time I think we are going to be driven to it. And one of the reasons why we are is the resentment of young Americans in footing the bill for wealthy Americans who, in their minds anyway, don't need it." [#1]

Representatives who believe all social insurance recipients are deserving are 25 percent more likely to support increased benefits for Medicare than those representatives who believe some recipients have needs and others do not (63 percent versus 38 percent). They are also more likely to report support than those representatives who do not use deservingness explanations to justify their decisions. In other words, beliefs about recipient deservingness seem to matter in relation to support for Medicare. However, regardless of how representatives see the needs of recipients, they support simply maintaining Social Security benefits. Thus, beliefs about recipient deservingness appear not to matter with respect to Social Security. Later we will discuss why this is. For now, let us look further at how congressional beliefs about recipient deservingness influence support.

Beliefs about recipient deservingness affect the way representatives support social insurance programs, and they also appear to influence the way they vote. Those representatives who see all Social Security and Medicare recipients as deserving are more likely to vote yes on legislation to benefit the elderly (mean = 8.3, on a scale from 0 [support none] to 10 [support all], as compiled by NCSC) than those who see only some recipients as needy and some as not needy (mean = 6.0, t(17) = 1.59, p = .13). Those representatives who do not mention recipient deservingness in explaining their support decisions are more similar to the representatives who believe only some recipients are deserving. The mean NCSC voting record for representatives not mentioning recipient deservingness is 5.5. Thus, deservingness is somewhat important to Congress members when making decisions about social insurance, but more important when discussing public assistance.

Deservingness and targeted groups for services.   In chapter 3 we found that representatives expressed different priorities from the general public when it comes to deciding who should receive targeted services. Congress members were more likely than the public to report wanting to help poor children and are less likely to report wanting to help the elderly. In the interview itself, after representatives had ranked groups for services, they were asked why they made the decisions they did. From their open-ended responses, we can examine the importance attributed to features of deservingness.

Table 4.3 shows that deservingness factors are more important in explaining support for the elderly than for children or nonelderly adults. Elderly are rarely chosen by members of Congress as the most important recipient group, but when they are, representatives rely almost exclusively on recipient deservingness to justify their responses. The data show that all Congress members use recipient deservingness to justify priorities for poor and disabled elderly for additional assistance. In addition, nearly three-quarters of those who rank the disabled elderly as a top priority for food and nutrition programs do so because they believe the recipients are most deserving. Except for the four representatives who elect to help disabled children through food programs, for no other group is the deservingness of recipients as important to representatives as it is with regard to the elderly. These findings are similar to the public responses.

Though representatives invoke deservingness to justify programs for the elderly, the particular form of recipient deservingness they use differs depending on the group and service in question. Representatives who give a high priority to the elderly are most

Table 4.3

Percentage of Congressional Respondents Choosing Recipient Deservingness Reasons to Justify First Choice for Services[a]

	No other sources	Entitled to help	Greatest need	Total	N
Poor elderly					
Nutrition	**	**	**	**	4
Additional help	53.3	46.6	0	99.9	4
Education	**	**	**	**	1
Disabled elderly					
Nutrition	50.1	0	23.3	73.4	11
Additional help	100.0	0	0	100.0	8
Education	**	**	**	**	2
Poor children					
Nutrition	37.6	0	0	37.6	34
Additional help[b]	48.7	0.6	0	49.3	35
Education	9.2	0	0	9.2	22
Disabled children					
Nutrition	100.0	0	0	100.0	4
Additional help	*	*	*	*	*
Education	19.0	19.1	0	38.1	8
Poor adults					
Nutrition	**	**	**	**	0
Additional help	**	**	**	**	0
Education	2.6	0	0	2.6	12
Disabled adults					
Nutrition	**	**	**	**	3
Additional help	0	0	0	0	3
Education	4.9	0	47.6	52.5	5

[a] Catastrophic Health Insurance is omitted from the table because so few differentiated between the various groups. A large proportion of congressional respondents (32%) chose a universal distribution.

[b] Category includes female-headed households.

* Respondents were not given an option of disabled children for additional help.

** Too few respondents selected the recipient group as their top priority for the type of service.

concerned with the fact that the poor and disabled elderly have no other sources of assistance available to them. However, they see the disabled elderly as having the greatest needs while they believe that programs should target the poor elderly because this group is entitled to governmental assistance. Thus, they conceptualize deservingness in terms of needs, availability of alternatives, or entitlement, depending upon the context.

The type of recipient deservingness they invoke is more akin to that applied to children and nonelderly adults. Nearly every representative who invokes deservingness and believes children and nonelderly adults should receive extra resources or maintain those they get, cites the unavailability of help from other sources as the major justification for their ranking. Entitlement and need are rarely mentioned. This is exactly what we find with the general public, who also define deservingness for children or nonelderly adults in terms of the availability of other sources of assistance.

Thus, deservingness appears to be an important concern both for the public and Congress, especially when considering services for the elderly. But because fewer representatives rank the elderly high for help when compared with the public, representatives are also less likely than the public to utilize deservingness as a justification for help. When evaluating current programs, both the public and representatives appear concerned that programs help those in greatest need who also try to help themselves.

Summary. It seems, then, that Congress members' beliefs about recipients' deservingness influence their support for social welfare programs and plays a role in decisions about targeting groups for services. Members of Congress who discuss the deservingness of recipients in a way that portrays them as deserving are likely to be more supportive both in their attitudes and in their votes than representatives who portray recipients as underserving. This is especially true with respect to public assistance programs but is also valid in discussions of Medicare. The one exception to this pattern is Social Security. There is nearly unanimous agreement among members of Congress that Social Security benefits should be maintained. Thus, because there is little difference in levels of support across Congress members, issues of recipient deservingness offer little useful information in predicting support.

The findings for Congress are consistent with the results from the public in three ways. First, deservingness is an important dimension in determining support for social welfare programs to members of both samples. Second, deservingness is more important to both the public and Congress when deciding about support for the two public assistance programs examined than when deciding about support for Social Security. Third, the principal ingredient of deservingness is a view that recipients have a legitimate and otherwise unmeetable need.

Program Effectiveness and Support

That the perceived effectiveness of a program would affect one's support for that program makes intuitive sense. After all, no one would argue that people should support programs that fail to achieve their goals or bring about other important social benefits. Americans all want programs that are both successful—however they choose to define successful—and efficient. In this section, we examine the relationship between individuals' beliefs about program effectiveness and their support for programs and services. We address four specific questions: 1) What do members of the public and Congress believe about the effectiveness of social welfare programs? 2) Do beliefs about effectiveness influence overall support for programs? 3) Do these beliefs affect choices in targeting groups for services? 4) Do beliefs about effectiveness influence support among members of the public differently from the way they affect congressional support?

The Public

Public beliefs about current programs.   In chapter 2, we outlined our criteria for describing a program as effective. The first criterion, which has traditionally been most important in discussions of public assistance programs, is that a program or service should promote independence and not perpetuate recipient dependence. Therefore, we first asked members of the public whether they agreed or disagreed that each program (e.g., AFDC, Medicaid, and Social Security) causes recipients to become dependent on it. Figure 4.2 shows that few respondents believe Social Security creates dependency since an overwhelming majority disagree with the statement (76 percent). Fifty-two percent believe that Medicaid does not create dependence, but only 38 percent hold this view about AFDC. In fact, just as many respondents feel strongly that AFDC does cause dependence (39 percent) as believe that it does not. The remaining 23 percent believe AFDC somewhat causes its recipients to become dependent. Thus, a sizable proportion of the public thinks that AFDC causes dependence.

An effective program should do more than prevent dependence, however; it should also work to promote independence. For example, when supporters proposed the Comprehensive Employ-

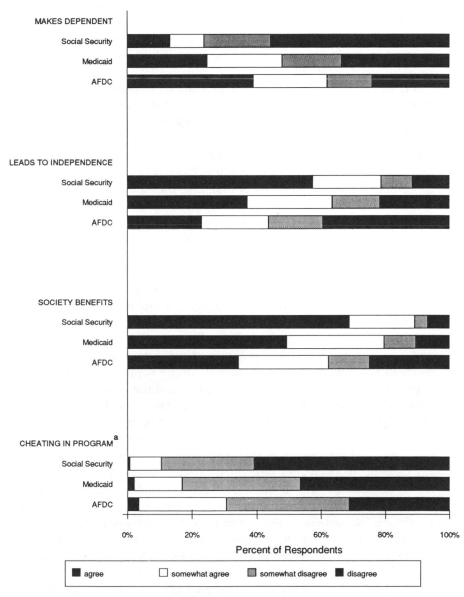

Figure 4.2
Public Responses to Questions of Program Effectiveness

MAKES DEPENDENT
- Social Security
- Medicaid
- AFDC

LEADS TO INDEPENDENCE
- Social Security
- Medicaid
- AFDC

SOCIETY BENEFITS
- Social Security
- Medicaid
- AFDC

CHEATING IN PROGRAM[a]
- Social Security
- Medicaid
- AFDC

0%   20%   40%   60%   80%   100%

Percent of Respondents

■ agree   □ somewhat agree   ▥ somewhat disagree   ■ disagree

[a] Response patterns are slightly different in this question: agree = almost all recipients cheat; somewhat agree = more than half cheat; somewhat disagree = less than half cheat; and disagree = only a few cheat.

ment and Training Act (CETA) to provide job training and place-
ment for the poor, they framed their discussions in terms of helping
recipients gain jobs that would make them and their families self-
sufficient. Whether CETA actually was effective in this way is not
an issue here. What interests us is that it was most often promoted
in terms of its ability to help recipients and their families become
financially independent.

Figure 4.2 shows that only 44 percent of respondents believe
that the AFDC program helps recipients become independent, but
the proportions are higher for Medicaid (64 percent) and especially
for Social Security (79 percent). Of course we must recognize that
independence may be thought of differently depending upon the
program. When people think of the "independence" of public
assistance recipients, more likely than not, they are concerned with
recipients earning wages rather than depending upon benefits from
the program. On the other hand, independence with regard to
Social Security recipients, the majority of whom are retired, often
denotes the ability to live at home and care for oneself rather than
depending on outsiders, such as nursing home providers. Thus,
although most Social Security recipients continue to receive their
benefits throughout the rest of their lives, members of the public
appear to see this as increasing independence.

Efficacious programs have a minimal amount of waste and abuse,
and it seems likely that any program plagued with perceptions of
waste or fraud will not receive overwhelming support. Public perceptions of widespread cheating within the three programs, however, are relatively low. Very few respondents report that "almost
all" recipients in the programs are cheating (4 percent in AFDC, 2
percent in Medicaid, and 1 percent in Social Security), but a larger
proportion believe that more than half of the recipients are cheating
(27 percent in AFDC, 15 percent in Medicaid, and 10 percent in
Social Security). Thus, a quarter of the respondents believe that
half or more of AFDC recipients are receiving benefits under false
pretenses. Nonetheless, the majority of respondents believe that
fewer than half of AFDC recipients are cheaters. No program is
perceived to be totally free of abuse, but Social Security and Medicaid are seen as having less cheating than AFDC.

The final element of an effective program is more abstract. We
contend that an effective program must be perceived as benefiting
society as a whole and not merely a small subgroup within society.
This does not imply that every individual within society benefits

directly. The benefit might be in terms of satisfaction in knowing everyone's material welfare is cared for adequately or that overall productivity is improved due to enhanced educational opportunities in some segments of society. We expect respondents to vary in the particular overall societal benefits they ascribe to programs, but the degree to which they think some larger benefit is achieved will, we argue, be related to their level of overall program support. When we asked respondents whether they agree or disagree that each social welfare program is a benefit to society as a whole, a large majority of respondents say they agree (62 percent for AFDC, 80 percent for Medicaid, and 89 percent for Social Security).

Summarizing the results concerning program effectiveness, we see that the general public perceives some social welfare programs to be more effective than others. Social Security receives the most positive evaluation and is widely perceived to be working to keep recipients independent, to be free of fraud and abuse, and to be a benefit to society as a whole. On the other hand, AFDC, and to a lesser degree Medicaid, is seen by some as helping recipients gain their independence but by others as actually making them dependent. More cheating is thought to exist in AFDC than in the other two programs, and AFDC is less widely believed to be a benefit to the entire society. Although no widespread belief that programs in general are ineffective, the image of AFDC in the public mind is considerably less positive than that of either social Security or Medicaid.

Program effectiveness and support for programs. The next question is whether beliefs about program efficacy influence overall support for programs. To test the hypothesis systematically, we performed regression analyses. We constructed a model for each program in which the dependent variable is program support and the independent variables are the measures of effectiveness. In some analyses we included the main and interaction effects of respondents' personal characteristics (of race, age, gender, income and education).

The results of the regression analyses are presented in table 4.4. They reveal that individuals' perceptions of effectiveness appear to influence their support for existing social welfare programs. This holds true for all programs and measures of support (adjusted R^2 for AFDC = .41, for Medicaid = .34, for Social Security = .20). Table 4.4 shows that respondents' characteristics such as age, in-

Table 4.4

Regression Coefficients for Models Predicting Public Support of Programs through a Model of Program Effectiveness

	AFDC[a]		Medicaid		Social Security	
	Effect	w/Demo	Effect	w/Demo	Effect	w/Demo
Society benefits	.233***	.263***	.289***	.299***	.339***	.334***
	(1.12)[b]	(1.26)	(1.40)	(1.47)	(1.90)	(1.97)
Leads to independence	.273***	.281***	.124**	.105*	.127**	.137**
	(1.31)	(1.35)	(0.51)	(0.43)	(0.58)	(0.65)
Cheating the program	-.277***	-.245***	-.193***	-.184***	-.033	-.054
	(-1.84)	(-1.64)	(-1.17)	(-1.11)	(-.21)	(-.35)
Makes dependent	-.081	-.073	-.189***	-.180***	-.113**	-.110*
	(-.38)	(-.35)	(-.77)	(-.73)	(-.51)	(-.51)
Demographic Characteristics						
Race (1 = black; 0 = white)		-.037		0.89*		-.008
		(-.71)		(1.49)		(-.12)
Age		-.047		-.061		-.044
		(-.02)		(-.18)		(-.01)
Income		-.027		-.113**		-.058
		(-.00)		(-.00)		(-.00)
Gender (1 = female; 0 = male)		.129**		-.025		.021
		(1.48)		(-.25)		(0.21)
Education		.019		.060		-.072
		(0.04)		(0.12)		(-.14)
Constant	(0.33)	(-1.12)	(1.20)	(0.72)	(-2.72)	(-.39)
Adjusted R^2	.406	.421	.342	.347	.196	.198

[a]To make the number of respondents comparable across the three programs, the AFDC analysis is based on 430 cases.
[b]Numbers in parentheses represent the unstandardized regression coefficients.
*p<.05; **p<.01; ***p<.001.

come, gender, education, and race add very little to how well program effectiveness predicts support, just as with deservingness (see table 4.1). Hence, we will not discuss respondent characteristics further, other than to draw the important conclusion that the American public seems to be homogeneous in its patterns of support preferences. In comparison to the role of attitudes toward program effectiveness, race, gender, age, income, and education are only weakly related to support.

The dimension of effectiveness that is most strongly related to support for Medicaid and Social Security is the perception that society benefits because of the program. This is especially the case with Social Security, where the staunchest supporters are those who believe most intensely that Social Security improves society. This component is also important for support of AFDC but is not the most important.

The perception that the program works to help recipients become independent is particularly important in influencing support for AFDC: those who think AFDC operates in a way that promotes independence and self-sufficiency are considerably more supportive, while those who think it has no such role are less supportive. This belief is less important in predicting support for Medicaid and Social Security. What is more important in the case of Medicaid is the belief that the program will not create dependence. There may be concern among some members of the public that government-provided medical insurance makes recipients dependent by forcing them to avoid jobs in order to keep medical coverage since many jobs that recipients qualify for do not offer medical benefits. Those who have this fear are less supportive of Medicaid.

Finally, believing that high levels of fraud and abuse occur in the AFDC and Medicaid programs is associated with lower levels of support, while perceptions of freedom from abuse are linked to higher levels of support. The level of abuse is not helpful in understanding support for Social Security, probably because so few respondents actually perceive any abuse occurring. With so little variance, this construct can hardly explain variation in support.

Overall, the data in table 4.4 show that beliefs about program effectiveness are important in determining an individual's level of support for social welfare programs. They explain 41 percent of the variance in support for AFDC, a third of the variance in support for Medicaid, and a fifth of the variance in support for Social Security.

Thus, beliefs about program effectiveness appear to affect support for public assistance programs and, to a lesser degree, support for Social Security.

Program effectiveness and targeted groups for services.   In addition to asking about effectiveness in the context of existing social welfare programs, we also asked if members of the public consider effectiveness criteria when deciding how to help others in need. After asking respondents which recipient groups they would most like to see helped in particular areas of the social services (food and nutrition, catastrophic health care, education, additional financial help), we then asked why they made their particular first choice selections. Responses are shown in table 4.5.

In considering program effectiveness we select two responses as representative of the underlying construct. Respondents who favor a program because they perceive the short-term costs worth the long-term gains (i.e., "investment in the future") are seen as choosing an effectiveness-driven principal, as are those respondents who favor a program because it leads to the greatest independence among its recipients. These two criteria are similar, respectively, to our previously discussed criteria of effectiveness as a benefit to society and as leading to recipient independence.

The first conclusion from table 4.5 is that, over all, effectiveness is not a major reason respondents invoke for choosing which groups should receive services. The second conclusion is that members of the public are more likely to show a concern with issues of program effectiveness when they rank children or nonelderly adults as a high priority to receive services than when they rank the elderly high. As we saw earlier, when respondents explain their reasons for ranking the elderly high, deservingness criteria are most important.

Looking at the third column in table 4.5 (total), we see that respondents are particularly likely to invoke program effectiveness criteria when they explain their decision to give children a high priority for educational services (71 percent invoke effectiveness for assigning educational programs to poor children and 64 percent invoke effectiveness for assigning education programs to disabled children). There is a difference in the criteria of effectiveness that respondents choose when they rank poor children high as compared to disabled children: they are more likely to use the effectiveness criteria "investment in the future" when justifying their

Table 4.5

Percentage of Public Respondents Choosing Program Effectiveness
Reasons to Justify First Choice for Services

	Investment in future	Maximizes independence	Total	N
Poor elderly				
Nutrition	1.8	8.3	10.1	168
Catastrophic ins.	1.5	12.1	13.6	66
Additional help	3.4	13.4	16.8	119
Education	1.5	28.4	29.9	67
Disabled elderly				
Nutrition	0.3	8.2	8.5	378
Catastrophic ins.	4.3	12.1	16.4	116
Additional help	1.0	7.5	8.5	518
Education	0.7	25.9	26.6	135
Poor children				
Nutrition	21.4	10.8	32.2	203
Catastrophic ins.	24.8	18.1	42.9	105
Additional help[a]	30.3	23.6	53.9	254
Education	45.7	25.6	71.3	164
Disabled children				
Nutrition	9.0	21.6	30.6	111
Catastrophic ins.	17.3	27.2	44.5	162
Additional help	*	*	*	*
Education	14.3	49.4	63.7	265
Poor adults				
Nutrition	**	**	**	18
Catastrophic ins.	**	**	**	15
Additional help	**	**	**	16
Education	26.2	57.0	83.2	149
Disabled adults				
Nutrition	0	8.3	8.3	24
Catastrophic ins.	4.2	41.7	45.9	24
Additional help	3.4	22.0	25.4	59
Education	6.3	59.1	65.4	176

[a]Category includes female-headed households.
*Respondents were not given an option of disabled children for additional help.
**Too few respondents selected the recipient group as their top priority for the type of service.

high ranking of poor children for education, whereas they are more likely to use "maximizing independence" when they justify their high ranking of disabled children for education services. Thus, they appear to want the goal of programs for disabled children to be to help them become more independent now, while the goal of education programs for poor children should be to make them more productive citizens in the future.

Those respondents who assign a high rank to poor adults and disabled adults for receiving education programs also use program effectiveness criteria to explain their decisions, and in both cases the particular reason they cite is to maximize independence. From chapter 3 we recall that few respondents ever give a high priority to nonelderly adults except for education ("rehabilitation and job training programs"). Thus, it is particularly instructive to note that respondents' rationale is clearly linked to the belief that education programs should achieve the goal of helping both poor and disabled adults achieve independence—presumably financial and physical independence through work.

In conclusion, we find that members of the public who favor helping the elderly for particular services tend to do so for deservingness reasons but not for reasons of program effectiveness. On the other hand, those who choose to target children and nonelderly adults justify their decisions with program effectiveness reasons, especially when the service is education.

Summary.   We can now answer three of the four questions asked at the beginning of this section on program effectiveness. First, what do members of the public believe about the effectiveness of social welfare programs? There can be no one answer, for the public has different perceptions about effectiveness, depending on what the program is. The image of Social Security is of a program that is effective in many ways: very little recipient abuse occurs; it does little to create recipient dependence but instead actively promotes independence on the part of recipients; and society benefits from its existence. The image of the effectiveness of Medicaid is also positive to the extent that respondents perceive very little recipient abuse occurring and think society benefits because from the program. However, the image of Medicaid is less positive than the Social Security image in that many respondents worry that, even though they believe Medicaid leads to recipients' physical independence, it makes recipients financially dependent and uninterested in paying for their own health care. Finally, the image of AFDC is the least positive of the three. On the positive side, close to two-thirds of respondents think that AFDC benefits society, and only a third think there is significant cheating by recipients. But on the negative side, almost two-thirds say it creates dependence among recipients and fails to promote independence actively.

Do these beliefs influence support for programs? The answer is quite clearly yes. Perceptions about program effectiveness explain more than a third of the variation in support for both AFDC and Medicaid and 20 percent of the variation in support for Social Security.

Do beliefs about effectiveness affect choices in targeting groups for services? The answer must be qualified in terms of which group is being considered. If the group that respondents want to target is the elderly, the answer is no because here respondents invoke reasons having to do with deservingness. If the groups that respondents want to target are children and working-age adults, the answer is more likely to be yes. For these groups, respondents invoke attributes of program effectiveness to explain their support.

The Congress

Members of Congress vote regularly on issues concerning social welfare services. As with the general public, we asked Congress members to consider changes in the appropriations for both existing and new programs. How much do members of the U.S. House of Representatives consider the effectiveness of a program when considering their support for it?

Effectiveness and support for existing programs. As described previously, representatives were asked whether they believe program benefits should be increased, maintained, or decreased. Following their responses, we probed the reasoning behind their specific decisions for both public assistance (AFDC and Medicaid) and social insurance programs (Social Security and Medicare). Earlier we noted that representatives often invoke the deservingness of recipients as a reason for their support. Even more frequently, however, for public assistance and especially social insurance programs, they bring up program effectiveness. In particular, they discuss: 1) the program's ability to help recipients become independent; 2) the efficiency of program administration (including allowing excessive abuse or waste); and 3) the overall importance of the program to society as a whole. When discussing social insurance programs, some members of Congress also bring up another aspect of program design—its political viability in the long or short term. We explored the importance of perceptions of program effectiveness in shaping overall supportiveness by analyzing what Congress members have to say about these criteria.

Program effectiveness is an issue of concern to members of Congress. Fifty-four percent invoke the concern when they discuss social insurance programs and 68 percent when they discuss their decisions about public assistance programs. About a third of the representatives (N = 20) express negative views about the effectiveness of social insurance programs and 44 percent (N = 25) express negative views about the effectiveness of public assistance programs. In other words, this means that about two-thirds of the representatives invoking program effectiveness to describe social insurance programs express negative views, and about three-fourths of those invoking rationales of effectiveness for public assistance programs express negative views. The remaining representatives are divided between those who hold positive positions (ten for social insurance and seven for public assistance) and those who suggest both positive and negative attributes of program effectiveness (two for social insurance and seven for public assistance). Clearly, therefore, there is no universally held belief among Congress members about the effectiveness of programs, but negative assessments are more often mentioned than positive ones. Before looking at the relationship of these attitudes to support, let us examine the characteristics of effectiveness that representatives bring up.

As with the public, representatives express concern lest social welfare programs cultivate long-term poverty. This point is brought out by a third of respondents with respect to public assistance programs (31.5 percent, N = 18), and most of these individuals believe that programs too often fail to offer the poor any real assistance for rising out of poverty (N = 16). In the words of three representatives from different parts of the country:

> Our current [public assistance] system has perpetuated dependency rather than moved people off of dependency. [#43]

> It [AFDC] is obviously not working because we are running into third and fourth generation people. The program was originally

designed to get people off it rather than to get more people on it. And we're getting more people on it so it isn't working. [#4]

There's something fundamentally, inherently wrong in the system because we don't break the dependency cycle. [#47]

The following representative tries to illustrate how he believes it happens that public assistance programs inadvertently result in dependence rather than independence:

I have a lot of young men and middle-aged men in my district who are unemployed. For them to accept a low-paying job, $5.00 an hour, without benefits, they sit down and they figure, "Look, I have a wife and three kids and they are all in school. If I take that job, I'm going to lose my Medicaid. I lose my food stamps. I lose my welfare payments. I now have to travel to work, and I gotta get a car and pay my car insurance. I can't afford to take the job." Rather than subsidize employment, we subsidize unemployment. And it should be reversed. . . . I think we should change the system. [#54]

On the other side, only a very tiny minority of representatives (N = 2) say they believe that public assistance programs help recipients become independent. One representative says that, although most of his colleagues and constituents believe AFDC to be a disempowering program, he thinks something quite different happens: "It seems to me that the major message in America's welfare system is that it has been successful in literally moving tens of millions of Americans out of poverty and into the middle class." [#48]

Promoting independence is only one feature of effectiveness, however. A second is that the program functions with minimal fraud and abuse. About 15 percent of representatives (N = 9) mention cheating and abuse within public assistance programs. Some of them argue that the accusations made in the mass media exaggerate reality. For example, responding to what he perceives to be misplaced criticism, one representative states:

Most of the criticisms that are directed at AFDC and welfare are really mythological criticisms. . . . You are talking about a one percent phenomenon. [#52]

However, his view is certainly not held by all his congressional colleagues who express an opinion of the issue. Although directed at the Food Stamp program, the following story told by a midwestern representative characterizes the image shared by some about the abuse in public assistance programs:

> I was in a little country grocery store one day, just visiting with the grocer, and a young child came in and got a couple of pieces of bubble gum. I didn't pay any attention at first as to the method of payment, but I saw the grocer gave him some change. . . . The kid went out of the store and came back and did this routine all over again. Finally I said to the grocer, "What's going on here? If that kid wants ten pieces of bubble gum, why didn't he just buy ten pieces of bubble gum?" He said, "Oh, he's not interested in the bubble gum. He's cashing Food Stamp coupons and what he's really trying to do is to get enough money to go to the skating rink and have enough money left over to buy a hamburger and a milk shake." Well, I observed that case but I know of scores of instances where similar things have happened. [#46]

Congressional blame for abuse is not focused on the recipients as much as on a "very, very cumbersome" administration of public assistance programs. That recipients have found creative ways to abuse benefits is seen as more a problem of program administration than a reflection on the moral flaws of individual recipients. The Congress member quoted above does not overtly blame the boy for wanting to go skating and raising cash this way. Instead, he is more concerned that Food Stamps can be used so easily in such unintended ways. The view that program management is inadequate is widely held with respect to public assistance (N = 20, 35 percent of the sample). Only a few say they believe that public assistance programs are well maintained administratively (N = 2).

A final definition of program effectiveness emphasizes the belief that the very existence of programs is a benefit to society (12.5 percent, N = 7). This is exemplified by the representative who says, "Theoretically, you're taking care of the next generation of Americans." [#22]

What is the relationship between beliefs about program effectiveness and support for public assistance programs? Representatives expressing positive evaluations about the effectiveness of public assistance were slightly more supportive (mean = 12, on a scale ranging from 5 [decrease all] to 15 [increase all]) than those who present negative evaluations (mean = 10.7), but these differences are not large enough to be statistically significant given our small sample size of representatives. The difference in the voting patterns on children's issues of the two groups is in the same direction but is again not significantly different (mean = 6.5 for those with positive evaluations and mean − 5.9 for those with negative evaluations, on a scale from 0 [vote for none] to 10 [vote for all]).

Thirty-two percent of the representatives do not discuss program effectiveness at all. Judging from their support and voting scores, we can conclude relatively little from their silence except that as a group they are no less supportive than their colleagues who spontaneously bring up issues of program effectiveness. In fact, if anything, they are somewhat more supportive than those who present negative evaluations, though the differences are again not statistically significant (support mean = 12.3 versus mean = 10.7 for negative views; vote mean = 7.2 versus mean = 5.9, t(41) = 1.48, p = .15).

From these analyses, we draw two major conclusions. First, program effectiveness is important to many representatives—roughly two-thirds discuss attributes of effectiveness when they explain their support for AFDC and Medicaid. Second, beliefs about effectiveness are not strongly related to level of support for public assistance programs, since those who discuss the ways in which programs are effective are only slightly more supportive than those who discuss the ways in which programs are ineffective.

How does it happen that the relationship between beliefs about program effectiveness and support is so low? Some members of Congress who think programs are ineffective favor decreases in benefits. Others, however, think programs are ineffective but believe the recipients are deserving and argue that the programs simply need to be reformed, not decreased. For example, we quoted a representative earlier as saying that "rather than subsidize employment we subsidize unemployment." He favors increasing benefits, not cutting them. He has an elaborate plan for "subsidizing employment" that includes providing medical benefits, Food Stamps, and transportation allowances to people who have low-paying jobs so that people "can afford to go to work." Similarly, another representative who is quite critical of the ineffective attributes of public assistance programs says, "Truthfully, I don't care if we spend more money or less money or the same money as long as we can come up with a genuine reform that will meet our social goals." [#17] Thus, program effectiveness appears to be important to members of Congress when considering public assistance programs, but it is not a powerful enough force to shape their support decisions in any way we could detect in our analyses with admittedly low statistical power.

We turn now to examine the role of program effectiveness in shaping representatives' support for the social insurance programs of Social Security and Medicare. As noted earlier, more than half (54 percent) invoke issues of program effectiveness when they respond to our question of whether benefits should be increased, maintained, or decreased for Social Security and Medicare. The representatives who discuss program effectiveness do so in terms of two major attributes: 1) the adequacy of the design of the programs for achieving their goals, and 2) the overall importance of the programs to society through the provision to the elderly of greater security. Of these two reasons, representatives most frequently discuss the adequacy of program design. About a third of those who discuss the adequacy of programs note how good designs promote the successful attainment of goals. One representative refers to Social Security as "the most successful and important of all the social programs." [#24] Several other legislators say that the most important accomplishment of Social Security's design has been to reduce poverty among the elderly:

> Well, we've had great success with Social Security, and now that success seems to have had a curious backlash. People are pointing to senior citizens and saying, "Gee, senior citizens are doing pretty well" as if that was accidental. That is because of social efforts, the leading one of which is Social Security. The purpose of Social Security is to give senior citizens some modicum of security in their later years. And Social Security has done that fairly well. I want to see Social Security continue to do that. [#48]

> Social Security has been the most successful program that we've ever devised in terms of lifting people out of poverty. It's the one program you can point to and say absolutely we have succeeded in ending poverty in a certain class of people and that is the elderly. . . . "Old" used to equate with "poor," and it doesn't anymore. [#17]

However, despite these positive views, the other two-thirds of those who invoke program design see Social Security and Medicare as inadequate. Their concerns fall into three major categories. First, some representatives are concerned about the long-term implications of an aging society on Social Security and Medicare that arise because more people are living longer and thus will need Social Security and Medicare benefits longer. This will mean dramatic increases in costs in the next century. For example, one representative describes Medicare as "a big smoking bomb" [#58], and another says of the program:

> You know the age of our population is going up in a rather dramatic fashion. We don't seem to pay an awful lot of attention to that. There are going to be fewer and fewer people paying for Medicare for more and more people, and if you think the problems we have now are something, wait until it comes down to the question twenty years from now of replacing hearts and curing cancer when these types of things are rather routine and you have a real dramatic increase in the proportion of people who are old! [#22]

Representatives especially worry about the effects that the huge baby boom generation cohort will have when they begin retiring in 2010. As one representative says about Social Security, "The system will bankrupt itself because all the post–World War II babies will come of age for Social Security at one time." [#53]

Congress members' second category of concern has to do with the threat to the long-term viability of the programs. This arises from what representatives perceive to be increasing resentment among young adults about the burden of the employment tax. Two members expressed it this way:

> My children, my daughters who are between 23 and 33, have no faith at all that Social Security will be there for them. . . . And the young people say, "Why should I be worried about my contribution to Social Security to pay recipients who are senior and improve their benefits when the program won't be there for me?" So you've got a kind of head-on collision here, and I hate to see this, you've got society pressure groups being created—senior citizens protecting their lot, junior citizens protecting what their lot is. [#42]

> I can see that it is going to get so bad that we are going to have an age split. Revolution, if you would. Maybe that's a little too strong a word, but the younger people are getting more and more fed up

with paying such high rates. The young people are, on an increasing scale, becoming more and more alarmed about how much they are paying into the system, and becoming less and less accepting of the fact that there will be anything for them. Getting downright cynical. They are paying in all this and they know that the system will never be there when they get ready to retire. [#13]

Third, some representatives are also concerned about the adequacy of the program to control costs even today. For Medicare, this translates into concern about the costs of medical technology, the heroic procedures that are available for prolonging life, and physicians' possible overuse of these two factors. As one representative explains,

> They've invented so many things that nobody heretofore has ever thought about. . . . What I am really trying to illustrate is the fact that there are a number of very expensive investigations doctors can give people today, and if you are already pretty elderly the question is, is it worth this in dollars, particularly if it is followed by an exploratory operation which could cost a lot of money, when you're likely to be dead before the thing ever overtakes you. [#6]

Those representatives who are particularly concerned about costs are likely to think Social Security and Medicare should be redesigned so that the wealthy elderly pay a larger share. The first comment below relates to Medicare, the second to Social Security:

> I would say my major concern is that we don't have wealthier elderly people paying what I consider their fair share. I'm not sure that I would go all the way to means testing Medicare. But I am for requiring different levels of input at least. . . . Rather than see level of benefits reduced or procedures eliminated, I would rather have more wealthy recipients participating in the support of Medicare closer to the extent they can afford to. [#35]

> I think the benefit structure should be changed. I mean, the fact of not much relationship to income just does not work in today's budget. . . . I support something approaching means testing (a term that I have learned not to use!), but I've always supported that through the proposal for what we call the tax back. That is the tax on Social Security benefits. I do not see why somebody with $20,000 income should be receiving tax-free benefits when a younger person's $20,000 income is being taxed. Taxing is the fairest means

test on Social Security. . . . Social Security is in some case a person's entire income, but in most cases it is less than half the income. [#13]

Thus, among Congress members we find frequent discussion of program effectiveness when considering both Social Security and Medicare, largely fueled by financial worries. We now turn to our next question. What relationship exists between attitudes about program effectiveness and support for these programs?

Though program effectiveness is often invoked, we do not find differences in support between those who mention it and those who do not. Individuals with positive assessments are no more likely to support programs attitudinally (mean = 10.9 versus mean = 11) nor behaviorally in their voting (mean = 6.4 versus 6.5) than those not mentioning effectiveness. Furthermore, those expressing positive assessments of the effectiveness of social insurance programs are not more supportive than representatives with negative opinions (mean = 10.6 for attitudes and mean = 5.5 for votes). Although there are many opinions about program effectiveness across members of Congress, these beliefs do not appear to influence support for social insurance programs, just as they did not for public assistance programs. Why might this be?

In the case of public assistance programs, representatives seem to perceive them as so crucial to the needs of recipients that they believe they have to support the programs, even though they need reform. A quite different explanation is relevant to the absence of a relationship between support and perceptions of the effectiveness of social insurance programs, particularly Social Security. Those representatives who support Social Security but harbor doubts about it do so, they say, because they hear more from the public about this program than about any other. The vast majority of the public is supportive, and the representatives know it. As one member of Congress puts it,

> The Social Security program has been safe for a long time. It isn't about to collapse. That's about the last thing Congress would let collapse. They would wipe out national defense before they did that. I hate to say it, but I think they would. [#6]

According to two others: "It's the mother lode; it's the Holy Grail around here. Nobody touches a hair on the head of Social Security"; [#12] and "When you talk about Social Security, that's motherhood, that's apple pie." [#53]

Because Social Security is very popular and because of the furor in recent years over suggested policy changes concerning Social Security, representatives critical of the program hesitate to express their concerns and are unlikely to suggest any modifications. As one representative from the south says:

> For the Congress, [Social Security] is politically too hot to address. . . . The Republicans were burned severely in '82 with the way the Democrats demagogued Social Security. So, consequently, you end up with a standoff. Nobody wants to address those issues that are so politically volatile. [#31]

A representative from the west puts it this way, "People are coming around and realizing that something has to be done . . . but politically Social Security is just dynamite." [#1] A midwestern representative comments, "[Social Security] is a political fact of life. . . . We are just virtually landlocked into maintenance. Politically, we have very little choice other than to maintain the program as it is." [#13]

What the preceding analyses show is that members of Congress are concerned enough about issues of program effectiveness to bring them up frequently, but their concerns about effectiveness do not appear to be strongly related to either their attitudinal support or their voting behavior in the social welfare domain. Unlike members of the public, representatives do not appear to support or reject social welfare programs according to beliefs about their effectiveness. The reasons for this lack of relationship are quite different depending on whether the programs in question are public assistance or social insurance programs. For public assistance, representatives' beliefs about the needs of the recipients often override their beliefs about the ineffectiveness of the programs, and so they make support decisions regardless of how effective they perceive a program to be. For social insurance programs, on the other hand, representatives anticipate a negative reaction from the public if they alter the program and this prevents them from seriously suggesting any revisions in Social Security. They thus make their decisions regardless of how they perceive program effectiveness.

Effectiveness and targeted groups for services. A second measure that can help illuminate the relationship between beliefs about program effectiveness and congressional support are the reasons Congress members give for targeting groups for services. As described earlier, we asked Congress members whom they would most like to see helped through specific services and then asked why they prioritized a particular group for each service. In this section, we explore how their beliefs about the potential effectiveness of a service influence their decisions about priorities.

Representatives cite two principal reasons for preferring certain groups for particular services. The first is that providing a specific service to one group benefits society in the long run. In other words, representatives see the assistance as an investment in the future. As table 4.6 shows, representatives are particularly likely to be concerned for the future when they place a high priority on helping children. For example, one representative offers as his reason for selecting poor children to receive governmentally funded school lunches:

> I think it bets on the future. . . . Unless you have well-nourished young people, it's not likely that they're going to be able to learn as well as they would otherwise. So, I think if you're going to be looking toward the future of the nation, you've got to [fund nutrition programs for poor children].

The second feature of effectiveness Congress members mention is a concern that a service help recipients become independent. In this case, representatives favor services that would only be used in the short term because it would help beneficiaries become self-sufficient. Program effectiveness defined in terms of leading to recipient independence is invoked most often with regard to non-elderly adults—the group most able to become self-sufficient in the view of members of Congress.

The results shown in table 4.6 are similar to those obtained from the public . Both members of Congress and members of the general public seem to be most motivated by concerns of program effectiveness when targeting children and working-age adults. In developing services for the elderly, both respondent groups pay more attention to deservingness characteristics.

Table 4.6

Percentage of Congressional Respondents Choosing Program
Effectiveness Reasons to Justify First Choice for Services[a]

	Investment in future	Maximizes independence	Total	N
Poor elderly				
Nutrition	**	**	**	4
Additional help	0	0	0	4
Education	**	**	**	1
Disabled elderly				
Nutrition	0	26.7	26.7	11
Additional help	0	0	0	8
Education	**	**	**	2
Poor children				
Nutrition	42.2	20.2	62.4	34
Additional help[b]	40.3	0.6	40.9	35
Education	79.7	11.2	90.9	22
Disabled children				
Nutrition	0	0	0	4
Additional help	*	*	*	*
Education	21.0	40.9	61.9	8
Poor adults				
Nutrition	**	**	**	0
Additional help	**	**	**	0
Education	20.3	77.2	97.5	12
Disabled adults				
Nutrition	**	**	**	3
Additional help	0	100.0	0	3
Education	0	47.5	47.5	5

[a]Catastrophic Health Insurance is omitted from the table because so few differentiated between the various groups. A large proportion of congressional respondents (32%) chose a universal distribution.

[b]Category includes female-headed households.

*Respondents were not given an option of disabled children for additional help.

**Too few respondents selected the recipient group as their top priority for the type of service.

Summary.   Representatives frequently bring up issues of program effectiveness—68 percent when discussing public assistance and 54 percent when discussing social insurance programs. However, whereas perceptions of ineffectiveness in programs can lead members of the public to be less supportive of public assistance programs and somewhat less supportive of social insurance programs, the same cannot be said of members of Congress. Although a number of representatives perceive program design problems in AFDC and Medicaid, they do not conclude that the programs should be decreased. Instead, they contend that programs they perceive as ineffective should be reformed, and some even suggest that they should be expanded. In addition, regardless of their personal beliefs concerning the effectiveness of Social Security, few Congress members will recommend any changes. This is not because they believe improvements cannot be made but because they fear public disapproval. Thus, exploring congressional beliefs about program effectiveness provides insight into their views of existing programs, but it offers little understanding of their probable voting behavior.

An Integrated Examination of Program-Based Explanations of Support

In this chapter, we have presented data about two possible explanations for public and congressional support of social welfare— recipient deservingness and program effectiveness—each of which has several different attributes. In general, both recipient deservingness and program effectiveness appear to be equally important in describing the public's support for public assistance programs. That is, when we compare the data from tables 4.1 and 4.4, we see that recipient deservingness and program effectiveness issues explain about the same amount of the variance in support for AFDC (adjusted R^2 = .40 and adjusted R^2 = .41) and for Medicaid (adjusted R^2 = .35 and adjusted R^2 = .34). This is not what we find for members of Congress. For them, beliefs about recipient deservingness are more important in shaping their support decisions than are beliefs about program effectiveness.

There are two ways that recipient deservingness and program effectiveness appear to play a somewhat different role in shaping the public's support for Social Security as compared to the public assistance programs. First, program effectiveness explains two times more of the variance in public support for Social Security than does recipient deservingness (respectively, adjusted R^2 = .20 versus adjusted R^2 = .09). Second, neither attitudes about deservingness nor program effectiveness are as powerful in shaping support for Social Security as in shaping support for the two public assistance programs. This weak relationship may in part be due to the lower variability in support for Social Security; nearly everyone supports the program. It may also be attributed to the low variability in the deservingness and effectiveness measures; views toward Social Security are more consistently positive than for the other programs. Given that we did not have a lot of variance to explain for Social Security, explaining as much as these variables do is noteworthy.

Comparing the findings for the public with those for Congress, we find that perceptions of recipient deservingness and program effectiveness play a different role in representatives' support for social insurance programs. For members of Congress, recipient deservingness is more important than perceptions of program effectiveness in explaining support for social insurance programs, but neither set of beliefs appears to be very powerful. Rather, their support for Social Security and Medicare appears to be driven by their fear of what they think the reaction of the public will be if they are not supportive.

Recipient deservingness and program effectiveness are both explanations of support that focus on the program and so may share explanatory power. It would be especially informative, therefore, to put them together into a single model to probe how they are related and whether one explanation is stronger than the other. To do this for the public, we will use the LISREL program for structural equation modeling (see Jöreskog and Sörbom 1989). This program allows for multiple measures of a single latent factor, or construct, such as we have with our various measures of recipient deservingness, our various measures of program effectiveness, and our various measures of support. Table 4.1 presents relationships between program support indices and a set of items measuring deservingness, while table 4.4 presents relationships between support indices and a set of items tapping into program effectiveness. These sets of items represent underlying latent constructs—one assessing recipient deservingness and the other program effectiveness. By using these two factors in our analysis rather than each individual item, we can better show the distinctive relationship between attitudes about recipient deservingness and program effectiveness and support, free of the distorting influence of measurement error.

Figures 4.3a–c display a program-based model of public support for AFDC, Medicaid, and Social Security. We did not include some of the original items assessing recipient deservingness and program effectiveness in the measurement of these two constructs. In some cases items were excluded because they did not improve the measurement of the factor, and in some cases they were highly

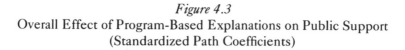

Figure 4.3
Overall Effect of Program-Based Explanations on Public Support
(Standardized Path Coefficients)

(a) AFDC

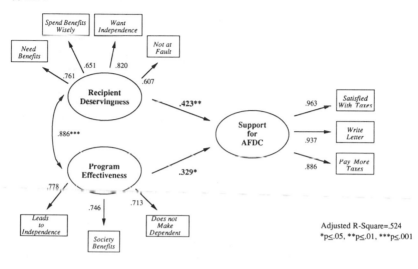

Adjusted R-Square=.524
*p≤.05, **p≤.01, ***p≤.001

(b) Medicaid

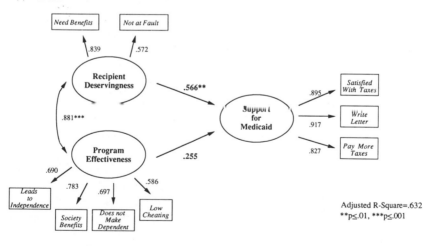

Adjusted R-Square=.632
**p≤.01, ***p≤.001

Figure 4.3 (continued)

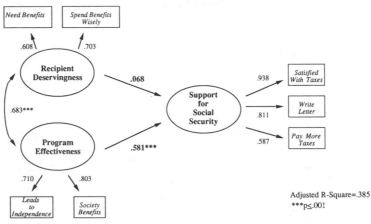

(c) **Social Security**

Adjusted R-Square=.385
***p≤.001

correlated with the other factor, despite also fitting well into their intended factor. Thus, to promote parsimony and discriminant validity, only the items shown in figures 4.3a–c entered the analysis.

Figures 4.3a–c provide the standardized path coefficients for the models tested. Looking first at the model describing public support for AFDC (figure 4.3a), the coefficients show that perceptions of both program recipient deservingness and program effectiveness are related to support for AFDC at approximately the same level, although recipient characteristics are more important. Furthermore, these two factors together explain a greater proportion of the variance in program support (adjusted $R^2 = .52$) than did either factor alone (adjusted $R^2 = .40$ and .41 for deservingness and effectiveness, respectively). But the figure also shows that these two sets of program-based attitudes are highly related and so they together do not explain as much variance as they would if they were independent.

The combined program-based model for Medicaid provides even higher prediction than does the model for AFDC (adjusted $R^2 = .63$). More explanatory power seems to come from beliefs about deservingness than program effectiveness. Knowing individuals' beliefs about the deservingness of recipients gives nearly twice as much prediction of support for Medicaid when compared to knowing about their beliefs concerning the quality of the program. Once again, however, the two predictive factors are highly correlated with each other.

Beliefs about the deservingness of Social Security recipients and the effectiveness of the Social Security program also correlate significantly with each other, although the relationship is not as strong as for the other programs. More interesting, however, is that respondents' attitudes about the deservingness of Social Security recipients have virtually no direct effect on program support, although the model combining both factors explains more of the variances in support than does either model alone (adjusted R^2 = .38).

All these analyses show that attitudes about program-related characteristics are important when trying to understand public support for social welfare programs. Interestingly, however, the usefulness of program characteristics differs depending upon the program. For the two public assistance programs (AFDC and Medicaid), support by members of the public seems to be related more to their perceptions of recipients than to their views about program goals and effectiveness. On the other hand, for the one social insurance program investigated in detail (Social Security), members of the public appear to be more concerned with program effectiveness than recipient deservingness. This partly reflects the fact that nearly all members of the public believe that Social Security recipients are deserving, limiting the variability that correlations need. Nonetheless, it is important to note the clear difference in results for models of these two types of programs.

The Differential Role of Deservingness and Effectiveness

How do we interpret the differences among the public and the differences between the public and the Congress? We find the public makes a sharp distinction between public assistance programs and social insurance programs. Most of our respondents said they currently contribute to Social Security or have contributed to it at some point in the past, and most know someone who receives benefits. Since all who receive Social Security benefits have in some way contributed to its funding, it is not surprising that the public finds beneficiaries deserving. Furthermore, Social Security has a simply stated goal; it exists to provide retirement income to past employees and their spouses.** There is little bureaucratic red tape involved with Social Security: one federal agency manages accounts and sends out benefit checks. Given the clarity of the goal of Social Security and the relative efficiency of its implementation, it is not surprising that the public is pleased with the program.

The contrast between these characteristics and those of AFDC and Medicaid is instructive. Few respondents receive AFDC and Medicaid, and only a small proportion know people who do. When they hear about recipients, it is often in negative terms. As a Republican representative notes, "Also to be candid, some Republicans and some conservatives, notably including our president [Reagan] who I am a great admirer of, have reaped votes in the past by telling stories about welfare queens. And that is unfortunate, and I hope we are past that day." [#17] With the abundance of negative portrayals of welfare recipients, we are surprised that perceptions of deservingness are positive on the whole. But we are not surprised to find a strong relationship between perceptions of deservingness and support for AFDC and Medicaid. Since the Elizabethan Poor Laws of 1601, notions of deservingness have informed the discussion about whom should be helped.

The goal of Social Security is fairly simple and the degree of its effectiveness easy to see. On the other hand, the goals of AFDC and Medicaid are complex. Are AFDC and Medicaid designed to help children directly, or are they intended to help children by helping parents? Is their purpose to provide essentials (e.g., money, medical care), or is it to reach a higher goal of recipient self-sufficiency? Any one of these characterizations is correct. Because there is no single, simply stated goal of these public assistance programs, their effectiveness is more difficult for the public to judge. Additionally, unlike for Social Security, most members of the public have little personal experience with the programs in question. Although we are surprised to find the public relatively pleased with the effectiveness of AFDC and Medicaid, we are not surprised that perceptions of effectiveness influence levels of support. Beginning in the 1960s, policy changes in the social welfare

** Social Security (OASDI) also provides benefits to permanently disabled workers and their dependent children and spouses, as well as to surviving children and spouses of deceased workers. Although these individuals comprise roughly 30 percent of Social Security beneficiaries (Levitan 1990), the traditional image of Social Security recipients centers around the elderly.

domain have focused on improving that which works (Schwarz 1988). For the public, perceptions of "what works" clearly helps shape support.

But perceptions of what works do not help explain the support of Congress members. Why? If social welfare programs do not work effectively, it is in part the responsibility of Congress to remedy the situation. Congress must enact programs and legislate modifications. We find that when programs do not work, Congress members feel that they must develop better designs, not withdraw their support or dismantle programs. Thus, despite the fact that many representatives believe public assistance programs are ineffective, they continue to support them while at the same time trying to reform them. Members of the general public feel no such responsibility. Consequently, those members of the public who believe programs are ineffective are much more likely than members of Congress to withdraw their support.

The analyses in this chapter have helped us elucidate more clearly the roles of recipient deservingness and program effectiveness in shaping public and congressional support for social welfare programs. The two factors are obviously important to both members of the public and of the U.S. Congress, but they have a greater influence over public support. In the next chapter, we look at the power of two other explanations in shaping support for social welfare.

5
Self-Interest and Political Predispositions as Explanations of Support

In the preceding chapter we showed how attitudes about recipient deservingness and program effectiveness contribute to shaping support for social welfare programs and for social welfare services. Deservingness and effectiveness are based on perceptions of program characteristics—how well the program works and whom it is designed to help—and can be altered by changing attributes of either the program or its beneficiaries. However, these two programmatic explanations ignore the personal characteristics of the individual respondent that some social scientists argue play a powerful role in affecting political behavior. Two of the central perspectives that have been used to explain a relationship between personal traits and political attitudes are economic self-interest and political predispositions. Past research on Americans' attitudes toward welfare has embraced each of these perspectives, most commonly using income as an indicator of self-interest and focusing on party identification as the most relevant political predisposition.

The self-interest approach to political behavior is best exemplified by the rational choice theory first presented in a political context by Downs (1957; see also Becker 1976). From this perspective, individual behavior is understood as actions rationally calculated to further one's own interests or goals. Within the social welfare arena, self-interest would be indicated if, for example, the elderly (who stand to benefit most from public retirement funds) are especially eager supporters of Social Security and Medicare, while the young (who must pay the cost through additional taxes) are especially strong opponents. Similarly, self-interest would be indicated if the poor (who stand to benefit the most from social welfare programs such as AFDC, Medicaid, and Food Stamps) are the strongest supporters of public assistance programs, while the middle class and the wealthy (who must pay a disproportionate amount of the cost) are the strongest opponents. Thus, self-interest among members of the public is a calculation of what one personally stands to gain or lose materially in the short term by espousing a particular course of action.

In considering the self-interest of members of Congress, we would expect representatives from higher-income districts (whose constituents must disproportionately pay the cost) to be much less supportive of public assistance programs such as AFDC, Medicaid, and Food Stamps than those from lower-income districts. Given the high voter turnout of the elderly and their greater tendency to be represented by interest groups (Day 1990), self-interest also predicts that representatives from districts with a high concentration of elderly persons will be more likely to favor programs for the elderly than will representatives from districts with a smaller proportion of elderly. Thus, self-interest for members of Congress focuses on actions that will lead to reelection—that is, actions that are targeted at benefiting those most politically active in the district who will in turn, representatives hope, vote for them and contribute to their political campaigns.

A second respondent-based perspective we consider that might help explain support for social welfare programs and groups for services is political predispositions. This explanation is closely linked to the "symbolic politics" position developed by Sears (1975, 1983), who argues that explanations of policy, politics, and politicians are linked more strongly to personal ideology—or "symbolic predispositions"—than to concerns of immediate material self-interest. Sears sees these predispositions typically manifest as party identification and as respondents' self-description as "liberal" or "conservative." Political predispositions are especially useful in predicting behavior because they tend to be relatively stable throughout most people's adult life (Sears and Funk 1990).

Past analyses of Americans' support for various policies have shown that both economic self-interest and personal predispositions influence support, depending on the policy issue in question. The explanatory power of the symbolic politics model has been confirmed in studies involving support for the busing of students to desegregate schools (Sears, Hensler, and Speer 1979), the war in Vietnam (Lau, Brown, and Sears 1978), and the death penalty (Tyler and Weber 1982). However, ideological predispositions do not explain support for tax policies. On the contrary, past research shows self-interest to be a much stronger predictor of support for paying taxes (Sears and Citrin 1982).

Why does self-interest predict beliefs about taxation but symbolic politics explains support for other policy issues? According to Sears and Funk (1990), it may be because of the "unusual clarity of the personal stakes" (p. 159) involved with taxation policy. If this is so, we might expect to find self-interest important in explaining support for social welfare programs. Social welfare programs are financed with tax dollars, but clearly go to help only specific subgroups within the general population. Thus, the stakes may seem fairly clear to those who will directly benefit from a particular program as well as to those who will not. They are clear to the taxpayers who are funding the programs in question and to Congress members representing larger proportions of wealthy taxpayers.

On the other hand, there is also reason to expect political predispositions—party identification and degree of liberalism or conservatism—to be influential in explaining support for social welfare programs. From Franklin Roosevelt's New Deal to Lyndon Johnson's War on Poverty to the present, Democrats have acted largely as the originators and the guardians of social welfare programs. Republicans traditionally have been the critics. Liberals take on the role of spokespersons and defenders of a strong social welfare state, while conservatives tend to advocate for a more limited role of government.

In this chapter, we examine the importance of both the self-interest and political predispositions perspectives in explaining support for social welfare programs among members of the public and the U.S. House of Representatives.

Self-Interest and Support

The Public

Self-interest can be conceptualized in a number of ways. We choose to define the concept through four personal characteristics likely to influence support for social welfare programs: 1) whether or not one is a recipient of a particular program, 2) whether or not one has close friends or relatives who are recipients, 3) whether one is poor or more well-to-do, and 4) whether or not one shares characteristics with the program's target populations (e.g., poor families with children). A fifth category that some have included in their analyses of self-interest is African Americans, although few find a simple and straightforward case for self-interest among blacks (see for example, Sanders 1988; Hasenfeld and Rafferty 1989; Shapiro and Patterson 1986). Because it is common to include blacks in any study of self-interest, we too have incorporated them in our analyses. However, as we will discuss in greater detail later, all blacks as individuals do not necessarily gain in immediate and material ways by supporting social welfare, and therefore we do not define high support among blacks as a group as indicative of self-interest.

The special interests of recipients, their families, and friends. We will first look at the personal interests of the recipients themselves. Respondents who receive benefits will naturally be more directly affected by changes in the program. Therefore, according to self-interest, program recipients should be more supportive of the programs in which they participate than should nonrecipients.

Although not direct recipients themselves, individuals who have close relatives or friends benefiting from social welfare programs depend on programs to care for their loved ones. Were the benefit levels reduced, many of them would then have greater personal financial responsibility for the care of their relatives. The children and adult grandchildren of Social Security recipients fit this definition of self-interest quite well. Respondents with elderly parents or grandparents receiving Social Security payments may feel as supportive of the program as the recipients themselves because they would likely have to assume some of the financial burden if government benefits stopped.

We asked respondents whether they or anyone in their household received benefits through each of seven major social welfare programs. We also asked if they had any friends or family members not living in the household who received benefits. Few respondents were themselves direct recipients of welfare programs, but the numbers were large enough for us to examine their responses: 32 respondents received AFDC; 32 received SSI; 58 participated in the Food Stamps program; 69 used Medicaid; 101 got unemployment insurance; 205 benefited from Medicare; and 295 received Social Security.*

Table 5.1 provides a breakdown of the responses about whether program benefits should be increased, decreased, or maintained. Looking first at the responses of recipients of each of the public assistance programs, the results demonstrate that an overwhelming majority of AFDC recipients (75 percent) favor increasing AFDC compared to 32 percent of nonrecipients. Similarly, Food Stamp recipients are more likely to favor higher payments (53 percent want increases) than are nonrecipients (24 percent), and more Medicaid recipients want to increase Medicaid benefits (64 percent) than do nonrecipients (47 percent). In the case of SSI, the trend is the same between recipients (69 percent) and nonrecipients (57 percent) although the differences are not statistically significant. Furthermore, even when we control for income and compare recipients with nonrecipients earning less than $20,000, we still find recipients more supportive. Thus, program recipients are not only more supportive than the public overall, but also they are more supportive than others who experience economic hardship.

These results clearly demonstrate a striking difference in support levels between recipients of public assistance programs and nonrecipients. Members of the public who are not themselves recipients but have family or friends receiving benefits also tend to hold more favorable views toward public assistance programs than those who do not have close friends and family members receiving assistance. The levels of support of friends and family tend to be

* Taking into account participation in more than one social welfare program, slightly more than one-third of the respondents in our sample (37 percent) received benefits from one of the seven social welfare programs about which we asked. Greatest participation occurred in the social insurance programs (33 percent received Social Security, Medicare, or Unemployment Insurance), while far fewer received benefits from public assistance programs (10 percent received Food Stamps, AFDC, Medicaid, or SSI).

lower than those of the recipients themselves but, nonetheless, generally higher than respondents not personally affected.

The case for self-interest among social insurance recipients is not as strong as that for public assistance recipients. Table 5.1 shows that recipients both of Social Security and Unemployment Insurance are more likely than nonrecipients to want increases in benefits and less likely to desire decreases. For the most part, however, the differences are not as large as those between public assistance recipients and nonrecipients. Moreover, Medicare recipients do not significantly differ from nonrecipients in their support

Table 5.1

Program Recipient Self-Interest and Support for Current Social Welfare Programs (Increase/Decrease Measure)

	N	% Increase	Increase/Decrease Scale % Maintain	% Decrease	Chi Square
Public Assistance Programs					
AFDC					
Recipient					
No	1101	32.4	51.2	16.3	25.48***
Yes	32	75.0	21.9	3.1	
Family/Friend					
No	921	31.9	51.5	16.6	7.54*
Yes	184	42.4	44.0	13.6	
Food Stamps					
Recipient					
No	1052	23.5	50.7	25.9	28.99***
Yes	58	53.4	39.7	6.9	
Family/Friend					
No	798	21.4	50.9	27.7	25.87***
Yes	294	35.4	46.9	17.7	
Medicaid					
Recipient					
No	1087	46.6	46.5	6.9	8.00*
Yes	69	63.8	33.3	2.9	
Family/Friend					
No	787	45.5	47.5	7.0	6.08*
Yes	325	53.5	40.0	6.5	
SSI					
Recipient					
No	1131	57.0	40.2	2.7	1.91
Yes	32	68.8	28.1	3.1	
Family/Friend					
No	184	62.5	34.2	3.3	3.22
Yes	940	56.1	41.3	2.7	

Table 5.1 (continued)

	N	% Increase	% Maintain	% Decrease	Chi Square
			Increase/Decrease Scale		
Social Insurance Programs					
Social Security					
Recipient					
No	901	54.8	41.0	4.2	12.19**
Yes	295	63.1	36.3	0.7	
Family/Friend					
No	365	54.2	40.8	4.9	4.48
Yes	822	57.8	39.5	2.7	
Unemploy. ins.					
Recipient					
No	1041	30.5	56.0	13.5	9.93**
Yes	101	45.5	45.5	8.9	
Family/Friend					
No	790	29.9	57.1	13.0	3.34
Yes	333	34.8	51.4	13.8	
Medicare					
Recipient					
No	976	68.4	28.6	3.0	4.39
Yes	205	68.8	30.7	0.5	
Family/Friend					
No	443	68.2	28.4	3.4	1.89
Yes	716	68.3	29.6	2.1	

*p<.05; **p<.01; ***p<.001

for Medicare. Medicare is one of the most strongly supported of the seven programs, and both recipients and nonrecipients urge legislators to consider increasing benefits (68 percent of both groups). That Medicare recipients are no more supportive than nonrecipients may be because all respondents consider themselves in some way potential recipients of the program, but it may also merely be evidence that the theory of self-interest does not always offer a viable explanation if it is expressed in terms of current beneficiaries.

Family members of social insurance recipients also do not differ greatly from unaffiliated respondents. Our working definition of self-interest is immediate material gain, and using this definition there is no apparent self-interest among family members of recipients of social insurance programs. However, it is difficult to disentangle immediate rewards from long-term benefits within the social insurance realm. Every worker pays into the system, and consequently every worker expects to get something out of it. Thus, nearly everyone is either presently a recipient or presently a contributor. Nonetheless, we can conclude that the immediate financial gains provided by Social Security and other social insurance programs do not appear to motivate greater support from family and close friends of program recipients.

So far, the results provide evidence that support, under some conditions, may be driven by concerns for the self. We can test the hypothesis further by examining the behavioral support measures for AFDC, Medicaid, and Social Security. Respondents were asked whether they would take actions (write letters, pay more taxes) to maintain each of the three programs. For all three programs, recipients express higher overall support than nonrecipients. On the 20-point scale (-10 to $+10$), AFDC recipients (mean $=$ 4.9) are more supportive than nonrecipients (mean $=$ 1.3); Medicaid recipients (mean $=$ 6.5) are more supportive than nonrecipients (mean $=$ 2.9); and Social Security recipients (mean $=$ 5.8) are more supportive than nonrecipients (mean $=$ 4.1). This is not true for indirect recipients. Individuals who do not themselves receive benefits but have family or friends who do are no more supportive than those who have no personal contact with the programs.

In the action-oriented support measure, respondents were asked how much more they would be willing to pay in taxes to support the programs. This is perhaps an unfair measure of recipient support since many recipients pay little, if any, taxes. Recipients can, however, write letters to their representatives in Washington, and the results indicate that they say they would do so if their program was under fire. While 33 percent of the respondents among the general public say that they would definitely write letters or sign petitions to protect AFDC from cuts, 59 percent of the recipients say they would write. The same pattern is true for Medicaid recipients (56 percent would definitely write versus 36 percent of nonrecipients) and Social Security recipients (69 percent would definitely write versus 50 percent of nonrecipients). Thus, not only are recipients more likely than others to say they would like to see benefits increased, but they are also more likely to report willingness to back their beliefs with actions.

As we have mentioned, pinpointing the self-interest of Social Security recipients is difficult since nearly all Americans hope one day to be Social Security beneficiaries. A number of researchers and policymakers have suggested a decreasing level of confidence

Table 5.2

Public Self-Interest and Support for Current Social Welfare Programs
(Increase/Decrease Measure)

	N	% Increase	Increase/decrease scale		Chi square
			% Maintain	% Decrease	
Elderly versus young					
Social Security					
Over 60	266	56.0	46.3	1.5	
31–59 years	603	58.7	38.1	3.2	8.75
Under 30	325	54.5	40.3	5.2	
Medicare					
Over 60	260	64.2	34.2	1.5	
31–59 years	591	69.2	27.6	3.2	6.53
Under 30	328	70.7	27.1	2.1	
Wealthy versus poor[a]					
AFDC					
Over $50,000	198	30.3	50.0	19.7	
Middle income	698	31.4	53.4	15.2	6.51
Under $10,000	152	39.5	46.1	14.5	
Food Stamps					
Over $50,000	200	18.5	51.5	30.0	
Middle income	674	23.6	49.4	27.0	12.90**
Under $10,000	127	30.7	54.3	15.0	
Medicaid					
Over $50,000	200	40.5	47.0	12.5	
Middle income	704	47.7	46.3	6.0	15.90**
Under $10,000	133	52.6	44.4	3.0	
SSI					
Over $50,000	204	52.9	43.1	3.9	
Middle income	714	56.4	41.0	2.5	7.67
Under $10,000	160	65.6	33.1	1.3	

[a] Recipients have been omitted from the analyses.
*p<.05; **p<.01; ***p<.001

among young adults toward the Social Security program (Goodwin and Tu 1975; Preston 1984). These commentators hypothesize that distrust is largely motivated by a fear that the program will fail to pay benefits in future years—that is, a fear that Social Security will become insolvent. If they are right, following a theory of self-interest, the young should be less supportive because they think they will not personally benefit from the program yet must contribute financially to it. Yet the results depicted in table 5.2 fail to bear out this hypothesis. Younger respondents (those under thirty years of age) appear no less supportive than older respondents (those over sixty) of either Social Security or Medicaid. The young are also no less likely to show their support of Social Security through actions (the means of 4.22 for young adults and 5.18 for older respondents using a scale from −10 to +10 are not statistically significantly different). Thus, the younger members of the public interviewed in this study do not appear to be driven by self-interest into opposing Social Security.

Self-interest of the rich and poor. For the most part, poor people pay little in federal and state income taxes. Thus, according to self-interest theory, it is in their best interest to favor increasing public assistance benefits since they will not lose much and may one day need assistance. On the other hand, middle- and upper-income citizens must provide the tax money necessary to sustain programs, and it is in their best interest to be less supportive. They do not directly receive benefits; yet they must pay for those who do. Table 5.2 shows the supportiveness of middle- and upper-income groups as compared to the poor. In order to control for the high support expressed by program recipients (whose views we have already examined above), recipients have been omitted from this analysis so that we can look only at the views of the poor who do not receive public assistance in comparison to middle- and high-income groups.

From the data (table 5.2) we see that poor respondents are more supportive of Food Stamps and Medicaid than middle-income respondents and that middle-income respondents are more supportive than high-income respondents. Although the trend in support for AFDC and SSI is the same as for the other two public assistance programs, the differences are not significantly different.

Using the second measure of support for programs the action oriented twenty-point scale—we find that low-income respondents report considerably more willingness to support Medicaid than do middle- and upper-income respondents (mean for low income respondents = 4.91, middle income = 2.92, and high income = 2.34, $F(2,418) = 4.76$, $p < .01$). The same trend occurs for AFDC (mean low income = 1.70, mean middle income = 1.32, and mean high income = 1.16), but this difference is not statistically significant. The clear tendency, though, is for the poor to be more supportive of Medicaid than the more well-to-do who must pay the actual taxes.

Reference groups and self-interest. So far we have defined a self-interested public as those individuals who actually receive benefits or whose friends or family members do, and as those who pay for benefits but do not receive them. Another group to consider are individuals who, although not necessarily recipients, share similar personal and financial characteristics with those who receive benefits. In other words, they are members of the programs' target population though not presently participating in the program. The AFDC program is targeted at low-income families with children, and benefits are directly linked to the presence of children in the household. We might then expect that individuals who have children or could potentially expect to have children (i.e., are married and of a childbearing age) and are poor (i.e., have incomes below $20,000) have some self-interest in maintaining programs for others like them. The results of our study fail to demonstrate any unique interest by these individuals. Poor adults with children are no more likely to support increases in AFDC benefits, are no more likely to take actions to support AFDC, and when asked to choose who to help through services, are no more likely than other poor nonelderly adults to rank children high for receiving services.

The unique interests of African Americans.   Throughout the discussion of self-interest, we have used a narrow definition of the concept. We have argued that only those who have more to gain in the short term both personally and materially should express higher support because of self-interest. A number of researchers have considered African Americans in their analyses of self-interest because, as Hasenfeld and Rafferty contend, they are "socioeconomically vulnerable and thus more likely to benefit from the welfare state" (1989:1041). In several ways, this is true. Roughly the same proportion of AFDC recipients are black as are white (40 percent versus 38 percent), but because African Americans represent only about 12 percent of the total population, a much higher proportion of blacks receive AFDC than the proportion of whites participating in the program.** In 1990, 10.7 percent of the non-Hispanic white population lived below the U.S. poverty line, while in contrast, 31.9 percent of African Americans lived in poverty. Further, 26.8 percent of white families headed only by women are poor com-

---

    ** A recent publication by the U.S. Department of Health and Human Services (1991) anchors AFDC recipients in two ways—either by parents or by children. Anchored by parents, 40.1 percent are African Americans, 38.4 percent are white, 15.9 percent are Hispanic, 2.7 percent are Asian, 1.3 percent native North American, and 1.5 percent are of unknown origin. Of all parents, 90 percent are mothers. Anchored by children, the comparable proportions are 41.4, 33.5, 17.1, 3.8, 1.3, and 2.9 (p. 6).

pared to 48.1 percent of black female-headed families (U.S. Bureau of the Census, 1991c).

Similar to the results from other studies (Hasenfeld and Rafferty 1989; Shapiro and Patterson 1986), the results from this study show that black respondents are more supportive than white respondents (because of limited sample size, we are not able to examine other racial and ethnic groups). In fact, black respondents are much more likely to favor benefit increases and oppose decreases than nonrecipient whites for each of the seven programs in question. They are also more likely to back their support with actions. On the twenty-point scale from -10 to $+10$, black respondents scored an average of 3.07 for AFDC, 5.42 for Medicaid, and 5.43 for Social Security. This compares to the scores by white respondents of 1.18 for AFDC ($t[1128] = 3.5$, $p < .001$), 2.96 for Medicaid ($t[452] = 3.3$, $p < .001$), and 4.51 for Social Security ($t[470] = 1.3$, n.s.).

Is this self-interest? It would be self-interest if the higher overall support scores of blacks result either from poor blacks being considerably more supportive than financially well-to-do blacks, or from black public assistance recipients being considerably more supportive than nonrecipients. In fact, since 31 percent of the black respondents in our sample have incomes of less than $10,000 compared to only 14 percent of the white respondents, it is conceivable that the support of these low-income respondents might drive up the mean support score for blacks in general. Yet when we examine the supportiveness of African Americans by income group, we find no differences. In fact, in some cases upper-income blacks (those earning greater than $50,000) tend to be more supportive than lower income blacks, although in no instance is the relationship statistically significant. For example, poor blacks are slightly less supportive of AFDC (mean $= 3.18$) and Social Security (mean $= 4.82$) than upper-income blacks (mean $= 4.12$ and 6.33, respectively).

Just as African Americans are more likely than other respondents to be poor, they are also more likely to be recipients of social welfare programs. Self-interest argues that black recipients should be more supportive than nonrecipients. However, the results fail to bear this out. We find no pattern of black recipients being consistently more supportive than black nonrecipients.***

Further, the same pattern of support exists between blacks and

*** On the other hand, white recipients of public assistance programs are more supportive than white nonrecipients in every case except SSI.

whites: both groups are more supportive of Social Security than Medicaid and are more supportive of Medicaid than AFDC. We argue, therefore, that the high supportiveness of African Americans is due to factors other than self-interest, such as shared ideology. As Shapiro and Patterson (1986) note, self-interest on the part of African Americans is difficult to disentangle from group interests or group consciousness and, more important, from normative concerns such as fairness to all citizens (p. 19).

Self-interest and the public.   As predicted, self-interest helps explain the greater support of some members of the public. Program recipients are especially supportive of social welfare programs when compared with nonrecipients. The poor also tend to be more supportive, although not to the extent of recipients. On the other hand, and contrary to predictions, family and friends of recipients—many of whom share similar characteristics to recipients—are not consistently more supportive than respondents with no direct contact to programs, especially when support is measured as willingness to take actions. Furthermore, recipients of any given program represent a small proportion of all Americans, so we can not expect this characteristic to be particularly useful in advancing our understanding of public support for social welfare. Most citizens do not have a personal and direct interest in maintaining programs, and yet many are nonetheless supportive.

How much variance in support does self-interest account for? We can answer this question through the use of regression analysis. Using our behavioral measure of support, we test the viability of self-interest in predicting support for public assistance programs with four independent measures: recipient status, recipient status of family or close friends, income, and being of childbearing age (under forty). Because so many of the variables are dichotomous, we used polychoric correlations rather than Pearson product-moment correlations in the regression matrix. Polychoric correlations allow for greater divergence from normality and thus are better able to detect relationships when using dichotomous or skewed variables. Despite this methodological advantage, the model of self-interest is able to explain only five percent of the variance in support for AFDC. However, it fares better in predicting support for Medicaid (adjusted $R^2 = .17$). The measures of self-interest for Social Security are slightly different than for the two public assistance programs. Income is omitted since Social Security is not means-tested, and the elderly replace adults of childbearing age as principal targets.**** Self-interest explains 16 percent of the variance in support for Social Security.

Nearly all of the explanatory power in predicting support for AFDC and Medicaid comes from knowing a respondent's status as a recipient. This variable alone is able to explain 16.5 percent of the variance in Medicaid (99 percent of all explained in the full model), and 4.5 percent of AFDC (87 percent of all explained). For Social Security the recipient status variable is also the most important, although not as strikingly so as for the other two programs. Recipient status alone explains 9 percent of the variance in support for Social Security.

Thus, self-interest explains little of the variance in support for AFDC but explains more of the variance in support for Medicaid and Social Security, although still relatively small amounts. Taking into account the findings discussed earlier in this section, it is not surprising to find that self-interest has only limited value in explaining public support for AFDC. Those respondents who support AFDC for what are likely to be self-interested reasons are simply too small in number to make a difference to overall levels of support among the public as a whole.

We can now draw several conclusions about the viability of the hypothesis that self-interest causes individuals to support social welfare programs. When self-interest is defined narrowly, in this case as recipients of existing programs, it clearly appears to influence support. Also, we see some degree of self-interest in the greater support of the poor for Medicaid and Food Stamps as compared to the support of middle- and upper-income respondents, though these differences are not so striking for support of AFDC and SSI. However, the usefulness of self-interest as an explanatory variable declines as the definition of self-interest is

---

**** The categories "Social Security recipients" and "elderly persons aged 65 and over" are not completely overlapping. For example, some persons younger than age 65 may be Social Security recipients because they elected to retire early and to receive reduced benefits beginning at age 62 or because they are survivors of a Social Security contributor. Likewise, some persons over age 65 may not be Social Security recipients because they are continuing to work full time after age 64 and thus cannot receive Social Security benefits until they reach age 72. And, of course, a very few elderly persons are not Social Security recipients because they never contributed to Social Security through their work and are not survivors of a spouse who contributed.

broadened. Individuals who share similar personal characteristics with recipients but are not themselves presently participating in a program (family and friends of recipients, low-income families with children) are not consistently more supportive than others with dissimilar backgrounds.

Given findings from past research, it is not surprising that recipients of program benefits should be more supportive than others. Sears and Funk (1990) argue that self-interest operates in political decisions when personal stakes are particularly clear and important. Both these conditions are present when recipients make decisions about support for social welfare programs. Benefits for most social welfare programs are low; for example, in 1989 the average AFDC mother of two children received $360 per month—only 46 percent of the federal poverty threshold, and no state pays benefits sufficient to keep AFDC families out of poverty, although the availability of Food Stamps helps alleviate the stress somewhat. The maximum value of both Food Stamps and AFDC benefits was $570 for a family of three in 1989—73 percent of the poverty threshold (Levitan 1990:49). Thus, we should expect that recipients would favor increased benefits that will significantly improve their quality of life.

The Congress

Self-interest is a popular theory for explaining the actions of elected officials. As Anthony Downs (1957) persuasively argues, members of Congress seek electoral success, and they will do what it takes to achieve it. Thus, they do not necessarily follow their own views about the merits of policies or respond to the most pressing problems and needs of members of the public. Rather, as outlined by Stigler (1971), representatives barter their political power for votes and campaign resources from groups wishing to gain particular policies. Similarly, according to the "electoral theory" of Congress developed by Mayhew (1974) and Fiorina (1977), representatives earn electoral rewards by supporting the needs or demands of organized interest groups. In return for favored policies or programs, interest groups promise representatives campaign money and votes.

The self-interest of members of Congress, then, can be operationalized in terms of that which will lead to more votes and more money for their campaigns. According to this explanation, representatives from high-income districts should be less likely than members from low-income districts to favor increases in social welfare benefits. This is because constituents from high-income districts are not likely to benefit from social welfare programs, although they will have to pay for them through their taxes. Favoring increased benefits (hence, increased taxation) would gain members of Congress representing high-income districts neither votes nor campaign contributions from those with the most money to spend.

Likewise, according to self-interest theory, representatives from districts with high proportions of elderly residents should be more likely to favor increasing benefits in programs for the elderly than would representatives representing districts with lower proportions of elderly residents. Studies have shown the elderly to vote in higher proportions than the nonelderly. Furthermore, the elderly are heavily represented by interest groups in Washington, D.C. (Day 1990). Thus, Congress members hoping to increase their electoral margins should cater to those most likely to lobby and to vote.

In our survey, we asked congressional respondents about their support for several major social welfare programs as well as about which target groups they prefer for specific services. We also coded information on the characteristics of the districts represented by each member of Congress in our sample. Thus, we can relate representatives' support for programs and groups to the characteristics of the constituents within their districts.

The interests of the well-to-do. If members of Congress make decisions based on self-interest, we would expect those who represent districts with larger proportions of wealthy citizens to be less supportive of public assistance programs than those representing districts with little wealth. To categorize districts by relative wealth, we combined two measures: median income of district residents (high, middle, and low) and proportion of district residents with incomes over $50,000 (high, moderate, and low proportions).*****
Thus, higher-income districts have both a high median income and

***** By combining these two measures, we can be sure we are really looking at high-income districts and not just districts that are solidly middle-income and only appear to have a high median income because there are no poor people in the district to bring down the median income. One-quarter of the districts have both higher median income and higher proportions of wealthy, and one-quarter have both lower median income and lower proportions of wealthy.

a larger than average proportion of residents with incomes over $50,000, while low-income districts have both a low median income and few, if any, residents with incomes over $50,000.

Examining the data in the first section of table 5.3, we find little evidence of self-interest in representatives' level of support for

Table 5.3

Congressional Self-Interest and Support for Current Social Welfare Programs (Increase/Decrease Measure)

	N	% Increase	% Maintain	% Decrease	Chi square
			Increase/decrease scale		
District wealth[a]					
AFDC					
High	15	23.0	77.0	0.0	
Medium	27	42.9	51.4	5.7	7.17
Low	15	24.1	55.1	20.8	
Food Stamps					
High	15	12.6	56.2	31.3	
Medium	27	24.1	63.7	12.3	6.59
Low	15	3.6	54.7	41.7	
Medicaid					
High	15	44.9	34.3	20.8	
Medium	27	56.1	43.9	0.0	18.16**
Low	15	12.6	87.4	0.0	
Proportion of elderly[b]					
Social Security					
High	23	6.8	93.2	0.0	
Medium	16	10.1	89.9	0.0	1.16
Low	19	19.2	80.8	0.0	
Medicare					
High	23	28.5	51.1	20.3	
Medium	16	33.7	66.3	0.0	4.28
Low	19	35.9	55.8	8.3	
District poverty[c]					
AFDC					
High	20	43.1	56.9	0.0	
Medium	20	25.4	51.2	23.4	10.44*
Low	18	29.6	70.4	0.0	
Food Stamps					
High	20	17.6	66.5	15.9	
Medium	20	18.4	50.4	31.2	1.90
Low	18	10.6	61.6	27.8	
Medicaid					
High	20	42.3	57.7	0.0	
Medium	20	34.5	65.5	31.2	9.60*
Low	18	49.5	32.9	17.7	

	N	% Increase	Increase/decrease scale % Maintain	% Decrease	Chi square
District unemployment[d]					
AFDC					
High	19	48.4	51.6	0.0	
Medium	17	41.7	49.3	9.1	10.22*
Low	21	8.1	75.8	16.1	
Food Stamps					
High	19	33.3	51.6	15.1	
Medium	17	12.2	68.3	19.4	10.61*
Low	21	0.0	59.7	40.3	
Medicaid					
High	19	59.3	33.1	7.5	
Medium	17	29.1	70.9	0.0	6.52
Low	21	34.3	57.7	8.1	
Unemploy. ins.					
High	19	25.0	66.7	8.3	
Medium	17	1.9	89.1	9.1	5.80
Low	21	8.1	75.8	16.1	

[a]High-wealth districts are those with a median income greater than $21,000 and at least 1.7% of the families earning more than $50,000; low-wealth districts have a median income no greater than $17,500 and no more than 1% earning over $50,000.

[b]Districts with high proportions of elderly are defined as those with greater than 17.2%; low elderly proportions have less than 14.4%.

[c]Poor districts represent those with more than 14% of the population living below the official poverty level; low-poverty districts have less than 10% below the poverty level.

[d]High unemployment defined as greater than 6.7%, low defined as less than 4.8%.

*p<.10; **p<.05; ***p<.01

public assistance programs. Members of Congress representing higher-income districts have similar levels of support for AFDC and Medicaid when compared with Congress members who represent lower-income districts. In terms of support for Medicaid, the differences in support are statistically significant, but the data tell a different story from the one expected if self-interest predicted support. Whereas self-interest predicts that representatives from higher-income districts will not favor increasing Medicaid benefits, in fact a larger proportion of these representatives favor increasing benefits than do representatives from lower-income districts (45 percent versus 13 percent). Thus, despite the fact that most Congress members recognize that "people who are fortunate enough to have a job figure that a big portion of the money they pay in taxes, . . . they would not have to pay . . . if it didn't go to these programs," [#41] representatives from wealthy districts are not moved to favor lower public assistance benefits solely because their constituents are disproportionately called upon to finance these programs.

This conclusion is not restricted to beliefs. In addition, Congress members' behaviors do not seem to be strongly affected by the income composition of their districts. The number of times that representatives from districts with higher proportions of wealthy residents vote for issues designed to help low-income children and their families is not significantly different from the voting patterns of their colleagues representing districts with little wealth. Respectively, the means are 5.5 and 6.6 on the Children's Defense Fund voting scale from 0 (in favor of no policies) to 10 (support all ten coded policies). We can conclude, therefore, that the socioeconomic status of the district does not motivate representatives either to believe public assistance programs should be reduced or to vote strongly against such programs.

The elderly as an interest group.   The elderly are often seen as a strong and powerful interest group with a higher percentage of people who turn out to vote (Jacob 1990). In the words of one midwestern Democrat, "You've got a very powerful lobby of senior citizens in the Social Security area who impress you with their importance." [#42] When we asked representatives from whom they hear the most among their constituents, an overwhelming number of Congress members mention the elderly and groups representing the elderly. For example:

> Let's say I average 200 people, a total of 200 people, at all four meetings [that I attend a month]. . . . Each month, 150 of them will be senior citizens worried about their Social Security checks and two or one might be there to talk about AFDC. [#37]

> I hear a great deal about these issues. I have a large elderly population. Many of the people in my constituency would be lost without these programs, and they are frightened about the erosion in support that has come about as a result of the cutbacks in these programs of the last five years. [#39]

> The seniors are much in the forefront [because] of their organization abilities and capabilities of contacting individually and through organizations. They have very active organizations—effective organizations. I think that they do represent a very large constituency in voting percentile. [#25]

If self-interest, defined here in terms of meeting the demands of the most vocal and powerful group, is an important criterion in explaining congressional support, we would expect representatives from districts with higher proportions of elderly to be especially concerned both with social programs that focus on the elderly (e.g., Social Security and Medicare) and with targeting future programs so that they will especially help the elderly. To test these hypotheses, we compare the views of members of Congress who represent districts with higher proportions of elderly to those who represent districts with lower proportions of elderly.

Table 5.3 shows no relationship between the proportion of elderly in the district and representatives' beliefs about support for elderly-targeted social insurance programs. Representatives from districts with larger proportions of elderly are no more likely to favor increasing benefits than are representatives with fewer elderly residents. This null relationship is replicated in Congress members' voting patterns. Those coming from districts with higher proportions of elderly voted for policies to help the elderly six out of ten times (votes calculated by the National Council of Senior Citizens), whereas those from districts with low concentrations of elderly adults voted for five of the ten bills. This difference is not statistically significant. In terms of serving the interests of the elderly as voters, these results give little evidence that members of Congress are driven by reelection-seeking self-interest in either their attitudes or their voting behavior.

We can also ask whether Congress members representing higher proportions of elderly constituents are more likely than others to give the elderly a high priority when asked to consider who should receive new services. The results are mixed and depend upon the type of program under consideration. Representatives from districts with higher proportions of elderly are no more likely than those representing districts with lower proportions of elderly constituents to rank the elderly high for receiving additional financial assistance (19 percent of representatives from districts with higher concentrations of the elderly give the elderly a high ranking versus 14 percent from districts with lower concentrations of the elderly). On the other hand, representatives from districts with high elderly concentrations are more likely to give the elderly top priority for nutritional and educational services than are representatives from districts with lower concentrations (34 percent compared with 16 percent for nutritional services; 17 percent versus 0 percent for educational services). These differences are statistically significant (Chi Square (4) = 13.4, and Chi Square (4) = 11.5, p < .05). Thus, self-interest appears to motivate Congress members to rank the elderly high for certain services but does not appear to cause them to differentially support existing programs either attitudinally or behaviorally.

The interests of potential recipients.   Earlier we stated that if Congress members are motivated by self-interest, those from a relatively wealthy district should not support social welfare because of the added financial burden to district taxpayers. The converse should also be true. In other words, those representing districts with higher proportions of constituents having incomes below officially determined poverty thresholds should be more supportive because social welfare programs benefit their constituents disproportionately.

In our interviews, some Congress members express concern with the plight of the poor in their districts. As this representative from the west coast states, "Low-income people suffer more in silence and are not a vocal constituency. While I know I have large numbers of low-income people in my district, they're not the ones I hear from particularly." Despite this, he goes on to explain, "I just have a feeling and a knowledge about what the impact [of cuts] would be on them." [#39] This individual is clearly concerned with meeting the needs of the poor, and he also represents a district with relatively high rates of poverty. Would he be as concerned if his district poverty level was lower? To answer this question, we compare the views of Congress members who represent districts with high proportions of poverty to those who represent districts with moderate and low proportions. In this study, we have identified high poverty districts as those having more than 14 percent of the population falling below the federal poverty line, and low poverty districts are defined as those with fewer than 10 percent living in poverty.****** Our measure captures the two extremes in a nation where 11.7 percent of the population had incomes falling below the federal poverty threshold.

****** The Census Bureau computes district-level demographic data only from the decennial census; therefore, these are the district data that were available for representatives to understand the characteristics of their districts at the time of our survey (U.S. Bureau of the Census 1983).

The results presented in table 5.3 show a pattern of greater support from Congress members who represent districts with high levels of poverty. For example, 43 percent of the representatives from high poverty districts support increased AFDC benefits and none favor decreased benefits, whereas only a quarter of representatives from districts with moderate levels of poverty favor increased benefits and another quarter favor decreased benefits. A similar pattern exists in support for Medicaid. However, the differences in support are not so clear-cut between Congress members representing districts with moderate and low levels of poverty.

District-level poverty also appears to influence congressional voting. Representatives coming from districts with higher proportions of constituents living in poverty are more likely to vote in favor of policies to aid poor children and their families (mean = 7.5) than are those either from moderate-poverty districts (mean = 5.3) or low poverty districts (mean = 5.7, $F_{(2,55)}$ = 3.43, p < .05).

A second group of constituents whom Congress members may be interested in helping are the unemployed. We examined the views of representatives from districts with high, medium, and low levels of unemployment. As the data in table 5.3 show, those representatives from districts with high levels of unemployment are more supportive of the various social welfare programs that could affect the unemployed than are those from districts with lower levels of unemployment. For example, almost half the legislators representing districts with high unemployment support increased AFDC benefits, compared to only 8 percent of representatives from districts with low unemployment. Likewise, a third of those representing high-unemployment districts favor increased food stamp benefits, whereas none of their colleagues representing low-unemployment districts favor such increases and 40 percent support decreases. The pattern is similar for Medicaid and Unemployment Insurance, though the effect of high unemployment is weakest with regard to the program affecting the unemployed most directly, namely Unemployment Insurance. That is, the level of unemployment in the district has a greater influence on congressional support for tax-supported public assistance programs than for Unemployment Insurance.

The voting behavior of representatives from high-unemployment districts also reflects their supportive attitudes (mean = 7.1

versus 6.3 for representatives from districts with mid-level unemployment and 5.0 for those from districts with low unemployment, $F(2,55) = 2.91$, $p = .06$. Thus, Congress members representing either larger proportions of people living in poverty or larger proportions of the unemployed pay greater attention than their colleagues to improving social welfare benefit levels.

Congressional self-interest and support.   Contrary to expectations, the wealth of the district does not appear to affect either congressional attitudes or voting behavior for public assistance programs. The wealthy have the power and money to put pressure on their representatives if they choose; yet this potential threat to reelection has little impact on support for public assistance programs. The other two measures of self-interest for public assistance programs—levels of district poverty and district unemployment—have a stronger effect on congressional attitudes and actions.

To what extent do these three measures of self-interest, when combined, improve our understanding of representatives' support for public assistance programs? To answer this question, we used regression analyses and include the following district-level characteristics as the independent variables: proportion of constituents earning over $50,000; proportion of constituents falling under the federal poverty standard; and percentage of constituents unemployed. With this model we are able to explain 22 percent of the variance in support for public assistance (AFDC and Medicaid combined) and 16 percent of the variance in voting on issues related to low-income children and families. We find, however, that the wealth of the district adds little useful information to the equation. In fact, it actually reduces the fit in the model of attitudinal support because it reduces the degrees of freedom while adding no information beyond what the other two measures offer (adjusted $R^2 = .23$ when wealth is excluded). For voting behavior, the model is virtually identical when district wealth is omitted (adjusted $R^2 = .15$). Thus, self-interest helps to explain level of support when it is defined as attitudes and actions that might assist in meeting the financial needs of poorer constituents, but it does not help to explain support when it is defined as attitudes and actions that might assist in meeting the financial desires of the wealthy to pay lower taxes by reducing benefits for programs.

We also conducted regression analyses to learn the extent to which the proportion of elderly in congressional districts explains representatives' attitudes about social insurance and their votes on elderly issues. As we described earlier, the elderly are especially well organized, and Congress members report hearing from their elderly constituents on a regular basis. Through such interest groups as the American Association of Retired Persons (AARP) and the National Council for Senior Citizens (NCSC), the elderly comprise a strong and vocal voting bloc. Despite this, the proportion of elderly in a district has only a limited effect on Congress members' attitudes and no effect on their voting. Specifically, regression equations using the proportion of elderly in the district explains only a small proportion of the variance in representatives' attitudes toward social insurance (adjusted $R^2 = 0.08$) and none of the variance in their votes for elderly issues (adjusted $R^2 = 0.001$).

Given the nature of congressional reelection-seeking motives, we expected Congress members to be most influenced by those constituents who can have the greatest impact on their campaigns: the wealthy, because of their ability to sponsor candidates, and the elderly, because of their influence and high voter turn-out. Instead, those constituents who have a stronger impact are the least politically influential—the poor and the unemployed. A number of representatives stressed in the interviews that they hear little from the poor. The comments below typify the views we heard from many:

> What you will find is that most of the people who are the recipients of social welfare are not your politically most active people. [#27]

> There is no kind of lobby efforts that goes on for [public assistance] programs. . . . And there are no groups that are really effectively organized to be concerned for poor people. [#38]

Although none of the Congress members commented on their lack of contact with the unemployed, previous research describes the low political involvement of the unemployed. Schlozman and Verba (1979) note that the results of a large national survey on the 1976 presidential election showed that 37 percent of the unemployed did not vote compared with just 25 percent of working citizens. Concerned that voting behavior did not adequately represent the political participation of the unemployed, Schlozman and Verba interviewed a number of government officials concerning their interactions with the unemployed. These interviews led the authors to conclude that "the unemployed are not an active force. They are, in the words of one government official, 'a political zero' " (p. 265). Thus, even though we have Congress members confirming that they hear little from the poor and past research describing the unemployed as politically inactive, we still find these groups have a great impact on representatives' support for social welfare. Why is this?

To the debate about congressional self-interest Kelman (1987) has introduced the concept of congressional "public spiritedness." Instead of seeing representatives as driven by their own personal reelection interests, Kelman argues that they are motivated by their "empathy with the situation of others" (p. 240). Congress members believe and vote as they do, not because they wish to improve their own positions, but because they share the concerns of their constituents and the public as a whole and wish to improve the public condition. Arthur Maass (1983) also contends that representatives are moved to devise policies that will benefit the nation as a whole as well as their own constituents. The public spirit hypothesis may help explain why Congress members are moved by constituent poverty and unemployment to support social welfare programs.

What is it about the experience of representing a district with large proportions of poor people that might make members of Congress more supportive, even though they do not hear from their low-income constituents and even though the poor are less likely than other socioeconomic groups to vote? A representative from the south says it is not what he hears but what he observes when he travels through his district:

> The area that I come from, people are very dependent upon [AFDC]. . . . Going out in the countryside and seeing these people and seeing how helpless they are and how defenseless they are, and how they need protection and—it's not going to be there if there is not some programs that are maintained to put the support mechanisms in place. [#2]

Such representatives are moved to help because they believe it is the right thing to do, not because they think the poor will vote for them. Is this self-interest? To some extent perhaps it is since some constituents who are poor will vote for these representatives and some nonpoor constituents who believe the poor need assistance will also vote for them. But in its purest sense—reelection-seeking behavior—such members of Congress hardly demonstrate self-interest. Instead, members representing large numbers of unemployed constituents and those representing large numbers of poor constituents are motivated to meet the special needs of poorer residents within their districts—a concept we shall label *district interest*. Thus, self-interest is not a strong predictor of congressional support within the social welfare domain, but district interest does influence attitudes and voting behavior.

Political Predispositions and Support

A second respondent-based explanation of support considers the long-held political values of individuals. Before human beings enter adulthood, they have already formed lasting ideological preferences about politics, politicians, and policy directions; and although adult experiences may alter one's earlier political predispositions, these dispositions tend to be fairly stable over time for most individuals (Abramson 1983). These preferences traditionally arise from family background, early experiences, and social relationships and commonly are manifested through party identification, ideology (measured as liberalism or conservatism), nationalism, and racial prejudice (Sears et al. 1980). Sears and his colleagues (Sears 1975, 1983; Sears, Hensler, and Speer 1979) have labeled the use of preferences to guide decisions *symbolic politics*. This befitting terminology denotes how, when faced with a new policy decision, people look for symbols in the new option similar to those held within their preference schemes. Thus, rather than delineating all the pros and cons of the novel selection, they rely on general preferences to help lead the decision and make the situation less unfamiliar. By using preference guides, people remain relatively consistent in their decisions and can spend less energy in the decision-making process.

Perhaps the most common "symbol" is political party identification. Political party represents for most a positive reference group, a group through which ideas and identity are defined and shared. Most individuals develop the same party affiliation as their parents and retain it throughout their lives (Abramson 1983). The strength of party cohesion, acting through the individual's commitment to the group, can be a strong influence on his or her expressed support for institutions, such as social welfare. Some people, of course, do not personally affiliate themselves with a single party and are therefore "independents." For these individuals, party cannot be a guiding factor in political decisions.

The Democratic party has traditionally advocated more government-sponsored social welfare programs than the Republican party, which maintains that government intervention in private affairs should be limited. Although members of political parties share attitudes similar to the party as a whole before they join, the party can also act to encourage certain opinions to flourish within its membership. Unfortunately, one cannot determine conclusively whether individuals affiliate with a party because of shared ideology or whether people affiliate with a party because of family influence and later develop similar ideologies. Most likely there is a little of both involved in the decision to affiliate with a specific party, but because research suggests that party affiliation is relatively stable from early adult life on, we take the position that party affiliation precedes attitudes toward specific issues (such as social welfare programs) rather than the other way around.

A second common predisposition upon which people base their attitudes and decisions about specific issues is their self-described level of liberal or conservative ideology. Liberal and conservative ideologies are related to political parties, of course, with Democrats being more liberal than Republicans. However, as we noted in chapter 2, ideology and party identification are not identical. In our sample of the public, 23 percent of Republicans labeled themselves as liberal, while 44 percent of Democrats characterized themselves as conservative. Ratings by various interest groups provides some insight into the liberalism or conservatism of Congress members. In our sample, 10 percent of the Democrats received high marks from the Americans for Constitutional Action—a conservative group—and 9 percent of the Republicans achieved high ratings from the Americans for Democratic Action—a liberal group (high is taken as ratings greater than 60 on a scale from 0 to 100). Thus, although ideological liberalism is closely associated with the Democratic party and conservatism with Republicans, the two measures do not overlap completely.

Sears and Citrin (1982) found that party identification and political ideology accounted for 7.3 percent of the variance in support for a tax revolt. In their study, both "symbols" of party and ideology were equally powerful in their predictive ability. The meaning of "liberalism" or "conservatism" can vary over time, but in the social welfare arena it has remained constant. Liberals espouse public intervention in helping those in need while conservatives promote the role of the private sector—business, charity, and the family. These distinctions have changed little over the years. What we now explore, therefore, is how the party identification and political ideologies of the public and Congress relate to their level of support for social welfare programs.

The Public

Party as a political symbol. Respondents affiliated with the Democratic party tend to be more supportive of social welfare programs than respondents who associate with the Republican party. In table 5.4 we present the proportion of Democratic and Republican respondents favoring increases, maintenance, or decreases in seven major programs. With no exception, regardless of whether the program is public assistance or social insurance, Democrats are more likely to favor increasing benefits. Likewise, in all but one instance—SSI—Republicans respond more often than Democrats that program benefits should be decreased.

Not surprisingly, these trends also translate into Democrats being willing to provide action-oriented support. On the twenty-point scale of support (-10 to $+10$) for AFDC, Medicaid, and Social Security, Democrats are consistently more supportive than Republicans. The difference in mean scores is greatest for Medicaid (mean Dem = 4.3, mean Rep = 1.9; F = 25.12, p < .001) and AFDC (mean Dem = 2.19, mean Rep = 0.7; F = 17.48, p < .001), but is also statistically significant for Social Security (mean Dem = 5.2, mean Rep = 3.8; F = 7.80, p < .01).

Despite the differences between Republicans and Democrats in level of support for existing programs, we find similarities in the patterns of support; that is, highest level of support for Social Security, next highest for Medicaid, and lowest for AFDC. In addition, Democrats and Republicans make similar choices of groups to receive specific services. Thus, political party does not appear to be of particular use in explaining patterns of support and prefer-

Table 5.4
Party Affiliation and Public Support for Current Social Welfare
Programs (Increase/Decrease Measure)

| | N | % Increase | Increase/Decrease Scale | | Chi Square |
			% Maintain	% Decrease	
Public Assistance Programs					
AFDC					
Democrat	488	41.8	46.7	11.5	33.84***
Republican	390	24.4	55.1	20.5	
Food Stamps					
Democrat	475	33.7	50.5	15.8	63.84***
Republican	386	14.8	49.7	35.5	
Medicaid					
Democrat	495	56.4	40.2	3.4	33.97***
Republican	401	39.4	50.4	10.2	
SSI					
Democrat	496	65.7	31.7	2.6	35.84***
Republican	402	46.3	51.2	2.5	
Social Insurance Programs					
Social Security					
Democrat	512	63.5	34.4	2.1	33.14***
Republican	413	45.3	49.2	5.5	
Unemploy. Ins.					
Democrat	497	41.4	51.2	7.4	50.86***
Republican	393	22.1	58.8	19.1	
Medicare					
Democrat	508	75.4	23.2	1.4	29.26***
Republican	403	59.0	37.0	4.0	

*p<.05; **p<.01; ***p<.001

ences for helping one group above another. There is only a clear
relationship between party and level of support for the current
social welfare system.

Ideology as a symbol.   A second component in the political predispositions explanation of support that we can test is a self-defined
measure of liberalism or conservatism. Respondents were asked
whether they considered themselves extremely liberal, somewhat
liberal, somewhat conservative, or extremely conservative. Not
surprisingly, the largest proportion of respondents define themselves with the less extreme terms: 32 percent report being somewhat liberal and 46 percent say they are somewhat conservative.
Only 5 percent define themselves as extremely liberal and 8 per-

cent as extremely conservative. Four percent offer voluntarily that they consider themselves moderate, 3 percent do not think of themselves in these terms, and 2 percent do not know how to classify themselves. Thus, the sample tends to fall in the middle of the spectrum, but there is a slight slant toward the conservative end.

The effects of political ideology are similar to those of political party, and the two measures correlate significantly with one another (r = .32). Extremely liberal respondents are much more likely than extremely conservative respondents to favor increases in the seven major social welfare programs, while extremely conservative respondents are more likely to prefer decreases. This is true for every program, but it is especially dramatic with regard to AFDC and Food Stamps. For these two programs, 71 percent and 60 percent of the self-declared extreme liberals favor increasing AFDC and Food Stamps, respectively; while only 29 percent and 21 percent, respectively, of the extreme conservatives prefer increasing benefits (Chi Square (8) = 82.08 and 59.38, p < .001, for AFDC and Food Stamps, respectively). The findings are similar, although less striking for the remaining five programs. The likelihood of favoring increases rises as ideology moves from conservative to liberal; thus, we find the somewhat liberal respondents more supportive than the somewhat conservative ones.

We see similar results for the three programs looking at the action-oriented support scores. Ideologically liberal respondents are more willing than conservatives to take action to support AFDC, Medicaid, and Social Security. The average AFDC action support score for the very liberal is 3.26; for the somewhat liberal the mean is 2.55; the moderate respondents score 1.15; somewhat conservatives register 0.76; and the very conservative are unwilling to take actions (mean = −0.15; F = 8.65, p < .001). This pattern of decreasing support with decreasing liberalism is similar, albeit less strong, with both Medicaid and Social Security. Thus, the results confirm our expectations. Political predispositions have an effect on political attitudes within the social welfare domain such that those who label themselves as liberal support social welfare programs more than those who consider themselves conservative.

Political predispositions and the public. There is no doubt from these results that Democrats tend to be more supportive than

Republicans. Nor is there reason to question that liberals are more supportive than conservatives. Both Democrats and liberals favor increases in program benefits more often than Republicans and conservatives, and they rarely prefer benefit cutbacks. In addition, Democrats and liberals say they would take actions to defend favored programs more often than Republicans report they would act. Despite the large differences in level of support between Democrats and Republicans and between liberals and conservatives, neither measure of political predisposition is especially good at explaining the variance in support scores. Regression models using party affiliation and political ideology to predict public support for AFDC, Medicaid, and Social Security explain 12 percent of the variation in support for Medicaid; 8 percent of the variance in support for AFDC; and just 5 percent of the variance in Social Security support scores. There is clearly more to understanding public support for social welfare than can be explained through political predispositions.

The Congress

Much has been written concerning the influence of political parties on congressional voting decisions. Studies have uncovered attitudinal and ideological differences between parties not explained by any other characteristic (including such things as age, gender, and income). Furthermore, these cleavages between parties tend to be largest among activist party members—those most likely to be in high leadership positions such as the U.S. House of Representatives (Page 1978). One of the traditional points of departure between Democrats and Republicans in the social welfare domain has been the view of the role of government in promoting the welfare of the nation's citizens. Throughout the years, Democrats have acted as the stronger advocates of social welfare programs.

Examining the responses of Democratic and Republican Congress members, we are able to confirm past findings about the importance of party. Overall, party affiliation correlates fairly well with level of support ($r = .39$). For five of the seven social welfare programs, a larger proportion of Democrats than Republicans report that they would like to see benefits increased. Furthermore, Republicans are more likely than Democrats to want benefits decreased.

Table 5.5
Party Affiliation and Congressional Support for Current Social
Welfare Programs (Increase/Decrease Measure)

	N	% Increase	% Maintain	% Decrease	Chi square
			Increase/decrease scale		
Public Assistance Programs					
AFDC					
Democrat[a]	32	31.6	68.4	0	7.67**
Republican	24	34.2	46.3	19.4	
Food Stamps					
Democrat	32	21.7	64.1	14.1	5.85**
Republican	24	7.4	52.8	39.8	
Medicaid					
Democrat	32	51.9	48.1	0	6.63**
Republican	24	27.8	59.3	13.0	
SSI					
Democrat	32	36.4	63.6	0	11.99***
Republican	24	6.5	74.1	19.4	
Social Insurance Programs					
Social Security					
Democrat	32	10.9	89.1	0	0.05
Republican	24	13.0	87.0	0	
Medicare					
Democrat	32	41.1	54.2	4.7	4.74*
Republican	24	20.4	60.2	19.4	
Unemploy. Ins.					
Democrat	32	16.6	78.3	5.2	3.74
Republican	24	6.5	74.1	19.4	

[a]Weighted sample.
*p<.10; **p<.05; ***p<.01

Table 5.5 shows that Republican and Democratic representatives differ much more in their support for benefits in the area of public assistance programs (SSI, Medicaid, Food Stamps, and AFDC) than in the area of social insurance programs. The pattern of differences between Republicans and Democrats is significant for every program except Social Security and Unemployment Insurance. With respect to Social Security, Republicans and Democrats appear to be strikingly similar in their support, and they share an almost unanimous view that benefits should be maintained; only a small proportion (11 to 13 percent) advocate increases in benefits. Social Security is indeed a nonpartisan issue, quite unlike the other major social insurance program for the elderly, Medicare, where 41 percent of Democrats favor increases and only 5 percent favor decreases, while 20 percent of Republicans favor increases and 19 percent favor decreases.

A strong relationship also exists between party affiliation and congressional voting behavior. Democrats are far more likely than Republicans to vote in favor of social welfare measures to benefit low-income children and their families (mean Dem. = 8.1, mean Rep. = 3.6; $F(1,56)$ = 7.9, $p < .001$). In addition, their votes on policies for the elderly reflect partisan differences (mean Dem. = 8.6, mean Rep. = 2.8; $F(1,56)$ = 113.2, $p < .001$). Thus, Democratic members of Congress are more likely to have positive attitudes toward both public assistance programs and social insurance programs than Republicans, and they are also more likely to vote in favor of social welfare legislation.

The overall patterns found in the attitudes of Congress members mirror those found among the general public. That is, just as Democratic Congress members are more supportive than those who are Republican, so too are Democratic citizens more supportive than Republican citizens. However, although the patterns are similar between Democrats and Republicans in the Congress and the general public, the degree of their supportiveness differs. While the support expressed by Democratic Congress members is similar to that of Democratic members of the public when considering three of the four public assistance programs, Democrats in the general public are more supportive of social insurance programs than Democratic representatives. For example, while only 11 percent of Democratic Congress members want to increase benefits for Social Security, 64 percent of Democratic citizens favor increases. Forty-one percent of Democratic Congress members favor increased Medicare benefits as compared to 75 percent of Democratic citizens.

Similarly, Republicans in the general public are also more supportive than Republicans in Congress. And again, the greatest differences between Republican representatives and citizens are over social insurance programs. For example, 45 percent of Republican citizens support increases in Social Security benefits, but only 13 percent of Republican leaders do. And 20 percent of Republican Congress members report they want to increase Medicare benefits as compared to 59 percent of Republican citizens.

Republican and Democratic committee leaders. The overall findings for Republican and Democratic Congress members are somewhat different for leaders of committees relevant to social welfare. Democratic committee leaders express more favorable attitudes toward both public assistance programs and social insurance programs (mean = 13.2 and 12.1, respectively) than do Republican committee leaders (mean = 10.7 and mean = 10.2, $F(1,20)$ = 16.4 and $F(1,20)$ = 8.9, $p < .01$, respectively). The party difference is less pronounced among nonleaders, although Democrats (mean = 11.4 and 11.2, for public assistance and social insurance, respectively) tend to be more supportive than Republicans (mean = 9.9 and 10.4, respectively). Furthermore, Republican representatives at large hold similar beliefs to their committee leaders, but Democratic leaders are somewhat more supportive of public assistance programs than Democrats at-large ($F(1,30)$ = 5.6, $p < .05$). The special importance of party to leaders is perhaps best expressed in the high correlation between party membership and support for public assistance programs ($r = .67$) and social insurance ($r = .56$). The relationships are stronger than with Congress members at-large ($r = .30$ and $r = .19$ for public assistance and social insurance, respectively).

As is true for the overall sample, Democratic committee leaders are more likely than Republican committee leaders to vote on behalf of social welfare policies for both children (mean Dem. = 8.9, mean Rep. = 4.8, $F(1,22)$ = 35.6, $p < .001$) and the elderly (mean Dem. = 9.0, mean Rep. = 3.9, $F(1,21)$ = 36.6, $p < .001$). The correlation between party and voting behavior is also quite high among committee leaders ($r = .79$ for children's issues and $r = .80$ for elderly issues). We find similar high correlations between party and voting among the random sample of Congress members ($r = .77$ for children's issues and $r = .82$ for elderly issues). Thus, while party has a stronger influence on social welfare committee leaders' supportive attitudes than on the attitudes of nonleaders, it correlates equally with the voting behavior of both groups. Furthermore, for leaders, party affiliation correlates strongly with both personal attitudes toward social welfare issues and voting behavior, while among nonleaders party has a more powerful relationship with votes than with attitudes.

In the congressional sample, Democrats respond with greater

support than Republicans. But we see now that committee leaders tend to be more supportive than nonleaders within the same party. Why might this be the case? One possibility relates to the amount of information on social welfare issues available to each group. Because leaders of both parties organize and direct informational hearings and visit program sites, they spend far more time than nonleaders on issues specific to social welfare and are likely to have a larger store of knowledge on social welfare issues than Congress members not directly involved with the topic area. This is what Heclo (1974) refers to as "policy learning." A number of committee leaders tell us their committee role brought them new insights into the problems of poverty and social policy:

> The difference [of being chair of a relevant committee] that has come to me personally is that I have become much better informed because of the myriad of details that is available to us, much better informed about the problems. [#48]

> [Being leader of a committee] certainly has broadened my knowledge of the different programs and some of the conditions that exist and so forth. . . . You don't realize what is going on out there in the world until you rub elbows and you find out. [#54]

Because committee leaders have more information, perhaps they see the specific needs of social welfare beneficiaries—and recognize the values of programs—more clearly.

A second explanation for the differences between leaders and nonleaders may relate to the fact that committee leaders are, in effect, the representatives of their party within the committee. The party expects them to advocate and vote the party line, and nonleaders within the party look to them for guidance on difficult decisions (Parker 1985). It is altogether possible, therefore, that attitudes may actually change as a result of this influential role, if not at least become stronger and more personal.

The committee leaders' deeper knowledge of social welfare issues, in turn, further emphasizes their party role by making them the party experts on these issues. When nonleaders of either party cast votes on issues pertaining to social welfare, they often look to party colleagues in leadership positions for assistance. Clearly, party affiliation is an important dimension in congressional attitudes and voting behavior, but just as important, it has a differential effect on leaders and nonleaders.

Party and Congress as a whole. Now that we have explored the differential effect of party on leaders and nonleaders let us return to the discussion of support among Congress members as a group. As with members of the public, we want to know how much information can be provided by party affiliation toward understanding congressional support for social welfare. To do this, we must once again weight respondents according to their party and position of leadership (for reference to the weighting procedure, see appendix A). For Congress as a whole, party affiliation is able to explain 35 percent of the variance in support for public assistance programs (AFDC and Medicaid) and 13 percent of the variance in support for social insurance programs (Social Security and Medicare). Social Security, and to a lesser extent Medicare, are nonpartisan issues and the low predictiveness of party exemplifies this. Although party does well in describing attitudinal support for public assistance, it is extremely useful in predicting voting behaviors. Party alone is able to explain 83 percent of the variance in votes for children's issues and 92 percent of the variance in votes for elderly concerns. Thus, party shapes congressional attitudes, but even more strikingly it affects voting decisions.

Respondent-Based Explanations of Support

So far we have examined the separate effects of self-interest and political predispositions on public and congressional support for social welfare programs. Looking first at public support, both self-interest and political predispositions have an effect, but neither play a powerful role. Specifically, as the summary of the results in table 5.6 shows, neither theory of support explains a large proportion of the variance in the public's support. Self-interest is more important in explaining support for Medicaid and Social Security than in explaining support for AFDC, but in no case does it explain more than 17 percent of the variance. As an explanation of support among the public, political predispositions does no better.

The results tell a different story for members of Congress. Political predispositions—measured as party alone rather than, as with the public, both party and ideology—are much more important for representatives than for the public. Party explains 35 percent of the variance in representatives' beliefs about supporting AFDC and Medicaid (combined) and 13 percent of the variance in their atti-

Table 5.6

Proportion of the Variance in Support Explained by Self-Interest and
Political Predispositions, Examined Separately

	Self-Interest[a]		Political Predispositions[b]	
	Attitudes Adj. R^2	Votes Adj. R^2	Attitudes Adj. R^2	Votes Adj. R^2
Public				
AFDC	.05		.08	
Medicaid	.17		.12	
Social Security	.16		.05	
Congress				
AFDC and Medicaid	.22	.16	.35	.83
Social Security and Medicare	.08	.00	.13	.92

[a]For the public, self-interest for AFDC and Medicaid is defined as program recipients, family of recipients, income, and being of childbearing age. In the case of Social Security, income and childbearing age have been omitted. For Congress, self-interest in the case of AFDC and Medicaid represents the proportion of the district earning over $50,000, the proportion of constituents below poverty, and the district unemployment rate. In the case of Social Security and Medicare, self-interest is the proportion of elderly in the district.

[b]For the public, political predispositions include party identification (Republican or Democrat) and reported ideology (very liberal to very conservative). For Congress, political predisposition is party identification alone.

tudes about supporting Medicare and Social Security (where, the reader will recall, there is less variance to explain). More dramatically, party explains 83 percent of the variance in voting for issues having to do with low-income children and their families and 92 percent of the variance in support for issues having to do with the elderly.

In contrast to the role of party in explaining representatives' support, the role of self-interest pales. The data fail to demonstrate that members of Congress believe and act in a self-interested manner when self-interest is defined in its narrowest sense (i.e., as that which is most likely to lead to reelection). However, when district interests are included, as in table 5.6, the explanatory power improves substantially. Thus, Congress members do appear to be motivated to support social welfare both attitudinally and through votes when their constituents are likely to be recipients of the added benefits.

Past researchers have pitted self-interest against political predispositions and tested the value of one over the other (see for example, Sears, Hensler, and Speer 1979; Lau, Brown, and Sears 1978; Tyler and Weber 1982; and Sears and Citrin 1982). Although one explanation may prove more important in the social welfare realm, we expect some overlap between individuals' political predispositions and their self-interest in this policy area. For example, since the poorest citizens have been traditionally affiliated with the Democratic party, at least since the election of Franklin D. Roosevelt, we would expect self-interest and political predispositions to interact in predicting support. We now put the two explanations together and examine their mutual ability to explain public and congressional support for social welfare.

We tested the efficacy of an overall respondent-based model of public support for social welfare using structural equation modeling and the LISREL software program. Unlike other programs, LISREL allows for multiple indicators of a single latent factor. Each model of public support (one for each of AFDC, Medicaid, and Social Security) includes two exogenous factors (self-interest and political predispositions) and one endogenous factor (support for the specific program). Because it is overwhelmingly the best measure of self-interest, we have chosen to use recipient status as our indicator of self-interest. Political predispositions are represented by the combination of party affiliation and self-reported political ideology. Support is conceptualized as satisfaction with paying current taxes, willingness to write letters or sign petitions, and willingness to pay higher taxes in defense of three separate programs—AFDC, Medicaid, and Social Security. Figures 5.1a–c provide the path coefficients for the three models.

We can draw three general conclusions from examining these models. First, each allows us to explain more of the variance in support than either self-interest or political predispositions alone. Second, in each case, self-interest and political predispositions interact, telling us—not surprisingly—that recipients of each of the three social welfare programs are more likely to be Democrats and liberals than are nonrecipients. Third, self-interest and political predispositions vary in importance depending on whether it is support for Social Security or support for AFDC and Medicaid being explained.

As figures 5.1a and b show, political predisposition has a greater effect on support for AFDC and Medicaid than does self-interest. Although the equations do not explain a great deal of the variance in support scores for either AFDC or Medicaid (adjusted $R^2 = .16$ and .22, respectively), political predispositions account for about

Figure 5.1
Overall Effect of Respondent-Based Characteristics on Public Support
(Standardized Path Coefficients)

(a) AFDC

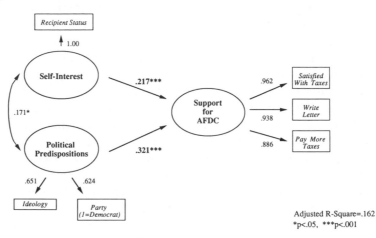

Adjusted R-Square=.162
*p<.05, ***p<.001

(b) Medicaid

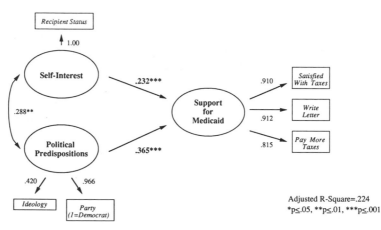

Adjusted R-Square=.224
*p≤.05, **p≤.01, ***p≤.001

(c) Social Security

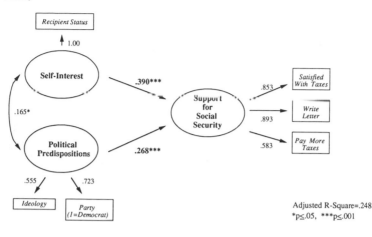

one-third more of that variance than does self-interest. Of course, it must be recognized that self-interest is a single indicator with limited variance; respondents are either recipients or not recipients, whereas political predisposition includes both party (coded as either Democrats or Republicans) and the five-point ideology scale. Thus, political predisposition may be better able to predict support merely because of the added variability in the measure.

However, this argument loses validity when we turn to support for Social Security. Figure 5.1c shows that the self-interest of Social Security recipients is more relevant to support for Social Security than whether an individual is politically predisposed toward liberallsm or conservatism. In this case, political predisposition accounts for less of the explained variance than does recipient status.

This overall analysis of public support demonstrates the unique contributions made by self-interest and political predisposition as well as by the interaction of the two explanations. Knowing an individual's political predisposition allows one to predict his or her support for social welfare programs. Furthermore, knowing whether an individual has personal stakes in a program tells us that he or she will also tend to be more supportive of the program. Although these two explanations are not completely independent of each another, when we look at them together we can gain a fuller understanding of public support for social welfare. Liberals and

Democrats are more supportive than conservatives and Republicans. Program recipients are more supportive than nonrecipients. But the most supportive members of the public are likely to have both personal stakes in the program and to be Democrats or to have predispositions toward liberalism.

How do these findings for the public compare to the findings for members of Congress? Earlier in this chapter, we demonstrated how pure measures of self-interest (district wealth for public assistance programs and the proportion of elderly for social insurance programs) fail to predict congressional support, but measures of needs in the district (e.g., poverty and unemployment) do predict support. Although representatives describe the lack of contact they have with their poorer constituents and note that these constituents rarely become involved politically, those Congress members from poorer districts and districts with higher levels of unemployment are nonetheless more supportive than others. Such representatives are not acting in a clearly self-interested manner in that the poor and the unemployed are not politically influential. However, they are paying particular attention to the needs of their district. We therefore add to a respondent-based model of congressional support the effect of district interests.

When we combine self-interest (district wealth), district interest (district poverty and unemployment levels), and party into a single model, we are able to explain 31 percent of the variance in congressional support for public assistance programs (AFDC and Medicaid). The same variables explain 85 percent of the variance in the voting decisions made by Congress members with regard to children's issues. While both these models are strong, and voting behavior is particularly good, neither is a substantial improvement over party alone. In fact, when adjusted for the added degrees of freedom, the full model explaining attitudes is less powerful than party alone (adjusted R^2 = .31 versus adjusted R^2 = .35 for party alone). As the path coefficients shown in figures 5.2a and b demonstrate, party is by far the more important factor in the model. We conclude that although Congress members from poorer districts tend to support programs more and to vote for them more often than other representatives, in the end, district interests are far less important than party alliances when considering assistance to the poor.

The same can also be said about Congress members' voting

Figure 5.2
Overall Effect of Respondent-Based Characteristics on Congressional Support

(a) Support for AFDC and Medicaid

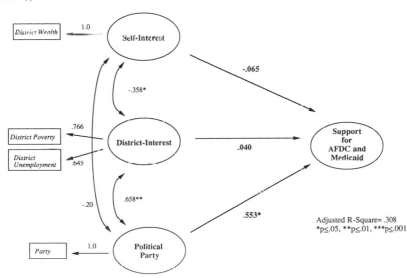

(b) Votes for Issues Regarding Low-Income Children and Families

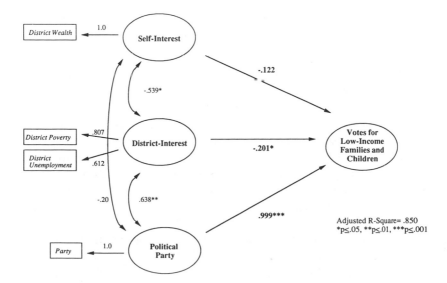

Figure 5.2 (continued)

(c) Support for Social Security and Medicare

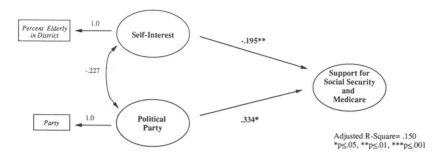

Adjusted R-Square= .150
*p≤.05, **p≤.01, ***p≤.001

(d) Votes for Elderly Issues

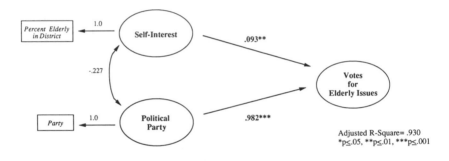

Adjusted R-Square= .930
*p≤.05, **p≤.01, ***p≤.001

behavior with regard to elderly issues (see figures 5.2c and d). Self-interest accounts for very little of the explained variance in votes when combined with party. Together the two variables explain 93 percent of the variance in votes, compared with 92 percent when party is considered alone. Neither party nor self-interest is particularly useful in describing the attitudes of Congress members concerning social insurance programs. The combined model (adjusted R^2 = .15) is not much more useful than either indicator taken separately (adjusted R^2 = .13 and adjusted R^2 = .08, for party and self-interest, respectively), and both factors play an equally weak role in the prediction.

Thus, we can conclude that Congress members believe and act in allegiance with their party before they consider self-interest or district interest. This is not so true with members of the public, who may at times be more concerned with personal gain than party loyalty or ideological consistency. Congress members are elected through the political party system, and their affiliations with the party are strong. Members of the public, on the other hand, largely use their party affiliations to help guide voting behavior but not to define their political identity. Thus, party affiliation plays a much larger role in the lives of Congress members than among the general public, and it is not surprising that party is better able to influence the personal attitudes of representatives than of the general public. Among both respondent groups, those affiliated with the Democratic party tend to be more supportive of social welfare than Republicans, but the predictive power of party is far stronger among members of the Congress than among members of the public.

In conclusion, political party has an effect on public attitudes but a far greater effect on congressional attitudes and votes. On the other hand, direct self-interest proves of little importance to Congress members, but has some influence on members of the public, albeit not large. Researchers have found self-interest to be more relevant in some policy areas than others (see Sears et al. 1980). Social welfare does not seem to be one of the realms in which self-interest has a profound influence. The influence of political predispositions, however, cannot be ignored.

6
Toward an Integrated Explanation of Support

Most of us have heard some version of the story of the four blind men and the elephant. Four men are asked to touch an elephant and describe its appearance. The first blind man feels the large front leg and decides that an elephant looks like a tree with a wide, rough trunk. The second touches the swinging tail and concludes that an elephant resembles a rope. The third feels a floppy ear and deduces that an elephant looks like a fan. The fourth blind man examines the massive body and decides that an elephant is something without beginning or end. Each blind man is, of course, describing a specific part of the same elephant. But because each man has only partial information, the depictions are all very different, and none of them bring to mind the true picture of an elephant.

In some ways, social scientists studying American support for social welfare programs are like the blind men. Some believe support is a product of self-interest and nothing else (e.g., Downs 1957). Assuming that personal gain is the driving force behind actions, researchers maintaining the importance of self-interest argue that members of Congress support programs in order to gain votes, and members of the public support programs that benefit them while disavowing programs for which they must pay taxes but receive no benefits. Other scholars look to political predispositions, or symbolic politics, to explain high and low levels of support. These scholars suggest that public and congressional support for social welfare programs is guided by political preferences learned early in life, the same preferences that led them to identify with a particular political party and to label themselves as conservative or liberal (e.g., Sears 1983). Still other scholars argue that to understand support for social welfare, one must examine citizens' unique beliefs and attitudes about specific program characteristics. This view contends that members of the public and of Congress decide which programs to support based on particular program characteristics, such as the deservingness of recipients and the effectiveness of the program (e.g., Macarov 1978; Stein 1971; Haveman 1987; Murray 1984; see also Kluegel and Smith 1986).

These explanations are at times portrayed as incompatible with one another. For example, Sears and his colleagues pit self-interest and political predispositions against each other to determine which better explains political judgments. More often, however, like the four blind men, theorists simply ignore competing explanations and concentrate on only one. Were researchers to combine the pieces, a fuller, more accurate picture of support for social welfare might emerge.

In previous chapters, we have presented four explanations of support. We depicted them alone and in sets of two (i.e., program-based explanations and respondent-based explanations), and argued that some explanations are stronger than others because of their ability to account for more of the variability in support scores. This approach showed that each explanation, when taken alone or in combination with one other, has some power to explain support. But should we not also consider the possibility of complex relationships between the four explanations? Taken together, could they provide us with a more complete picture of the determinants of support? Or are they so highly related that little information is gained by combining them? Can we construct and test a model that puts all four explanations together and, if so, does such a model help us understand more about support than any one explanation alone?

We will now take a different approach from that in earlier chapters. We assemble the four individual explanations into a larger, integrated model of support for social welfare. What can we expect to find in constructing a more complex model? First, assuming that each explanation offers some unique perspective on support, we can expect that the full model will explain a larger proportion of the variance in support scores. Second, we expect to find some relationships among the four separate explanations. For example, political predispositions may well be related to perceptions of recipient deservingness and program effectiveness. Once a child or adolescent is provided with a particular ideological context for viewing the world—be it conservative or liberal—this ideological perspective should begin to shape beliefs about what kinds of people he or she thinks deserve help and what types of programs he or she thinks are effective.

Our integrated model is depicted in figure 6.1. The first stage of the model postulates that self-interest and political predispositions directly shape views about recipient deservingness and program effectiveness. This assumes that self-interest and political predisposition are causally prior to attitudes about recipient deservingness and program effectiveness. Research on political socialization shows that one's political ideology and party identification are shaped predominantly in adolescence and young adulthood (Easton and Dennis 1969; Jennings and Niemi 1974; Weissberg 1974). Furthermore, although specific opinions may change with maturity, studies have shown that general ideology and party membership remain relatively stable (e.g., Dawson, Prewitt, and Dawson 1977; Searing, Wright, and Rabinowitz 1976). Such findings suggest that political predispositions and self-interest are firmly rooted well before one is exposed to notions of recipient deservingness and program effectiveness. Although it is possible for the causal flow to go in the opposite direction (e.g., for one to switch party allegiance because of agreement or disagreement concerning perceptions of program effectiveness), the former direction is more probable than the later. Given the temporal precedence of ideology and self-interest, it is less plausible that beliefs about deservingness and effectiveness directly shape one's choices about political predisposition, and even less likely that they impact upon self-interest.

Second, the model postulates that self-interest and political predispositions affect judgments about support through both direct and mediated causal paths. Here we make the assumption that self-interest and political predispositions are causally prior to judgments about support. In earlier chapters we provided justification

Figure 6.1
Disposition-Attribution Model of Support for Social Welfare

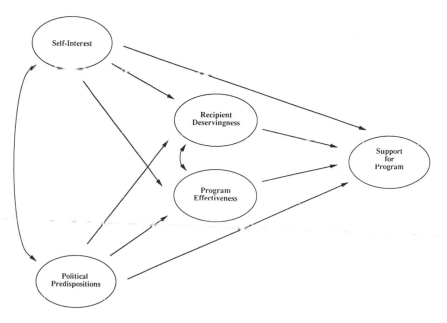

for the contention that respondent characteristics should influence levels of support. The literature provides no justifiable reason to suggest that the only effect of ideology and self-interest on support is mediated through program-specific attitudes, although there is reason to believe some of the effect goes through program attitudes. The model, therefore, depicts self-interest and political predispositions as both directly shaping American views on support and indirectly affecting views on support by altering program-based attitudes. For example, one path shows that political predispositions influence beliefs about recipient deservingness, attributions which in turn affect support, and another path shows that political predispositions have a direct effect on support.

Third, the integrated model suggests that attitudes about recipient deservingness and program effectiveness directly shape judgments about support for social welfare programs. Here the underlying assumption is that respondents make attributions about the deservingness of recipients and about the effectiveness of programs and that they make these attributions before framing their judgments about support. The justification for this assumption arises from experimental research. In these studies, researchers were able to change respondents' support levels by varying characteristics of recipients in hypothetical vignettes, thus altering respondents' attributions of deservingness (Cook 1979; Ponza et al. 1988; Periera and Rossi 1985). The research to date has only been performed under controlled conditions, but there is little reason to suspect findings would differ in real-life settings.

An overarching assumption of the integrated model is that the hypothesized predictors of support are conceptually distinct. Although they may be correlated, this correlation is not expected to be so high as to deny the validity of the four unique constructs. In chapter 2 we discussed the historical and scholarly traditions that gave rise to the four explanations of support we examine, showing that each originates from a different body of literature. Recorded conceptions of deservingness began with the Elizabethan Poor Laws of 1601, which dictated who should and should not be helped through public aid. Concern with program quality and effectiveness, on the other hand, did not become an important political issue until the 1960s when the search for excellence in social welfare programs led to the development of program evaluation— now a discipline in its own right (Shadish, Cook, and Leviton 1991). As for self-interest, Adam Smith (1799 [1776]) wrote of its role in newly developing capitalist society, and nearly two hundred years later, Downs (1957) reintroduced the concept into political science theory. Since then, debate on the merits of self-interest has remained lively (see Mansbridge 1990). Research on political predispositions, especially as it relates to party politics, is as old as the field of political science, and it continues to provide important information on political behavior (Carmines and Stimson 1989; Sears et al. 1980; Campbell et al. 1960). Each theory has been introduced into the literature as conceptually distinct from any other. At issue now is the extent to which the concepts are in fact empirically distinct and how they together affect public and congressional support for social welfare.

In summary, the integrated model shown in figure 6.1 proposes that citizens make decisions about their level of support for social welfare based on personal dispositions (i.e., their self-interest and political predisposition) and by the attributions they make about recipient deservingness and program effectiveness. Thus, the model can be aptly called a *disposition-attribution model of support*. Such a model allows us to test all four explanations of support together and to probe the extent to which the relationships we find among them differ by the program being considered. Finally, we can explore similarities and differences between the model describing public support and the model that best describes support among members of the U.S. House of Representatives.

The Public

Many members of the American public are far more supportive of social welfare programs—even public assistance programs—than recent political campaigns would lead one to think. On the other hand, not all people are supportive. Regardless of one's level of support, individuals tend to be more in favor of Social Security, a social insurance program, than AFDC and Medicaid, both public assistance programs. Individuals also tend to be more supportive of Medicaid than of AFDC. An integrated model can help pinpoint reasons for these differences.

Figures 6.2a–c present the standardized path coefficients for the disposition-attribution model of public support for AFDC, Medicaid, and Social Security. These maximum likelihood coefficients were computed using LISREL, a structural equation modeling program developed by Jöreskog and Sörbom (1989). Perhaps one of the greatest benefits of LISREL is that it allows for the use of multiple indicators of each explanatory construct, as outlined in previous chapters. (The factor loadings for recipient deservingness and program effectiveness are presented in figures 4.3a–c; for self-interest and political predispositions in figures 5.1a–c; and for the support items—satisfaction with paying taxes, willingness to sign petitions or write letters, and willingness to pay higher taxes—on both sets of figures.)

In every case, the disposition-attribution model explains a greater proportion of variance in support than any of the predictive factors taken alone or in sets of two. Even after we account for the increased number of predictors (by adjusting the R^2 to the decreased degrees of freedom), the model is able to explain 56 percent of the variance in support for AFDC as opposed to 52 percent with the program-based model (see chapter 4) and 16 percent with the respondent characteristics model (see chapter 5). For Medicaid,

Figure 6.2
Disposition-Attribution Model of Public Support for Social Welfare Programs
(Standardized Path Coefficients)

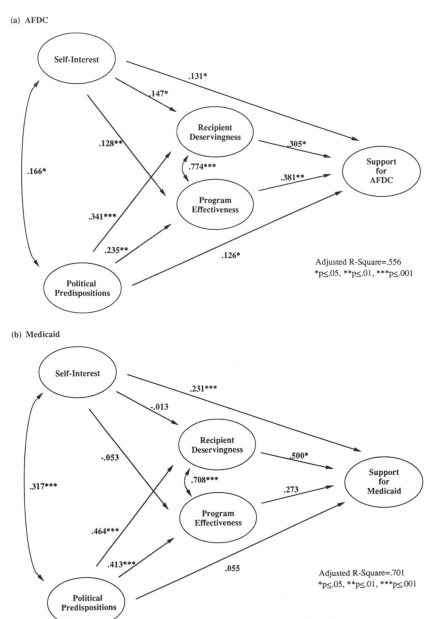

(a) AFDC

Self-Interest

.131*

.147*

Recipient
Deservingness

.128**

.305*

Support
for
AFDC

.166*

.774***

.381**

Program
Effectiveness

.341***

.235**

.126*

Political
Predispositions

Adjusted R-Square=.556
*p≤.05, **p≤.01, ***p≤.001

(b) Medicaid

Self-Interest

.231***

-.013

Recipient
Deservingness

-.053

.500*

Support
for
Medicaid

.317***

.708***

.273

Program
Effectiveness

.464***

.413***

.055

Political
Predispositions

Adjusted R-Square=.701
*p≤.05, **p≤.01, ***p≤.001

(c) Social Security

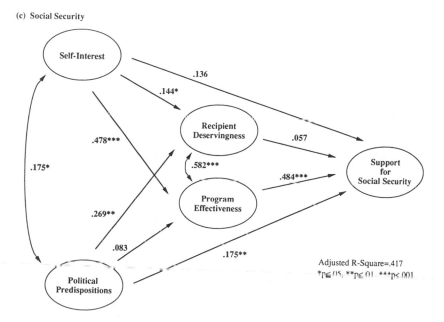

the integrated model accounts for 70 percent of the variance in support as compared to 63 percent and 22 percent with the program-based and respondent-characteristics models respectively. Finally, for Social Security the new model achieves an adjusted R^2 of .42, which is higher than either the 38 percent explained by the program factors alone or the 25 percent explained by respondent characteristics alone. In summary, then, the four factors combined offer more useful information toward understanding public support for public assistance and social insurance programs than any one or two factors considered alone.

Despite the higher predictive power of the disposition-attribution model, it is not an overwhelming improvement over the program-based model presented in chapter 4. Indeed, there is clear evidence that the four factors are not completely unique and that some of the information provided by one factor overlaps with that offered by another. First, we find that the proportion of the variance explained in the disposition-attribution model is less than the sum of the two smaller models combined, which suggests that although the disposition-attribution model improves upon the smaller models, it is not a great improvement. Second, the model shows complex intercorrelations among the four explanations, further suggesting a lack of total independence between the four factors. Specifically, in all the models, the recipient deservingness and program effectiveness factors are very highly related, and the self-interest and political predispositions factors are consistently but more weakly associated. We now turn to explore these relationships, first for public assistance programs and then for social insurance programs.

Explaining Support for Public Assistance Programs

Let us look first at public support for AFDC, the least supported of the three programs. Figure 6.2a demonstrates that respondents who believe that recipients are deserving and that AFDC is effective are more supportive than those who hold contrary views. Neither factor is much more important than the other in predicting support, but the two factors are highly correlated. Some of the correlation is probably due to measurement bias, since both sets of attributions were measured using the same agree-disagree format. Still, measurement bias alone cannot account for all of the shared variance. Some of the shared variance probably stems from the fact that each explanatory factor taps into the same domain of program-specific beliefs. Nonetheless, because attributions about recipient deservingness and program effectiveness are conceptually distinct and have been addressed separately in the literature, we maintain them as unique items in the model. The empirical case for their uniqueness is not strong. They would appear to be alternate measures of the same program construct were it not for two facts. First, in a pilot study to prepare for the nationwide survey of the public, we conducted a focus group session in which respondents from the general public clearly differentiated between the deservingness of recipients and the efficacy of programs. Second, in our separate survey with members of the House of Representatives, representatives spontaneously discussed both recipient deservingness and program effectiveness and clearly differentiated their support as linked to one of these program-based factors but not necessarily the other.

In addition, as figure 6.2a shows, both self-interest (that is, being an AFDC recipient) and political predispositions shape support. These two dispositions are also correlated with each other but not to a degree that would lead us to question their being measures of the same underlying construct. The relationship is no doubt influenced by the high probability of AFDC recipients identifying with the Democratic party, a fact that addresses the niche of caring for the poor that Democrats have carved out for themselves.

Political predispositions and self-interest have both direct and indirect causal links to support. Indeed, about half the influence of these two dispositions on support is indirect (42 percent of self-interest and 61 percent of political predispositions). AFDC recipients are more likely than nonrecipients both to believe themselves deserving of benefits and to see AFDC as a well-managed and effective program. Likewise, Democrats and political liberals hold more positive views about recipient deservingness and program effectiveness, which in turn motivate them to support AFDC.

The determinants of support for Medicaid are somewhat different from those for AFDC. Attributes about recipient deservingness are important, but beliefs about program effectiveness are less so— a result consistent with the model presented in chapter 4 showing that beliefs about program effectiveness no longer influence support once recipient deservingness issues are added to the equation. In other words, the predictive power provided by attributions about effectiveness overlaps to such an extent with the predictive power offered by recipient deservingness that the two together add little new information. What the data suggest is that whether one believes that Medicaid is effective has less influence on overall support than whether one believes that Medicaid recipients are deserving. As we will see later, this is very similar to the views of Congress members.

Medicaid recipients are self-interested enough to support the program more than nonrecipients. Furthermore, nearly all of the effect of self-interest on support is direct (only 10 percent of the influence of self-interest on support is indirect). On the other hand, the effect of political predisposition on support is nearly all indirect (86 percent of the influence of political predisposition is filtered through recipient deservingness and program effectiveness). Thus, while every one of the paths we have considered is relevant to modeling support for AFDC, several paths can be ignored in the best-fitting model of support for Medicaid.

Explaining Support for a Social Insurance Program

With few exceptions, the American public holds positive views toward Social Security. This is good news for proponents of Social Security, but it reduces our ability to model support because there is less variability in support scores. Despite this caveat, the distribution-attribution model is able to account for 42 percent of the variance, from which we can draw several conclusions about public support for Social Security. The two most notable findings from the distribution-attribution model are that support for Social Security, unlike support for either of the two public assistance programs, is largely influenced by attributions about program effectiveness, and it is not greatly affected by views of recipient deservingness. We discussed this earlier in chapter 4, but what we did not know at the time was the strong influence of self-interest on views about program effectiveness. In fact, 64 percent of the effect of self-interest on support is indirectly mediated through program-specific attitudes, primarily through the link between self-interest and program effectiveness.

To a lesser, but still statistically significant level, political predispositions also predict support for Social Security. However, political predispositions have their greatest effect on support directly rather than indirectly through program-specific attributions (24 percent indirect). Thus, the overall picture of support for Social Security shows a direct effect from attributions about program effectiveness and from political predispositions; and an indirect effect from self-interest through effectiveness, since recipients clearly hold more positive views about the effectiveness of the program than those who are not recipients.

Comparisons Across Programs

The disposition-attribution model reveals both the similarities and differences between the explanations of public support for the public assistance programs of AFDC and Medicaid and the social insurance program of Social Security. Perhaps the most significant similarity is that across all three programs, the disposition-attribution model is an improvement over any individual explanation taken alone. Thus, each component offers additional prediction to our understanding of public support for social welfare. Another similarity across all three programs is the relatively high proportion of the variance in support that is explained. At first glance, the model seems better at predicting public support for AFDC and Medicaid than for Social Security. But given the high support levels for Social Security and the limited variability this entails, our ability to account for even 42 percent of the variance in support for Social Security is striking.

Although the disposition-attribution model offers superior predictive power over individual explanations, the power gained from the addition of various factors is sometimes small. This is especially true of the respondent dispositions: self-interest and political predispositions offer far less information to the model than attributions about programs and recipients. However, such a description is somewhat misleading because it fails to take into account another similarity between explanations of support: while the dispositional variables affect support both directly and indirectly, they often have their strongest influence on support indirectly through beliefs about deservingness and effectiveness. Thus, considering only the direct effect of self-interest and political predispositions underestimates their total impact. Nonetheless, it is still true that their influence is less than that of beliefs about program effectiveness and recipient deservingness.

Just as prominent as these similarities, however, are the differences in what explains support for each program. The most obvious is the role that beliefs about recipient deservingness play in shaping support. Attributions about program recipients and their deservingness greatly influence support for both AFDC and Medicaid, but they add little to our understanding of public support for Social Security. Most members of the public see Social Security recipients as worthy, and the few who believe otherwise are either no less supportive or too few in number to have an impact on the explanation of support.

The significance of self-interest also varies across programs. For AFDC and Social Security, recipients tend to be more supportive of programs 1) because they see themselves, the program beneficiaries, as more deserving, and 2) because they see program effectiveness as being of higher quality. For Medicaid, however, recipients do not hold more positive views than nonrecipients about program effectiveness, and they are only slightly more likely to believe themselves deserving. While our data cannot provide an explanation for this finding, we speculate that it probably relates to the type of benefits provided and to the unequivocal dependence of Medicaid recipients on the program. Health care is a commodity not available through any other means, and it is something that people cannot easily live without. AFDC and Social Security offer cash assistance that may be a less critical necessity than medical care, given that financial assistance is sometimes available from savings, friends, family, and public or private agencies. Thus, self-interest directly motivates Medicaid recipients to support the program because, regardless of its quality or the legitimacy of their deservingness, they need the assistance.

In conclusion, the disposition-attribution model of support for social welfare programs demonstrates that the four factors taken together are more powerful than any one or two taken alone. It also shows the interesting and complex ways the four explanations interact with one another. The results from the disposition-attribution model instruct us in the importance of combining explanations rather than placing them in opposition with one another. Because each explanation is not mutually exclusive, the best picture is derived when they are combined. The story of the four blind men and the elephant reminds us that to see the elephant as a whole, we must consider each piece of information as being related to every other and then explore all of the possible connections among them.

Members of Congress

We now turn our attention to an explanation of Congress members' support for programs by integrating the four explanations into one overall model. We begin by examining congressional support for public assistance programs, then we look at support for social insurance programs. In each case, we propose that Congress members make their support decisions based upon their attributions about recipient deservingness and program effectiveness, which to some extent have been shaped by their self-interest and political predispositions. We expect both self-interest and political predispositions to have a direct effect on support as well.

Because of the differences in survey design, we cannot perform complicated LISREL analyses on the congressional data similar to those of the general public. Members of the public were asked

close-ended questions regarding their attitudes about recipient deservingness and program effectiveness. The opinions of Congress
members, on the other hand, were probed through open-ended,
qualitative questions intended to explore relationships rather than
confirm or negate preconceived hypotheses. The responses to the
congressional questionnaire provide important insights into the ways
members of Congress reason about social welfare, but unlike with
data from the public, we cannot easily quantify Congress members'
responses.

Explaining Support for Public Assistance Programs

Figure 6.3 presents a disposition-attribution model to explain Congress members' support of public assistance programs. A plus along
any path indicates evidence of a relationship between the variables
connected by the path. No sign along a path indicates that there is
not an obvious relationship between the two factors in question.
This model should not be interpreted as a traditional path diagram;
rather, it is a heuristic device within which to present our explanatory findings.

The five factors shown in figure 6.3 are defined exactly as they
were in chapters 4 and 5. Support represents the attitudinal support
of Congress members for AFDC and Medicaid combined. As described previously, attitudinal support correlates quite highly with
behavioral support (i.e., voting scores), but because votes are rarely
simple and specific to particular social welfare programs, we have
chosen to use attitudes alone in order to be most comparable to the
public measures. In the disposition-attribution model, we define
self-interest as those actions rationally calculated to further representatives' own reelection success. It follows, therefore, that within
the public assistance domain, representatives act in a self-interested manner when they choose not to support public assistance
programs in order to please higher-income constituents. Higher-
income constituents are most likely to be politically active, to
donate money to political campaigns, and to pay the highest taxes
for the programs. Thus, self-interest is operationalized as the level
of wealth within a Congress member's district (as defined in chapter 5, we combined median income of district residents with the
proportion of district residents earning incomes greater than $50,000).
Political predispositions are measured by the member's political

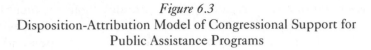

Figure 6.3
Disposition-Attribution Model of Congressional Support for
Public Assistance Programs

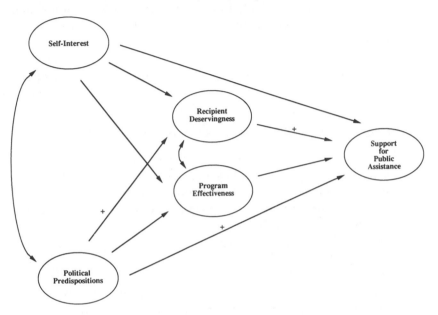

party affiliation. Finally, attributions about the deservingness of recipients and the effectiveness of programs are derived through extensive coding of responses given by representatives when asked about AFDC and Medicaid (see chapter 4 for greater detail on these measures). No new measures have been added; instead, the model incorporates the indices used in previous discussions into a single model.

We will focus both on interactions between the factors and on the indirect effects of these factors on support. In earlier chapters we showed that political predispositions and beliefs about recipient deservingness relate directly to support for AFDC and Medicaid, but self-interest and beliefs about program effectiveness do not. Still unexplored are the indirect effects of self-interest and political predispositions on support.

Self-interest and recipient deservingness. The comments of members of Congress fail to demonstrate any relationship between the wealth of a representative's district and his or her attributions about deservingness of AFDC and Medicaid recipients. The responses of two Congress members illustrate this point. Cited below are two equally supportive members of Congress, but the first member represents a very wealthy district while the second represents a district with relatively little wealth:

> As we find there are people who can't hold a job, or the jobs aren't available or can't be made available for them, then it seems to me that their benefits have to be forthcoming. . . . America's welfare system [has pulled] tens of millions of Americans out of poverty and into the middle class. [#37]

> In my own district, I can see these people who are on aid. . . . [They] have children, and most of them are women all by themselves, with their husbands gone. . . . They are scraping the bottom of the barrel most of the time. They hardly have enough to live on. They feel uneasy about their [public aid] status. Very uneasy and very apologetic. Well, it's no crime to be poor, and I suppose it's no crime not to be married. [#40]

In comparison to the first representative quoted above, the second appears to have more first hand knowledge of AFDC recipients, holding views that appear to be grounded in an understanding of their lives. He sees them "in my own district." But despite this, both representatives argue that public assistance recipients are deserving, and both are supportive of programs. Thus, the wealth of the district seems to have little effect on Congress members' beliefs about the deservingness of program recipients, and consequently, little indirect effect on support.

Self interest and program effectiveness. Here we again find no striking differences between representatives from districts of various levels of wealth and their corresponding beliefs about program effectiveness. Congress members from high-income districts are slightly less likely than those from low-income districts to discuss effectiveness, but when they do discuss it, they are just as likely as their colleagues to describe it in a positive way as in a negative fashion. Below is an example of a comment from a representative from a very wealthy district. He expresses negative views about the effectiveness of AFDC yet is still quite supportive:

> [The AFDC program has created] a no-win situation for a person on AFDC right now. If they try to improve themselves, they lose

benefits. . . . If they don't try to improve themselves, they're obviously stuck in an unsatisfactory situation for a many-year period. [#44]

Representatives' discussions of program effectiveness fail to show that self-interest has any meaningful effect on congressional support, whether it be a direct path to support or an indirect path via beliefs about recipient deservingness or program effectiveness.

Political predisposition and recipient deservingness. A relationship appears to exist between political party membership and attributions about recipient deservingness. Democrats talk more often about deservingness in a positive way than do Republicans. Conversely, Republicans are less likely than Democrats to bring up issues of deservingness at all; and when they do, they are more likely than Democrats to express negative or mixed feelings about recipient deservingness. To illustrate, the first comment regarding deservingness is from a Democrat and the second is from a Republican:

> [I go] out in the countryside and see these [poor] people and see how helpless they are and how defenseless they are and how they need protections and . . . [the protection isn't] going to be there if [welfare] programs [aren't] maintained to put the support mechanism in place. [#2]

> [I was talking to a woman on AFDC in my district.] I said, "How old are you?" She said, "I'm 31." I said, "When is the last time you worked?" She said, "Well, I was 16." I said, "What have you been living on during that time?" In the meantime I found out that there wasn't a man in the house and these were illegitimate kids. She says, "ADC." I said, "Do you mean to tell me that you have been on taxpayers relief rolls for fifteen years and you haven't had a job?" She said, "No, I haven't." Well, knowing something about that area, there is no excuse for that. There is no excuse for that. I know lots of people who are similarly situated. . . . I'm blaming her for not taking her own initiative and going our and getting something to supplement her income. We've got too many cases like that. [#51]

The two comments illustrate another interesting difference between Democrats and Republicans: the style in which they present their beliefs about recipient deservingness. Republicans are much more likely to present single case examples of recipients from which they generalize to all recipients. Democrats, on the other hand, are more likely to discuss recipients as a group than to single out the individual case. Thus, Democrats differ from Republicans in their more positive views about recipient deservingness, and in the ways they describe recipients.

Political predisposition and program effectiveness. Despite the differences between Republicans and Democrats in their beliefs about the deservingness of recipients, the data fail to show any consistent relationship between party membership and attributions about program effectiveness. Republicans are slightly more likely to speak negatively about program effectiveness than Democrats, but the relationship is marginal. Instead, representatives from both political parties are more likely to express negative views about program effectiveness than positive opinions. More important, though, negative attributions about program effectiveness do not lead representatives to be any less supportive of public assistance programs. The following demonstrate the lack of distinction between party members. Both the Republican (the first quote) and the Democrat express negative views about the effectiveness of AFDC yet both remain supportive of the program:

> [The AFDC cycle] is a graphic illustration of the sickness of the welfare state mentality. It is a program dedicated to keeping people on welfare rather than making them independent. It's a program designed to make them dependent on government. [#5]

> Right now, it's a very logical thing for a person on public assistance not to take a risk on entering the economic system because they have to place their children's health and safety . . . all at risk so that they can get an entry level job. . . . Therefore, they don't do it. [#36]

In summary, we find both a direct relationship between party and support, with Democrats significantly more supportive of public assistance programs than Republicans, and an indirect relationship between party and support through attributions to recipient deservingness. Specifically, Democrats are more likely to believe recipients are deserving, and Congress members with more positive feelings about deservingness are, in turn, more likely to be supportive of public assistance programs. On the other hand, party membership does not seem to influence support indirectly through attributions about program effectiveness. Both Republicans and Democrats are openly critical of these programs, and both are quick to offer suggestions for reform; their criticisms, however, appear to have little influence over levels of support.

We have seen, then, that Democrats clearly hold more positive views about the deservingness of recipients and are more supportive of public assistance programs than Republicans. However, representatives from both parties offer critical comments about program effectiveness. Despite their criticisms, none of the representatives interviewed is willing to scrap public assistance programs altogether. As they describe their support and offer suggestions for reform, they keep in mind their beliefs about the deservingness of recipients.

Explaining Support for a Social Insurance Program

Exploring the reasons behind congressional support for Social Security is difficult because nearly all members of Congress are solid supporters of the program (85 percent would maintain benefits at their current levels). There is, however, more variation in congressional support for Medicare, another social insurance program. Thus, in this section we examine the ways self-interest, political predispositions, and attributions about recipient deservingness and program effectiveness explain support for Medicare rather than for both Social Security and Medicare. Earlier analyses presented in chapters 4 and 5 failed to show any relationship between support for social insurance programs and representatives' self-interest (defined as having a high proportion of elderly residents in their districts) and their beliefs about program effectiveness. The discussion did demonstrate, however, a strong link between support and party membership. Democrats are consistently more supportive of Medicare than Republicans. Additionally, we also found that representatives who believe that Medicare recipients are deserving of benefits are also more likely to be supportive of the program.

Looking first at the relationship between self-interest and attributions about recipients and programs, we find that Congress members representing districts with high proportions of elderly are no more likely than members representing districts with low proportions of elderly to believe that Medicare recipients (the vast majority of whom are elderly) are deserving and that Medicare is effective in achieving its goals. Neither finding is particularly surprising. The elderly are an important presence in the country: articles about aging in America are seen frequently in the mass media; the elderly are well represented by interest groups in Washington; and both the House and the Senate have special committees devoted to examining elderly issues (Jacob 1990). Therefore, it is not unexpected that regardless of whether members come from districts with many elderly persons or few, all should share similar views on the deservingness of the elderly and on the effectiveness of programs that serve the elderly population.

Although self-interest does not influence beliefs about recipient deservingness, party does: Democrats are more likely than Republicans to think Medicare recipients are deserving of their benefits. However, party has no effect on attributions about program effectiveness. Thus, Democratic representatives are more likely than Republicans to believe Medicare recipients are deserving, and Democratic representatives are more supportive of the program overall. But members of the opposing political parties are equally likely to find fault in the effectiveness of the program and to suggest possible reform measures. Nonetheless, their feelings toward program effectiveness do not influence their level of support.

In summary, Congress members appear to base their support decisions for Medicare on the attributions they make about recipient deservingness, which in turn are strongly influenced by their political party. There is some evidence as well of a direct effect of political party. The comments representatives give do not provide evidence that their beliefs about program effectiveness influence their decisions or that they are motivated to support Medicare because of self-interest in seeking reelection.

Summary

The factors that influence representatives' support for public assistance programs (e.g., AFDC and Medicaid) are the same as those affecting their support for social insurance programs (e.g., Medicare). The key to explaining their support lies in their political party affiliation and their attributions regarding the deservingness of recipients. Political party affects support both directly and indirectly through its influence over program-based beliefs. Interestingly, neither self-interest nor attributions about program effectiveness appear to motivate Congress members to be more or less supportive of social welfare programs.

Regardless of the program under consideration, Democrats are far more likely than Republicans to see recipients as deserving, and thus to support social welfare programs. How can we explain this consistent finding? We contend that it can be traced to the basic philosophical difference between the two parties. Janda, Berry, and Goldman (1987:246; 1989:284) outline these fundamental differences through an analysis of the platforms adopted during national party conventions. The Democratic platform of both the 1984 and the 1988 national conventions stressed justice, while the Republican platform in both years stressed freedom. The following excerpts demonstrate the Democratic party's emphasis on justice:

> Fulfilling America's highest promise, equal justice for all: that is the Democratic agenda for a just future. . . . As Democrats and as Americans, we will make support for democracy, human rights, and economic and social justice the cornerstone of our policy. (1984)

> We believe that all Americans have a fundamental right to economic justice. (1988)

With a similar degree of clarity, the Republican party emphasized freedom as the platform's basic premise in both years:

> From freedom comes opportunity; from opportunity comes growth; from growth comes progress. . . . If everything depends on freedom—and it does—then securing freedom, at home and around the world is one of the most important endeavors a free people can undertake. (1984)

> Freedom works. This is not sloganeering, but a verifiable fact. . . . Our platform reflects on every page our continuing faith in the creative power of human freedom. (1988)

The Democratic party's goal of human justice leads the party to support government-funded social welfare, while the Republican desire for individual freedom suggests less government involvement. This was evident when in 1988 the Democratic party suggested that the role of government is to "help us solve our problems" while the Republican party wrote that government's role is to "empower people to solve their own problems" (Janda, Berry, and Goldman 1989:284). If one starts with a premise of "equal justice for all" and believes government should "help us solve our problems," then it naturally follows that those in need are seen as deserving of publicly funded social welfare programs. On the other hand, starting with a premise that "everything depends on freedom" because "from freedom comes opportunity," leads one to find fault with those who have failed to use their free choices wisely. Logically, if one believes that those in need are not deserving and that "government should see to it that people should solve their own problems," then it is unlikely that one will want to increase government's role in social welfare programs. Issues of social welfare policy bring the basic philosophical differences between the Democratic and Republican parties into sharp focus. It is from these core belief structures that Democrats and Republicans draw when they consider the deservingness of recipients and when they make decisions about their level of support for social welfare programs.

Comparing Models of Support for the Public and Congress

A number of similarities and differences between the public and Congress emerge when we compare the results of the disposition-attribution model of support. The most noticeable similarity is the important role played by political party. Democratic members of the public are more supportive than Republicans, and Democratic Congress members are more supportive than their Republican colleagues. For members of Congress, party is perhaps the most important factor explaining differences in level of support. It has both a direct effect and an indirect role through its influence on beliefs about recipient deservingness.

Party is not as important for the public as it is for Congress, but it nonetheless plays a significant role. Public support for AFDC is both directly and indirectly affected by party membership (i.e., Democrats are more supportive than Republicans, and Democrats are more likely than Republicans to believe that AFDC recipients are deserving and that the program is effective, thus leading them to be more supportive). For the other two programs we examined—Social Security and Medicaid—the effect of party is less complex. Party has only a direct effect in explaining public support for Social

Security (i.e., Democrats are more supportive of increases than Republicans), and has an indirect effect in explaining support for Medicaid (i.e., Democrats are more likely to believe recipients are deserving and thus are more supportive). These relationships may be difficult to keep in mind without a formal figure, but the underlying story is that political predispositions play an important role in determining one's support for social welfare programs. The differences in core principles between the Democratic and Republican parties appear to be as important to members of Congress as to the general public.

A second similarity between the disposition-attribution models of public and congressional support is the importance of attributions about the deservingness of recipients as predictors of support for public assistance programs. Those who maintain that program recipients are deserving of help are more supportive than those who believe otherwise. This finding has important implications for any group hoping to change levels of support among Congress and the public. It tells us that when recipients are seen as being in need, as having no other sources of help, as wanting to be independent, and as not being at fault for their condition, support will be forthcoming. Support for public assistance programs depends a great deal on images of program recipients.

The most striking difference between the model of public support and the model of representatives' support lies in the role of attributions about program effectiveness. Among members of Congress, beliefs about effectiveness play no part in predicting support. For example, representatives who think AFDC is ineffective and in need of reform are no less likely to be supportive than those who think it is effective. However, among members of the general public, beliefs about program effectiveness make a difference in support for AFDC and Social Security. Those citizens who think AFDC and Social Security are ineffective are considerably less likely to support them than those who believe the programs to be effective. Why do Congress and the public differ? We speculate that members of Congress feel responsible for the effectiveness of programs to some degree. Rather than try to decrease funding for program beneficiaries when they think a program is not effective, they are driven to improve the program design or management through reform legislation. On the other hand, members of the general public are not policymakers and they feel no such personal responsibility to improve programs. The public's response to their perceptions of ineffectiveness is to recommend a decrease in benefits in order to reduce the potential dollars wasted.

There are also differences in the role of self-interest between the public and Congress. While self-interest—as measured in this study—is somewhat important in predicting support among members of the public, it is not at all important in determining support among members of Congress. However, this comparison is not as clear-cut as it seems. For both the public and Congress, self-interest is construed as rational, calculated action designed to further their own interests or goals. But the measure of self-interest is different for the two groups: self-interest for members of the public involves pursuing those actions that will improve their financial well-being, while self-interest for representatives involves increasing their chances for reelection (Fiorina 1977; Tufte 1978). Specifically, the model of self-interest for the public suggests that a program's beneficiaries should support a program more than those who are not beneficiaries, whereas the model of self-interest for Congress suggests that Congress members representing high- and middle-wealth districts (whose constituents must therefore pay the costs) should be less supportive of social welfare programs than those representing low-income districts, and that Congress members representing districts with high proportions of elderly should be more supportive of programs targeted at the elderly (e.g., Social Security and Medicare) than Congress members representing districts with few elderly people. In the domain of social welfare, we think that self-interest should play only a minor role in future discussions of public and congressional support. We conclude this because support for a program does not necessarily depend on whether one receives benefits from that program. As we saw in earlier chapters, many people who are not recipients nonetheless empathize with recipients and the goals of social welfare. Furthermore, self-interest has virtually no observable effect on the level of support expressed by members of the U.S. House of Representatives.

We began this chapter by asking whether it was possible to construct integrated models of public and of congressional support.

The answer is yes, and the findings are revealing. When the four explanations of support are put together in a single model, we discover a number of interesting relationships between them.

The disposition-attribution model we have proposed suggests that citizens make decisions about support for social welfare based on their attributions about recipient deservingness and about program effectiveness. The personal dispositions of the individual evaluator—his or her self-interest and political predisposition—influence support as well, both directly and through a modification of beliefs about program characteristics. Additionally, the integrated model has shown that explanations for support differ depending on the program being considered and depending on whether it is congressional representatives or the public doing the ratings.

The disposition-attribution model explains public support for AFDC, Medicaid, and Social Security quite well, but the relevant relationships in the model differ across the three programs. Support for AFDC is the most complex, with the four factors both directly and indirectly influencing levels of support. Support for Medicaid and Social Security are somewhat simpler. For Medicaid, beliefs about program effectiveness are relatively unimportant when other factors are taken into account. Respondents reach decisions about their support for Medicaid based on the attributions they make concerning recipient deservingness, attributions that have been shaped by their political predispositions. In addition, self-interest has a direct influence on support for Medicaid, though it has no separate effect on attributions about program effectiveness and recipient deservingness. Conversely, for Social Security, beliefs about recipient deservingness are unimportant when other factors are taken into account; self-interest acts upon support only indirectly; and political predispositions function directly rather than indirectly through program-based beliefs.

Among members of the public, the relationships between the factors within the disposition-attribution model of support differ across the three programs. However, for Congress, the relationships between the factors is similar across programs. Given the constraints of limited variability in support scores, we find the best model for explaining representatives' support includes attributions about the deservingness of recipients and political party membership; factors of self-interest and program effectiveness offer little useful information toward predicting congressional support.

7
Social Welfare in America: Here to Stay

The welfare state was seriously called into question in the 1980s, but efforts to dismantle or substantially erode existing social welfare programs have met with failure. To understand why, one must look in part to the beliefs and values of the American public and its policymakers, especially their beliefs about the role of social welfare programs in a democracy. In this final chapter, we summarize the answers to the questions we raised in chapters 1 and 2 and examine their implications for both theory and policy.

The American Public and the Future of Social Welfare

Chapter 1 outlined the debate over a crisis of legitimacy in the American welfare state. By probing the American public's support for the current social welfare system, we have examined the extent to which such a crisis actually exists. The evidence now seems clear: social welfare in America is firmly rooted. Overall, we find relatively high levels of support for the current version of the American welfare state.

The majority of respondents in our national survey say they want either to maintain or increase benefits for seven of the most important programs of the American welfare state. These seven programs include both social insurance programs (Social Security, Medicare, and Unemployment Insurance) and public assistance programs (AFDC, Medicaid, Food Stamps, and SSI) and represent the broad array of programs within the American social welfare system. When we selected three of these programs (Social Security, Medicaid, and AFDC) for a more in-depth examination of public commitment to the welfare state, the majority of respondents again demonstrate their support by expressing satisfaction that their taxes go to support social welfare programs. Further, a third or more of the respondents go so far as to say they are willing to write their Congress member or sign a petition or pay higher taxes in order to prevent cuts in each of these programs.

Our second purpose has been to examine whether some aspects of the social welfare system are supported more than others and, if so, to learn which parts are most and least supported. Our data show that Americans do not see the welfare state as an undifferentiated, homogeneous entity. They distinguish between social welfare programs, and they support some more than others. For example, while a majority favor increases for Medicare, Social Security, and SSI, and about half favor increases for Medicaid, only a third want increases for AFDC and Unemployment Insurance and even fewer favor increases for Food Stamps. In fact, unlike for any other program, the same proportions prefer cuts in Food Stamps as favor increases (i.e., one-fourth).

Just as respondents differentiate between programs in their preferences for increasing, maintaining, or decreasing benefits, so too do they differentiate in the behavioral commitments they are willing to make to keep programs intact. Although a majority say they are satisfied with the fact that their taxes maintain current programs, this support falls when respondents are asked what actions they would be willing to take to keep programs from being cut. Fewer respondents are behaviorally committed to programs than are attitudinally committed, but like attitudes, behavioral support levels are greater for Social Security and Medicaid than for AFDC. In fact, Social Security appears to be doubly blessed with both a strong majority of actively committed supporters who say they are willing to contact their congressional representatives and pay higher taxes in order to keep the program from being cut, and with a very small minority of active opponents. Conversely, AFDC appears to be doubly cursed with less active supporters and more active opponents. Although a majority of all respondents say they are satisfied their tax dollars support AFDC, these supporters are simply not as likely to say they will act to demonstrate their support as are Social Security supporters.

The programs that the public are most likely to support—Social Security, Medicare, and SSI—are different in many ways. Two are social insurance programs (Social Security and Medicare) and one is a public assistance program (SSI). One provides benefits in kind (Medicare), whereas two provide benefits as cash (SSI and Social Security). However, they share one similarity: all focus on the needs of the elderly. Is the public more supportive of helping the elderly, regardless of the program in question? To learn more about the public's support within the social welfare domain, we asked respondents to rank which potential groups of recipients should receive assistance for each of four services—additional financial assistance, food assistance, educational-type services, and catastrophic health insurance. The findings show that respondents distinguish among potential recipients of assistance and support some groups more than others depending on the social service in question. The elderly are not chosen universally for assistance. For additional financial assistance and for food services, respondents give the elderly a high priority. But when considering educational services, members of the public are more likely to favor helping adults under age sixty-five, whether they be physically disabled or able-bodied but poor. Children receive highest priority as potential recipients of catastrophic health insurance. Thus, as these findings show, the public does not have a single universal preference for the elderly, nor for any other group, regardless of the service in question. Instead, people try to match their perceived needs of the group with the benefits offered through the specific service. In order to understand the high support attributed to Social Security, Medicare, and SSI, we must look at the relationship between perceptions about the program and perceptions about the recipients.

These findings have three implications that strike us as particularly noteworthy. First, they allow us to understand more clearly the extent to which there is a crisis of legitimacy in the welfare state. Second, they allow us to address claims concerning the types of programs most and least favored by the American public. And third, these findings have implications for arguments that the public is indiscriminate in its opinions, thus serving as a poor source to consult during the formulation and assessment of policy.

The Crisis of Legitimacy Rhetoric

In the 1980s, and continuing into the 1990s, discourse about the welfare state in both the scholarly and the political communities has been imbued with presumptions that many members of the public are not willing to continue to support social welfare programs with their tax dollars. Yet the reports issued in the past decade addressing the state of the welfare state have paid scant attention to public support (e.g., White House Domestic Policy Council 1986; California Department of Social Services 1986; Washington State Department of Social and Health Services and the Employment Security Department 1986; American Enterprise Institute 1987; American Public Welfare Association 1986; National Governors' Association 1987; Ford Foundation, 1989). In this book, we have attempted to correct that imbalance.

One of the clearest conclusions we can draw from the data presented in this book is that there is no crisis of support. Judging from the beliefs expressed by respondents in this study, the crisis rhetoric of the 1980s seems to have been based on the eloquent speech of a vocal few, and an overreliance on responses to a single yearly survey question about support for "welfare." Although citizens do not always unanimously agree about whom they want to help and how best to do so, there is a shared belief that the major programs of the welfare state should be at the minimum maintained.

This strong consensus for a national welfare state would not have been found among Americans at the beginning of the twentieth century. Then the prevailing belief was that the problems brought on by unemployment, disability, poverty, and old age should be handled through family, friends, the church, or private charities. It was not the legitimate role of the federal government to "promote the general welfare" by providing government-backed guarantees against losses due to old age, unemployment, disability, and sickness (as social insurance programs now do), nor should the federal government provide assistance to those who could not care for themselves and their families because of a lack of financial resources, ability, or job skills (as public assistance programs now do).* How is it that in less than one hundred years the American public has come to accept the federal government's role in insuring against the risks of modern life and in assisting those in need?

In a seminal essay, English sociologist T. H. Marshall (1950) answered this question. According to Marshall, the conception of democratic citizenship has changed and with it beliefs about the proper role of government. Marshall depicted the twentieth-century welfare state as "the latest phase of an evolution of citizenship which has been in progress for some 250 years." The first phase in the evolution of citizenship came in the eighteenth century when civil rights were granted to most citizens; these rights included trial by jury, representation in a court of law, and freedom of speech. The second phase came in the nineteenth century with the granting of political rights, encompassing the right to vote and the right to run for office (as is well known, of course, the right to vote was not granted to women until the 19th Amendment to the Constitution passed in 1920 and was not assured to African Americans until the Voting Rights Act of 1965).

During the first two centuries of U.S. history, citizens saw many rights extended to them, but social rights were excluded. In those early years, the federal government did not guarantee all citizens a minimum standard of living. Marshall's third phase of evolution of citizenship did not occur until the fourth decade of the twentieth century when the federal government became concerned with such issues as citizens' access to medical care, adequate food, and sufficient income. The enactment of the Social Security Act in 1935 set in motion the incremental development of the American welfare state—a patchwork quilt of social insurance and public assistance programs. If we consider these programs as social rights of citizenship, as Marshall did, then the data in this book show that a majority of the American public and their representatives to Congress support such rights.

It would be naive to suggest that the development of social rights of citizenship is complete. One need only look at the prob-

---

* As nearly all American readers will recognize, the phrase "promote the general welfare" comes from the preamble to the Constitution of the United States. In addition, Article I, Section 8 of the Constitution stipulates that Congress may levy taxes for the promotion of "the general welfare." In 1937 the Supreme Court invoked this clause as the basis for upholding the constitutionality of the Social Security Act.

lems of the 1990s to see the evidence: clashes over who should shelter and house the homeless and disputes over the rights of women to abortion. Opinions are sharply divided over exactly what these legitimate rights should be, and the results of our research cannot give answers to all the specific policy issues. We can argue from our findings , however, that the public supports federal guarantees of certain basic social rights, namely the right to medical care, to food, to protection from the risks of unemployment, old age, and sickness—rights that did not exist at the beginning of the twentieth century and that are now provided through the seven major programs we have examined. Thus, we find no evidence of a crisis in support for the current American welfare state, and we find the American public willing to support its government in continuing to guarantee certain basic social rights.

Differentiation Between Programs

Social scientists have offered different claims about which social welfare programs or types of programs the public supports most enthusiastically. Katz (1986), for example, suggests that the public is not supportive of any mandatory tax-financed social welfare programs. Others contend that the public is willing to support social insurance programs but not public assistance programs (e.g., Skocpol 1990; Hasenfeld and Rafferty 1989).** Yet a third perspective maintains that the public supports programs that target the elderly but not programs aimed at other groups (e.g., Preston 1984; Hewlett 1991).

The first claim is clearly incorrect given the results of our survey. Quite the opposite, we find that no less than three-fourths of the respondents want to maintain or increase benefits for each of the major social welfare programs. How could such an incorrect claim arise in the first place? It is probably in part due to the overreliance by social researchers on a single survey question asking about support for "welfare." Every year since 1972 the National Opinion Research Center (NORC) has asked, "Do you think we're spending too much money on welfare, too little money, or about the

---

**Although Skocpol (1991) uses the terms *universal* and *targeted* to describe programs, and Hasenfeld and Rafferty (1989) draw the distinction between "contributory" and "means-tested" programs, they are all nevertheless talking about social insurance versus public assistance programs.

right amount?" Because no program called "welfare" actually exists, respondents must construe their own referent for the term. It is impossible to determine whether a respondent is thinking about a specific program, about the poor in general, or even about recipients getting "something for nothing" (Popkin 1985; see also Smith 1987b). Despite the inexactness of the question, scholars and commentators have continued to use the responses to gauge public support for the American welfare state in its entirety (e.g., Stoesz and Karger 1992; AuClaire 1984).*** Plainly, the results of this study show that to understand support for the welfare state, we need to ask specifically about the individual programs that make up the welfare state.

The second contention about public opinion—that people prefer social insurance to public assistance—has a stronger justification, but it is not universally true. Two of the programs receiving the highest levels of support are in fact social insurance programs— Medicare and Social Security. However, one of the programs receiving the lowest levels of support is also a social insurance program—Unemployment Insurance. Thus, it does not appear that social insurance programs are the sole "magic bullet" with which to gain public support.

Finally, the third perspective—that programs for the elderly receive the most support —appears to be accurate, at least on the basis of answers to questions concerning benefit levels. In fact, of the seven programs in question, only the three programs targeting the elderly receive a majority favoring increases and a minority preferring decreased benefits. However, lest we conclude that targeting the elderly is the way to garner support, we must recall that the public did not consistently give the elderly top priority for receiving assistance in the four service domains we examined. Although the elderly were chosen as the most important group to receive additional financial assistance and food assistance, they were not preferred for either educational services or for catastrophic health insurance.

***AuClaire (1984) used the NORC General Social Survey data to analyze the question on spending for "welfare" but in his article he erroneously overgeneralized and labeled the domain in question "social welfare," implying to readers that that term was used in the survey question. In addition to the problem of definition, researchers have tended to project support only as the response that "we're spending too little" rather than also including "about the right amount," thus defining support only in terms of growth and not maintenance.

What do these results mean in terms of the aforementioned claims about support? They show that the answer to building public support does not lay solely either in the particular target group nor in social insurance versus public assistance. Rather, it lays in the particular combination of the target group and the program.

Consistency of Public Opinion

Early work on mass attitudes suggest that the general public has no consistent opinions. Converse (1964) argued that when researchers try to discover mass public opinions they are likely to find "a jumbled cluster of pyramids or a mountain range, with sharp delineation and differentiation in beliefs from elite apex to elite apex but with the mass bases of the pyramids overlapping in such profusion that it would be impossible to decide where one pyramid ended and another began" (p. 256).

Our findings suggest quite the opposite. We find the public holds consistent and discernible ideas about social welfare. Respondents who favor increasing benefits for a program at one time in the interview, later reiterate their support with a verbal willingness to perform actions in defense on that program. Likewise, those favoring decreases maintain that belief throughout the questionnaire. Additionally, we find consistent reasons given for prioritizing elderly, children, and nonelderly adults. This regularity in reasoning shows a clear and consistent pattern of beliefs.

Certainly the arguments made by Converse in the 1960s and 1970s have been met with criticism by others. For example, Pierce and Rose (1974) arrive at a contradictory conclusion when they reanalyze Converse's data, and Judd and Milburn (1980) show that mass and elite opinions are similar rather than different as Converse argues. The results given throughout this book show that the public has consistent and understandable opinions. These new findings, in combination with past evidence, demonstrate that members of the public, regardless of the level of their political involvement, have coherent beliefs about social welfare issues and that these beliefs are predictable when additional information is available, such as political predispositions and personal attributions about the world.

Explaining Public Support for Social Welfare

A major question that this book has addressed is why there are differences in level of support. We examined four possible explanations—perceptions of recipient deservingness, perceptions of program effectiveness, self-interest, and political predispositions. We find that each explanation taken alone contributes to an understanding of how support is shaped, but it is the combination of all four into one integrated model that most powerfully explains support. From this finding, we argue that support is complexly determined both by the personal dispositions that respondents bring to their support decisions and by the attributions they make about the deservingness of recipients and the effectiveness of programs.

In chapter 6 we presented what we labeled the *disposition-attribution model of support* in which the causal effects of self-interest and political predispositions have both a direct influence on support and an indirect influence mediated through attributions about the deservingness of recipients and the effectiveness of the particular program in question. In addition, we find that attributions of deservingness and effectiveness also have direct influences on support that are independent of personal dispositions. Our theory of support, then, is one of contingencies: how support is determined is contingent upon the particular program being considered for support, the political and self-interested dispositions of the person who is considering what level of support is appropriate, and the attributions that he or she makes about the program and the recipients of the program.

We have demonstrated that any model of support for social welfare must be complex. Support cannot be explained by only one predictive factor, as social scientists and social historians have done in the past, but must be viewed as an integration of several components. As we find in our analyses, the greater an individual's self-interested stake in program benefits, and the more he or she identifies with the Democratic party and with a liberal ideology in general, the more likely he or she is to see social welfare recipients as deserving and social welfare programs as effective. In turn, those who perceive recipients as deserving and programs as effective are more likely to support the particular social welfare program in question. The disposition-attribution model explains almost half the variance in support for Social Security and more than half the variance in support for Medicaid and AFDC.

The most parsimonious model for explaining public support for AFDC and Medicaid includes all four factors. In other words, members of the public decide whether to support public assistance programs based on a combination of reasons, including self-interest, political predispositions, attributions of recipient deservingness, and attributions of program effectiveness. On the other hand, fewer factors are important to understand public support for Social Security: self-interest (though only indirectly through attributions), political predispositions, and attributions about the effectiveness of Social Security. Beliefs about recipient deservingness have little effect on levels of support for Social Security. Why might this be the case? First, most members of the public make very positive attributions of the deservingness of Social Security recipients. Consequently, there is not much variability in the measure, and therefore it cannot help in the model of prediction. A second, and we think more important, reason, however, has to do with the eligibility requirements for Social Security. Receipt of AFDC and Medicaid is not determined by any past or future action; it is based strictly on financial need. Social Security recipients, however, have actively contributed to the program's financing and are receiving, many believe, a return on their past payments. Thus, because recipients of Social Security have directly contributed to the maintenance of the program, the public disregards issues of deservingness when determining their support; questions of recipient need, availability of alternative sources of help, and fault are assumed to be irrelevant.

Implications for Theory

These findings considerably progress our understanding of why the public supports some social welfare programs, and they have implications for theory development. The social welfare literature and the research on political preferences cite four principal reasons for support but deal with each separately. We have tried to take the discussion one step further by exploring the interrelationships between these four explanations. As Mackie (1980) argues, full theories of deterministic causation are probably impossible, but good approximations can be achieved through multiple contingency theories that specify the conditions under which an effect will occur.

In the natural sciences, researchers often appear to strive for the single causal agent that results in an effect, but in fact the process of change can usually be broken down into a set of multiple conditions that are needed to activate an effect. The important words here are *set*, *multiple*, and *conditions* as opposed to *single causal agent*. It is such a set of multiple conditions that we have tried to understand here in relation to support within the social welfare domain. The result has been to develop a multiple contingency theory of support, showing the conditions under which public and congressional support is forthcoming.

Three advantages accrue to our development of such a multiple contingency theory as compared with a theory with a single causal agent. First, the disposition-attribution theory of support improves our ability to make predictions. We showed that this integrated model explains a greater proportion of variance in support for each social welfare program we examined than any of the predictive factors taken alone or in sets of two. Second, the theory facilitates comprehensiveness by specifying how a system of causal agents interrelates. That is, rather than debate whether one factor (say, for example, self-interest) is more important than another (say, political predispositions), a multiple contingency theory reflects the broader view that both factors may be operating and seeks to understand how. Third, as a theory of support, the disposition-attribution theory is transferrable from the domain of social welfare to other domains. For example, we see no reason why it would not predict support for different types of foreign policy or for economic policy. From our readings of these types of policy arenas, support for government intervention might well be predicted by one's political ideology and level of self-interest and by one's attributions of program effectiveness and recipient deservingness. As an example, in his study of American support for foreign policy, Wittkopf (1990) observed numerous factors influencing preferences for U.S. intervention in foreign affairs. Key among the factors were a number of personal dispositional issues, including political ideology and region of the country where one resided, and several attributional concerns, such as beliefs about the threat of communism, evaluations of policymakers' foreign policy performance, and the appropriate use of force. Although the precise measures differ, the constructs are similar to those presented in the disposition-attribution model.

Is Social Insurance the Answer?

Recent welfare theorists have suggested universal programs as a way to gain public support for reforming public assistance programs within the social welfare system (Skocpol 1990; Ellwood 1988; Wilson 1987). The principal appeal of universal programs such as Social Security is that over time everyone becomes both a contributor and a potential beneficiary. Universal programs address the needs of low-income residents as well as those of middle-income taxpayers. By such reforms, programs would gain a larger group of stakeholders who would in turn be more supportive. Skocpol (1991) uses Social Security as her example of a universal program and shows that it gives proportionately higher retirement benefits to formerly lower-income workers. She calls this strategy "targeting within universalism" (p. 428), while Heclo (1986) calls it "helping the poor by not talking about them" (p. 325).

This strategy is appealing to us, but we must add a cautionary note gleaned from our findings. In our survey, we asked respondents about three universal social insurance programs—Social Security, Medicare, and Unemployment Insurance. Although all three programs are similar in that contributors, regardless of their income, can receive benefits at the time when they become eligible, all three programs do not receive similar levels of support. Both members of the public and Congress favor Social Security and Medicare far more than Unemployment Insurance. This variability in support prompts us to examine the differences between the programs. At least two obvious differences exist. First, Social Security and Medicare both primarily target the elderly, while Unemployment Insurance primarily helps those nonelderly adults who are out of work. Second, whereas all three are contributory programs, Social Security and Medicare require contributions from both the employer and the employee during the employee's working life, but Unemployment Insurance only requires contributions from the employer. In other words, the employee is not directly contributing to Unemployment Insurance and is thus a step removed from the contribution structure.

What can this tell us about universal programs? Although they may be a possible approach to gaining support for social welfare programs, we cannot necessarily expect them to be unanimously accepted. Universal programs address the issue of self-interest—everyone is a potential beneficiary and thus is personally concerned—but they do not necessarily address concerns of recipient deservingness and program effectiveness.

Congress and the Public: Convergence and Divergence of Opinions

One of the most important questions that we have addressed deals with the extent to which the views of members of the public and Congress are similar and different. We found their views to be similar in a very fundamental way: both groups want the major programs of the American welfare state to continue, and only a relatively small minority want to see any programs cut. Thus, this book shows that there is no crisis of support either from the perspective of the public or the Congress.

Representatives are supportive whether they be committee leaders or nonleaders, Democrats or Republicans. However, levels of support are not equally high among these different groups of representatives. Leaders of committees that have strong relevance to social welfare express more support than their colleagues who are not social welfare committee leaders. Committee leaders' greater support occurs among both Democrats and Republicans, with Democratic committee leaders being more supportive than Democrats in the House at large and Republican committee leaders more supportive than Republicans in the House at large. In no case do we find members at large more supportive than leaders of committees responsible for social welfare legislation. Since members of Congress who are not specialists in a particular area often take their cues from their colleagues who are specialists, the support levels among committee leaders bode well for the continuing stability of social welfare programs.

Despite the basic and important similarity in support between the public and their representatives, there are a number of striking differences. First, members of Congress are more likely to want to maintain programs at current benefit levels keeping up with inflation, while members of the public are more likely to want to increase benefit levels. For six of the seven programs about which we asked, a larger proportion of the public than Congress said they thought benefits should be increased. In not one case did a majority of representatives favor increased benefits for a program, whereas a majority of the public favored increased benefits for three of the programs (i.e., Medicare, Social Security, and SSI).

Does this mean that representatives do not care as much as the general public about social welfare? Not according to what representatives told us in our interviews. They are quite clear about why they are loath to say "increase" despite the fact that many frequently say they would like to see some of the benefits increased in an ideal situation. Their major reason for maintaining rather than expanding is cost. The massive U.S. budget deficit dominates representatives' thinking about benefit levels. According to one southern Democrat, "I'm going to sound like I'm just for the status quo, but the reason I favor maintaining the current levels . . . is not that I don't think we should do more, but just taking into account the economic realities, I think that's about all we can do." [#8] A Democrat from the west coast made a similar point about wishing he could increase benefits and went on to explain, "Everything that you ask me is going to be colored by the fact that we have a budget deficit and that we are struggling to try and get a handle on that." [#38] Members of the public do not appear to see as clearly as members of Congress the connections between increasing program benefits and increasing the deficit, or at least they are not as concerned.

A second difference between members of the public and Congress has to do with the programs to which they assign highest levels of support. Both groups are likely to express relatively high levels of support for Medicare; but whereas members of the public are more likely to support Social Security and SSI than other programs, representatives are more likely to support Medicaid and AFDC. Despite their concern over the deficit, a number of Congress members say they believe that it is the responsibility of the federal government to provide certain kinds of assistance. One is clearly medical care, according to representatives such as these:

> I realize that we have tight budgetary restrictions. I realize that we have high budget deficits, but if we can't take care of our people relative to medicine, then we are not worth the sand we walk on. [#15]

This government is broke, but what you're talking about is trying to cover the cost of adequate medical care for people who can't afford to pay for it out of their pocket or don't have outside insurance . . . it's our responsibility to pay for it. [#22]

Those who support AFDC also emphasize the responsibility of the federal government to help, despite budgetary restrictions. Ultimately, as this representative from the east coast explains, it is the federal government's responsibility to help children break out of the poverty cycle:

I think AFDC payments ought to be increased. . . . We talk about being pro-family. Certainly if we're going to be pro-family, we need to give to those [very poor] families, particularly in this nation where we see an expansion of female-headed households which have increasingly fallen below the poverty line during the last eight to ten years. I think it's necessary for us to expand that program so that we can not only assist the heads of the households, but insure that the children in those households live in an environment in which they can break out of the cycle of poverty. [#14]

The third difference between the views of the public and Congress is in the target groups that respondents rank highest for social services. Representatives are most likely to give children top priority for services (i.e., for three of the four services about which we asked), whereas the public is more likely to assign top priority to the elderly (i.e., for two of the four services). Representatives who rank children first tell us they are aware of statistics that show children to be more likely than other age groups to be living in poverty. They say that the problem of poverty among children is growing and that additional help is needed. As one west coast representative put it:

The group that has gotten worse off, relatively speaking, has been poor children. . . . What it really comes down to is that children get the hind end of the deal. What we are talking about is welfare mothers—a group of the poor who receives less sympathy. All that ends up coming to children. Whether it was [the fault of] their mothers or a terrible family situation, the child—of all people!—suffers the most. What has happened with children lately has just been terrible. [#33]

Further, representatives rank children above the elderly because they argue that the problem of poverty among the elderly is diminishing while the problem of poverty among children is increasing. They tell us of data showing the elderly, as a group, to be much better off than they were in the early 1960s before Medicare, Medicaid, SSI, the Older Americans Act, and the introduction of Social Security COLAS. For example, in the view of one representative from the south, "We are pretty well taking care of the elderly through various programs that we have. I think statistics, according to what I've been told, bear that out in the last year. But for the same period of time, I've seen children drop through the net, so to speak." [#31] A representative from the east made a similar point:

> We have successfully, to a degree, eradicated the problem of poverty among the elderly. We've turned that around. In 1950, almost 30 percent of elderly Americans lived in poverty. Today, only 12 or 13 percent live in poverty. And we are still fighting on that score. And, so, while we—here we are—making tremendous strides against povertization of our elderly, nobody is paying attention to the children. That is why this year should become the year of the children. . . . I think the increasing statistics, the information that comes to our budget committee through our hearings, bear me out about the growing povertization of American children. [#52]

Representatives are not saying that federal resource distribution between the young and the old is a zero-sum game such that giving to the young entails taking from the old. Rather, they are simply saying that federal efforts since the 1950s. have had the effect of reducing poverty among elderly Americans and that the need now is to give a higher priority to children, the age group most likely to live in poor families. When we look back at the census poverty data presented in figure 1.1, we see that these members of Congress are indeed correct. It may well be that if members of the public had access to the same detailed information on poverty rates as do members of Congress, they too would favor helping children. It is certainly true that representatives have access to rich information— from such sources as hearings, the Congressional Budget Office, the General Accounting Office, the Library of Congress' Congressional Research Service, and their legislative assistants who summarize in easily digestible form important media articles and research findings. We can only guess that similar poverty-rate information would affect the priority decisions of the public as it seems to do for members of Congress.

The fourth difference between the public and members of Congress is in the number of factors that explain support for social welfare programs. Although the disposition-attribution model is useful in explaining support levels among members of both groups, a simpler variation of the model explains representatives' support. Rather than all four factors playing a role in the explanation of representatives' support, only one disposition factor—political party—and only one attribution factor—recipient deservingness—are important. Political party, by far the most important factor, has both a direct effect on support and an indirect effect mediated through attributions about recipient deservingness. Thus, not only are Democratic representatives more supportive than Republican representatives, but they are also more likely to believe recipients are deserving. Similar to Democrats, supportive Republicans are more likely than their less supportive colleagues to believe recipients are deserving.

The effectiveness of programs appears to be considerably less important in explaining support among Congress members than among the public. This is not because members of Congress are not as concerned about fraud, abuse, and mismanagement in social welfare programs as members of the public; they are. Instead, we think that the reason Congress members do not base their support on effectiveness has more to do with the way they define their role as policy overseers than with the importance they attribute to effectiveness. Members of Congress are elected not only as representatives of the public in order to develop new policy, but also to oversee existing programs. Thus, when representatives perceive problems in a program, they seek remedy by reforming the program rather than by completely discarding it. The public, on the other hand, has no control over program management and therefore often chooses to cut back programs they perceive to be ineffective.

The similarities and differences between the views of Congress and the public have a number of important implications for thinking about the future of representative democracy as well as about the role of political parties in the social welfare domain.

Implications for Representative Democracy

The differences in opinion between Congress and the public place extra importance on understanding the meaning of a representative democracy. As Backstrom (1977) reminds us, "Representative government should be representative," but "the principle is easier to state than define and to measure" (p. 411). Part of the difficulty with defining and measuring representativeness is that Americans are not sure what "representation" should mean. In fact, according to Janda, Berry and Goldman (1987), the debate over whether legislators should be "delegates" and represent the majority views of their constituents or "trustees" and vote according to their consciences has never been resolved. A second debate is over which form of representation is more important—dyadic representation (i.e., the extent to which a legislator accurately represents the majority of his or her constituents) or collective representation (i.e., the extent to which legislators taken as a group collectively represent the entire American public [Weissberg 1978]). Although it is not our intention to resolve the debate, we chose in this book to look at collective, not dyadic, representation because the issue of support for social welfare has been framed in a national and collective way.

Should elected officials be spokespeople for their constituency or should they use their additional knowledge to make information-based decisions? Given that attitudes do have some influence over actual roll-call voting decisions (Barrett and Cook 1991; Wilson and Caldwell 1988), is there a threat to representative democracy when Congress members have different views from the general public? Thomas Jefferson believed that political decisions must represent the morals and values of the general public, and although the extent to which political philosophers agree with Jefferson varies, the fact remains that the long-term support a social policy receives from the general populace is important to its continuation.

We have clearly seen that, in general, Congress and the public differ in which programs they support most and which groups they would target for assistance, but do they really differ in their attitudes toward social welfare as such? Are they not using the same rules to decide which programs to support, but because of differences in information and perspective, they reach different conclusions? When Americans argue that Congress should be "representative" of the public, are they implying that the policy choices must be the same, or that the values reflected in the policies should match those held by the public? By looking at the disposition-attribution model that describes support, we see that Congress and the public are not so different after all.

Our data demonstrate that factors of recipient deservingness and program effectiveness are extremely important to both members of the public and Congress. Attitudes toward the deservingness of recipients—such as the legitimacy of their needs, availability to them of alternatives, and self-responsibility—influence the degree to which Americans, both the public and members of Congress, will support public assistance programs.

Program effectiveness is also extremely important. The public is far more likely to be supportive of programs they perceive to be addressing a problem in a useful manner and that are managed well and not burdened with waste and abuse. Congress members are keenly aware that these are important factors to the public. They make such comments as:

> I really think average Americans are compassionate about their fellow human beings, and they are not going to leave them out there in the middle of the ocean without at least some help. I think they want programs to work. They want them to work efficiently. They want to make sure that they are not getting ripped off. [#38].

> I think American people are compassionate but don't want to be taken advantage of. [#39].

> The general public wants people to work . . . they are not willing to tolerate job training programs that they believe are worthless or that don't accomplish the purpose, or that are subject to corruption in any way. . . . But they are certainly willing to support programs that actually give people skills. [#55]

Members of Congress hear the public lament the inefficiencies in social welfare programs, and they too are clearly concerned with the quality of social welfare programs. On the other hand, and most likely because of their role as elected officials, Congress members are not willing to discount programs just because of problems. They seek improvement but not abandonment. Thus, both members of Congress and the public form support decisions about social welfare based on attributions of deservingness, and both are moved by impressions of ineffectiveness. Although Congress and the public do not always agree on who should be helped or which programs should be expanded, both groups seem to be following similar reasoning in coming to their conclusions. An important question for future research is whether members of the public and Congress would reach more similar conclusions if the public were given the same information as Congress.

A second aspect of representative democracy one ought to consider is whether Congress sees itself as being directly responsive to the desires of the public. The degree to which representatives see themselves as delegates of the public can be seen in such comments as:

> I think Congress generally does what the public wants, and I'm more convinced of that the longer I'm here. It is a rare occasion when Congress leads the public. Now it happens, but I think generally Congress responds to what the public wants. [#44]

> I think the reason Congress has resolved itself in the past two or three decades to make a firm attack on poverty and all the issues surrounding it, is because of the insistence of the American public based upon the public's generosity and caring. [#48]

On the other hand, our findings that some of the policy preferences of the public differ from those of Congress suggest that Congress serves more of a trustee role than as a delegate. Although representatives and the public share similar concerns that recipients be deserving and programs be effective, they arrive at alternate policy outcomes because of differences in information. We do not find this particularly troubling. The cornerstone of most normative theories of democracy is that the beliefs of the public should somehow influence legislators' decision making (e.g., Dahl 1956). But exactly how these opinions should affect policy is a more contested question. Some maintain that the desires of the public should be the driving force behind governmental decisions, since in its simplest manifestation, democracy means government by the people. Others argue that the public should be responsible for setting the agenda, but experienced policymakers should be responsible for the intricate details because they are more knowledgeable and better equipped. The answers given by the representatives in this study demonstrate a Congress responsive to the needs of Americans and consistent with the values of the majority of the public. Returning to the debate described at the beginning of this section about whether legislators should vote according to their conscience or their constituencies, our interviews lead us to question whether the debate should be resolved in favor of one approach or the other for all policy issues. When asked how he made decisions, a representative in our survey replied, "I decide based on the three C's: Constitution, Conscience, and Constituency." He went on to say that depending on the issue, the mix between the three changes. It is perhaps this mix that we see when we examine the similarities and differences between the views of the representatives and the public in the social welfare domain.

Political Parties in the Social Welfare Domain

According to some classic arguments in political science, political parties are the institution that makes democracy possible (e.g., Schattschneider 1942). For presidential elections, each political party builds a platform that lays out its philosophies and programs. It submits these to the public and pursues them when its presidential candidate is elected. Thus, in Schattschneider's view, parties state the propositions to which the voters may respond with approval or disapproval. The problem is that the public has only two choices. As Schattschneider pointed out, "The people are a sovereign whose vocabulary is limited to two words, 'yes' and 'no' " (p. 52).

This "limited" vocabulary at the polls is a problem for public policy to the extent that political leaders often take electoral victory as their mandate to initiate all the policy changes in their platform. Specifically, at the beginning of the 1980s, the Reagan administration believed it was elected with a mandate to change the fundamental direction of American social policy. David Stockman, Reagan's first director of the Office of Management and Budget, put his conception of the mandate this way: "The Reagan Revolution . . . required a frontal assault on the American welfare state" (Stockman 1986:8).

The Reagan administration was wrong about its mandate to change the direction of social welfare policy. The election of Ronald Reagan did not demonstrate a "swing to the right" on every policy issue, as Reagan and his administration assumed, but rather it represented the public's "lost confidence in the answers and performance of the Democratic/Keynesian approach to the political economy" (Ladd 1984:248; see also Shapiro and Patterson 1986; Ferguson and Rogers 1986). The 1970s had been a period of persistent high inflation and diminished economic growth, and by the 1980s the public was ready to "try something different" in order to control inflation and promote economic growth. In the closing days of his 1980 campaign, Reagan dramatically urged Americans to ask themselves whether they had become better or worse off during the four years of Jimmy Carter's Democratic presidency. How people voted was closely tied to their perceived financial well-being. Ladd (1984) used CBS election-day poll data to show that the Democratic party suffered its greatest losses among voters who thought their financial situation was worse than in the previous year. Carter was preferred to Reagan by 53 percent to 37 percent among citizens who thought they were better off, but Reagan was preferred by 64 percent to 25 percent among those citizens who believed their personal economic condition had declined (Ladd 1984:229).

Reagan's mandate from the people was to improve the economy, and not, as he and members of his administration perceived, to change the course of the welfare state. Just as California voters had interpreted a vote for Proposition 13 as a message to cut taxes but not services (Sears and Citrin 1982), so too did the American public believe that Reagan would improve the economy without dismantling the welfare state. Nonetheless, the Reagan administration saw its victory as a clear mandate. Because of this misinterpretation, Reagan's efforts to dismantle or even seriously erode social welfare programs were unsuccessful. These findings prompt two questions: How did Reagan so misinterpret the desires of the public? How can such misinterpretations of public opinion be prevented in the future?

Reagan's failure to make substantial changes in the American welfare state was due primarily to the refusal of Congress members to go along with his proposals after their initial compliance in 1981 (Greenstein 1991:440). Members of Congress, who tend to be closer to the preferences of the public than the president, believed that social welfare should be maintained. This belief, as we have seen, was held by both Republican and Democratic legislators. Despite the widespread rhetoric about a crisis of support for the welfare state, members of Congress supported social welfare programs. From our findings, we see that in so doing and in refusing to follow the president's proposals, they represented the views of the public.

Despite an agreement that social welfare should not be scrapped, Republicans and Democrats are not equally supportive. As is accepted knowledge and was confirmed through our survey, Democrats are much more supportive than Republicans and are much more likely to be actively committed in their support. The Reagan administration faced a Democrat-dominated House of Representatives throughout its tenure and a Democratic majority in the Senate for two of those years. Given the greater supportiveness of Democrats over Republicans, it seems safe to conclude that had Republicans dominated the Congress during the 1980s, the welfare state would have experienced greater cuts than it did. On the other hand, from the relatively supportive responses given by Republican representatives, it is also unlikely that the welfare state would have been dismantled to the significant degree desired by the Reagan administration.

The Reagan administration perhaps miscalculated the willingness of Congress to agree with its proposals, but it also appears to have misunderstood public opinion. In part, this misinterpretation arose from a too heavy reliance on answers to a single question about support for "welfare." As we have tried to show, there is no such program called "welfare" and no reason to assume that because one dislikes "welfare" one therefore dislikes individual programs within the welfare system. Second, misinterpretation arose from extrapolating assessments of low support from the complaints of citizens, policymakers, and the media about program ineffectiveness. It is true that criticisms of social welfare programs abound, but the fact that Americans are critical and would like to see reforms does not mean they want to eliminate programs or are unwilling to finance them through their tax dollars. Third, the misinterpretation of public sentiments can probably be attributed in part to the media. For whatever reasons, the media have a tendency to paint dramatically and with broad brushstrokes policy issues as policy crises. An example of this is the ways Social Security has been depicted in the popular press. In the early 1980s, the Social Security program was portrayed as experiencing a "crisis" because it was claimed that the trust funds were about to go bankrupt. A few years later, in 1988, a second "crisis" was described with regard to Social Security, but this time the culprit was a rapidly growing financial surplus in the trust fund (Marmor and Cook 1988). Finally, and related to the second and third reasons above, misinterpretation may have arison from a phenomenon akin to Noelle-Neuman's "spiral of silence" (1984). According to this notion, when one view comes to dominate the public scene, another sometimes slips from public awareness because its proponents become silent. Thus, criticisms of social welfare programs may have been so dominant that proponents of social welfare may have felt outnumbered and retreated to silence.

The answer to the second question—how such misinterpretations of public opinion can be prevented in the future—is difficult to address. Preventing misinterpretations in the future will not be easy, but there are ways to decrease the likelihood of mistakes. The very nature of the polling enterprise is to ask many diverse questions about a range of issues in a single survey. Yet if one wants to understand public opinion accurately, one must ask numerous in-depth questions within each policy domain. Questions that ask about "welfare" tell little that can be clearly interpreted. Instead one must ask about specific social welfare programs. Finally, politicians and researchers might look for information about public opinion in forums bringing together citizens and policymakers in order to speak, listen, and learn (Yankelovich 1991). Such forums can offer useful insights into public beliefs. In the social welfare domain, we have seen that political party is the most powerful predictor of support for social welfare programs among members of Congress, and although parties play a less significant role among members of the public, they nonetheless represent an important means for citizens to communicate to leaders. By sponsoring public forums, political parties can open the discourse between the public and policymakers, and such citizen-representative policy forums might lead both parties to see better ways to make social welfare policies and programs express the consensus in support that exists.

After more than fifty years of expansion, the American welfare state faced a serious threat in the 1980s when the Reagan administration proposed a dramatic scaling back of the federal role in financing programs. Although the Reagan administration did not succeed in all its attempts, it did prompt many American citizens to rethink their support for social welfare. After a watershed decade of questioning the direction of the welfare state, the answer is clear. The public and their representatives in Congress support the social welfare state. They do not want any more cuts in the fabric of protection provided to all citizens by social welfare programs. Thus, it appears that the American welfare state is here to stay.

Surveying the Public and U.S. Congress: The Research Design

Opinion research has a long and varied history. Though scholars have suggested that interest in public opinion dates back four thousand years (Bauer 1934), even if we limit our discussion to this century we find times of great interest in public opinion alternating with periods when public opinion was virtually ignored (for a brief review see Weissberg 1976). In recent years, with increasing statistical sophistication, public opinion research has begun to enjoy a well-respected place in certain policy circles. The results of public opinion polls can redirect political campaigns, and politicians pay very close attention to poll results.

Opinion research is not without its critics. In our research design we have tried to address some of the flaws and limitations sometimes attributed to survey research. One common criticism is that respondents will provide "socially desirable" responses when queried by strangers. DeMaio (1984) defines social desirablity as "the notion that some things are good and others are bad, and the notion that respondents want to appear 'good' and answer questions in such a manner as to be perceived that way" (p. 258). From an extensive review of the research on social desirability, DeMaio concludes that "the problem is not as overwhelming as it appears to be" (p. 279).

In regard to the research reported in this book, two points are relevant. First, considering the definition of social desirablity given here, it is not clear what would be socially desirable responses in relation to welfare state issues. That is, with all the criticisms of welfare state programs by the Reagan administration at the time of this interview (Stockman 1986), it is not completely clear what was a "good" way to answer the questions and what was a "bad" way. Second, the very early work of Cantril (1944) showed that when interviews are conducted with total anonymity, as was our study of public attitudes, respondents are far more likely to give non-socially desirable responses. A computer program generated random telephone numbers, and at no time was the respondent asked to give his or her name or place of residence. Interviews with members of Congress were conducted in person, and of course were thus not anonymous to the interviewer. However, the confidentiality of responses was stressed throughout the entire process, from the initial letter (from a member of Congress to his House colleagues), introducing the first author, to the conclusion of the interview. Though some surveys may yield socially appropriate responses, we believe the results presented throughout this book reflect the true beliefs of the interviewed members of the American public and of Congress.

A second criticism, posed most often by ethnographers, is that public opinion polling cannot give the full picture; it is too superficial. In order to understand the views of the American public, they contend, one must conduct in-depth interviews and observe the behaviors of respondents in natural settings. We agree that this is a potential flaw of public opinion surveys. Too many surveys attempt to address numerous, unconnected issues in a short period of time and thus spend only a minute or two on each. In contrast, our survey dealt only with issues of social welfare in the United States. Members of the public spoke with interviewers for roughly forty-five minutes, all on a single topic. Though the interviews with members of the public were structured, they were anything but brief. Interviews with members of Congress averaged fifty minutes in length, were conducted in person, and were less structured than those with the public.

A third criticism questions the very nature of understanding attitudes. The objection is that attitudes are not important, it is behaviors that matter. Public opinion surveys measure attitudes and not the more important behaviors. We disagree that attitudes are universally unimportant, but we agree that behaviors are significant. Thus, we have tried to measure behavioral intentions in our survey. We asked members of the public what they would do in defense of programs, and we look at how representatives vote.

A final criticism is that many members of the public do not have consistent political beliefs and thus often randomly choose a response in order to be able to answer an interviewer's questions (Converse 1964). As a result, survey researchers end up with opinions that are basically "non-attitudes." Smith (1984) reviews the research on non-attitudes and concludes that "there is an appreciable amount of both instrument error and nonattitudes in many opinion questions" (p. 244). Nonetheless, on the individual level, consistent responses depend on whether an issue is salient, important, and comprehensible to the respondent. If it is, then an individual's attitudes should be consistent and "real," whether or not he or she is educated or informed (Arrington 1976). Unlike for many other political issues, social welfare is one about which nearly every American has an opinion. It is an often discussed topic and is close to home. We believe, therefore, that the contents of our interviews contain few, if any, non-attitudes.

Public opinion research has had to contend with strong criticism. Oftentimes the criticism is appropriate. But if it is well-crafted, public opinion research can provide useful information to both researchers and policymakers. Through survey research one can learn of underlying values held by the general public, and when dealing with salient issues (such as social welfare) one can see the broad picture of public beliefs. In addition, as we discussed in chapter 1, policy decisions often mirror public opinion. Thus, exploring public opinion, especially in conjunction with the opinions of political elites (in the case of this book, members of the U.S. House of Representatives) proves helpful in expanding our understanding of the strength of the American welfare state.

The findings reported in this book are based on the results from two separate surveys. The first survey involved personal interviews with fifty-eight members of the U.S. House of Representatives and took place in the spring and summer of 1986. The second survey was conducted in the fall of 1986 and contained telephone interviews with 1,209 residents of the United States. To ensure comparability, both groups of respondents were asked similar questions.

In this appendix, we will discuss the survey sampling procedures, the achieved response rates, and the representativeness of the samples.

The Samples

The Public

From October 27 to December 2, 1986, the Northwestern University Survey Laboratory contacted by telephone 1,209 residents of the United States. Specially trained interviewers asked the respondents a number of questions concerning their beliefs about the present national social welfare system and options for change. The interviews lasted an average of forty-five minutes.

Respondent selection.   To select the potential respondents, the Survey Research Laboratory used a one-stage random-digit-dialing design. The sampling frame consisted of the AT&T Long Lines Division NPA-NXX Vertical and Horizontal Coordinator tape that lists the 48,000 working area code-exchange combinations in current use. To these six digits were added the final four digits randomly generated by a computer. The interviewers attempted at least six calls for each selected telephone number and kept a record of the disposition of each call.

Although the random-digit-dialing technique will produce a random selection of telephone numbers, it will not ensure a random sample of individuals within households. In many homes, there often are one or two residents who are more likely than others to answer the telephone. Because we want to avoid only hearing from the most talkative citizens, to insure a random sample within households, we used the "last birthday" method to select the appropriate respondent. Other methods of respondent selection require time-consuming enumeration of all household members and often also ask personal, intrusive questions. The last-birthday method, on the other hand, requires only that the interviewer speak with the adult member of the household who celebrated the most recent birthday. Because birth dates are randomly distributed, all household residents have an equal probability of being selected. Research by Salmon and Nichols (1983) comparing this method to three other frequently used methods (the Troldahl-Carter method, selecting alternate males and females, and using no selection procedure) showed it to be an efficient means for selecting a representative sample of all household members.

Response rate. Determining the response rate is fairly simple in door-to-door surveys when the researcher knows the total number of eligible sample units. It would also be simple to determine the response rate in telephone interviews if the researcher could rely on numbers listed in telephone books to represent the entire population from which a sample could be drawn. However, because a sizable proportion of the American public has unpublished or unlisted telephone numbers, it is not possible to rely on telephone books as a guide to sampling. The random-digit-dialing technique of household selection eliminates the bias caused by failing to reach those with unlisted telephone numbers and has been shown to be an effective method to achieve a representative sample of a population (Groves and Kahn 1979). A drawback of this method, however, is the impossibility of knowing the exact number of eligible sample units because of our inability to determine whether a selected telephone number is that of an eligible respondent. Not only can numbers be nonworking (in some cases the caller gets a recording, but often only a ringing or busy signal occurs), but they may also belong to businesses. In our study, 6,140 of the numbers called by the Survey Research Lab were nonworking numbers and 929 were nonresidential (i.e, businesses, pay phones, or car phones).

Table A.1 presents the distribution of attempted calls. If we exclude the phone numbers screened ineligible and those for which eligibility could not be determined, the proportion of completed interviews to the total number eligible is 69 percent. If we do not count the partially completed interviews as nonrespondents but rather omit them from the formula, the response rate increases to 71 percent. These relatively high percentages are comparable to response rates achieved in other national telephone surveys (Salmon and Nichols 1983; Czaja, Blair, and Sebestik 1982; Kluegel and Smith 1986).

Representativeness. In any survey one of the most important concerns is that the respondents be representative of the population from which they are drawn. If our respondents are not representative of the adult population of the United States, we cannot generalize our findings about beliefs, attitudes, and support for social welfare to the U.S. public as a whole. Table A.2 compares the sociodemographic characteristics of respondents in our survey of the public to the characteristics of respondents in two other surveys conducted during the same year. The two surveys chosen for comparison are the 1986 General Social Survey (GSS) conducted by the National Opinion Research Center (NORC) and the 1986 U.S. Census Bureau's Current Population Sur-

Table A.1

Dispositions of Attempted Telephone Calls

	Frequency	Percent of Category
Screened eligible (N = 1,744)		
Completed interview	1,209	69%
Respondent refusal	256	15
Household refusal	192	11
Partial interview: refusal to complete	57	3
Partial interview: willing to complete, but unavailable	30	2
Screened ineligible (N = 1,133)		
Nonresidential (business, pay phone)	929	82
Number changed/new number given	136	12
Number changed to unlisted	42	4
Noncitizen, no one 18 or over	26	2
Eligibility undetermined (N = 799)		
Not able to contact after 6 + calls	631	79
Unable to participate (ill, deaf, religious beliefs, out of town for extended period)	104	13
Non-English speaking	64	8
Nonworking numbers (N = 6,140)		

vey. The GSS survey was similar to our survey in population coverage and sample size but it differed from ours in length (it took longer to complete) and in style of interviewing (face-to-face rather than by telephone). Unlike the decennial census, mid-decade surveys, such as the 1986 U.S. Census Bureau Survey, are not complete enumerations of the population. Instead the surveys gain demographic information from approximately 10,000 residents, a number that can provide a more useful representation of the population than the typical national survey with 1,200 to 1,400 respondents.

The close similarities between our sample and others, as demonstrated in table A.2, lead us to feel confident that our sample is fairly representative of the American public. The respondents in our sample

Table A.2

Comparison of Public Survey with Census Data and NORC's 1986 General Social Survey

	Public survey N = 1209	NORC GSS N = 1470	U.S. Census[a] N = 10,000
Age			
18–34	38.9	35.2	40.5
35–54	33.0	33.4	30.5

	Public survey N = 1209	NORC GSS N = 1470	U.S. Census[a] N = 10,000
55–64	13.1	11.9	12.8
65 +	15.2	19.5	16.1
Gender			
Female	57.2	57.8	52.3
Male	42.8	42.2	47.7
Race			
White	86.1	85.0	86.3
Black	9.2	12.5	10.9
Other	4.6	2.5	2.8
Marital Status			
Married	57.4	56.2	59.5
Widowed	10.7	11.6	7.7
Divorced	10.1	10.1	7.8
Separated	2.7	4.1	3.4
Never married	19.0	18.0	21.6
Region			
New England	5.5	5.9	5.3
Mid-Atlantic	14.6	14.8	15.6
EN Central	17.9	18.4	17.4
WN Central	9.8	9.1	7.3
South Atlantic	17.9	17.1	16.8
ES Central	6.4	7.9	6.3
WS Central	8.4	8.1	11.1
Mountain	5.7	6.0	5.3
Pacific	13.8	12.8	14.7
Income			
Median income (1986)	$25,000	[b]	$24,897
Under $5,000	4.4		7.4
$5,000–9,999	9.7		11.6
$10,000–19,999	22.3		21.4
$20,000–34,999	27.0		26.2
$35,000–49,999	18.2		16.5
$50,000	18.4		16.8
Education			
Less than High School	15.0	27.0	24.6
High School Graduate	59.6	54.0	57.9
College Graduate	15.9	13.0	10.6
Post-College	9.6	6.0	7.0
Household Size			
Mean Size	2.8	2.8	2.6

[a]Census data provided by Chuck Nelson, U.S. Census Bureau. The information is published in Current Population Reports, Consumer Income, series P-60, N-151. Money Income of Households, Families, and Persons in the United States. Income data are at the household level.

[b]NORC interviewers read respondents a list of income groupings and ask respondents to report the category into which their income falls. Thus, it is not possible for NORC to report median incomes. The income groupings that NORC uses differ from the census, and in this table we have chosen to present census results.

closely approximate the Census Bureau data with respect to age, race, marital status, region of residence, and household size. In only two respects is our sample not representative of the U.S. population as reflected by Census Bureau data. First, both our respondents and the respondents in NORC's General Social Survey are about 4 or 5 percent more likely to be female than Census Bureau data suggest of the true population. Second, a larger proportion of our sample is college-educated and a smaller proportion has less than a high school education than the proportions that the larger Census Bureau study suggest exist in the United States. Groves and Kahn (1979) note that this underrepresentation of the less-educated sector of the population is not atypical for telephone surveys. They suggest this is perhaps because citizens with less than a high school education are loath to risk themselves in answering questions without the nonverbal cues and support that face-to-face interviewing offers. Although these problems with our data cannot be lightly dismissed and must be considered in every analysis, on the whole the sample appears similar to the population at large.

The Congressional Sample

The second survey we conducted involved members of the U.S. Congress. Between May and August 1986, the first author interviewed fifty-eight members of the U.S. House of Representatives. The interviews usually took place in the Congress member's office, but some occurred in an inner office adjoining a committee conference room, in the congressional dining room of the Capitol, in a congressional conference room adjoining the House floor, or in hallways while the Congress member walked from his/her office to the House floor. The interviews ranged in length from fifteen minutes to two and a half hours, with a modal time of approximately fifty minutes.

Gaining access to members of Congress can be a difficult—and sometimes impossible—task for a researcher. Congress members' time is sought by many people: constituents who "drop in" and want their pictures taken with their representative; lobbyists who want to present their side of an issue; journalists who want to interview the Congress member for anything from a cover story for a major magazine to an article for the "down home" newspaper; other Congress members who want to discuss important issues coming up for a vote; or a staff person in the Congress member's own office who wants sometimes to "educate" his/her boss on a bill that's on the floor and other times to "get educated" on how to follow through on an assignment. Spending time with people such as these has a payoff for the Congress member, while spending time with a researcher has relatively little payoff. In fact, we were told by three appointment secretaries, "I'm sorry, but the congressman(woman) doesn't grant interviews to professors doing research."

With such resistance, special entree is important. Ours was provided by a Congress member who chairs one of the most influential Committees in the House of Representatives. He wrote individualized letters to each member of Congress in the sample introducing the interviewer (Fay Lomax Cook), detailing her background, explaining what she was doing, and asking his colleagues to spend time talking with her. Without this letter of introduction, we are certain that many members of Congress would not have granted interviews so willingly.

Sample selection. The total sample of Congress members consisted of two distinct subsamples: a random sample and a purposive sample. The purposive sample was composed of those representatives who were chairs (if Democratic) or ranking minority members (if Republican) of committees and subcommittees having jurisdiction over social welfare policy issues. These selected social welfare committees and subcommittees included:

Appropriations Committee (2; both chair and ranking minority member were asked to participate)
    Labor, Health, and Human Services Subcommittee (2)
Budget Committee (2)
    Health Subcommittee (2)
    Human Resources Subcommittee (2)
    Income Security Subcommittee (2)
Ways and Means Committee (2)
    Public Assistance and Unemployment Compensation Subcommittee (2)
    Social Security Subcommittee (2)
    Health Subcommittee (2)
Education and Labor Committee (2)
    Employment Opportunities Subcommittee (2)
    Health and Safety Subcommittee (2)
    Human Resources Subcommittee (2)
Energy and Commerce Committee (2)
    Health and the Environment Subcommittee (2)
    Select Committee on Aging (2)
    Select Committee on Children, Family, and Youth (2)

In 1986 the House of Representatives was composed of 435 members. In drawing the samples, we first selected the 34 Representatives who were either chairs or ranking minority members of social-welfare-relevant committees or subcommittees. These comprised our purposive group. From the remaining 401 members, we drew a random sample of 35. When we discuss members of the House of Representatives as a group—i.e., "Congress at large"—we will be referring to the entire sample of representatives, weighted such that the purposive sample represents its actual proportion in the House of Representatives. The actual weighting procedures are discussed below.

Response rate.   Despite our letter of introduction, we were unable to obtain interviews with all the members of Congress who were chosen for our study. As table A.3 shows, 60 percent of the representatives contacted as part of the random sample completed the interview process, including 62 percent of the Republicans and 59 percent of the Democrats contacted. Despite the fact that the letter of introduction came from a Democratic Congress member, Republicans were no less likely to comply than Democrats. In fact, the reasons for refusals were similar—prolonged illness (one potential respondent died during the time period of the interviews), absence from Washington due to family problems or due to running for another office (governor in one case, senator in two cases), or a "policy" never to grant interviews to researchers (some stated they'd been "burned" in the past). Among the first thirty-five contacted, fourteen Congress members were unable or refused to be interviewed, so an additional fourteen names were ran-

Table A.3
Congressional Response Rate

	Attempted	Achieved	Response Rate
Random sample	N	N	
Total	35	21[a]	60%
Republicans	13	8	62%
Democrats	22	13	59%
Purposive sample	N	N	
Total	34	24	71%
Republicans·	17	10	59%
Democrats	17	14	82%

[a]To replace the 14 Congress members who were unable or unwilling to be interviewed, others were randomly drawn. 13 of these 14 agreed to be interviewed, therefore the final random sample consists of 34 Congress members.

domly drawn to replace them. Thirteen of this second group completed an interview. Thus, the final random sample consists of thirty-four Congress members.

The response rate for the purposive sample was 71 percent—59 percent for Republicans and 82 percent for Democrats—leaving a final purposive sample consisting of fourteen chairpersons and ten ranking minority members. The response rate for purposively sampled Republicans is very similar to that for Republicans in the random sample. However, the rate of completion by Democratic chairpersons is considerably higher than for Democrats in the random sample. We can only speculate as to why Democratic committee leaders were so much more willing to be interviewed than both Republican leaders and the Democratic Congress members in the random sample. Our sense is that they were extremely interested in the fact that someone was doing a study of both the opinions of the general public and of Congress members. These members of Congress might also have believed the results of the study could eventually be useful to them in their committee work. They were curious about the research, asked numerous questions, and requested copies of the results. A final reason might stem from the fact that the letter was signed by a fellow Democratic chair. The chairs in our sample might have felt a stronger obligation or motivation to listen to their colleague.

Representativeness. One important characteristic of a sample is that it be representative of the population from which it is drawn. If our sample of Congress members is not typical of the population of the House of Representatives, the survey results will yield biased estimates of the beliefs and preferences of Congress members. To provide a sense of the potential for such bias, table A.4 compares selected sociodemographic and political characteristics of our 1986 congressional sample to characteristics of the actual membership of the House of Representatives in 1986.

The comparisons displayed in table A.4 show that our sample mirrors very closely the composite membership of the House. The percentages of Republicans (41.3 percent) and Democrats (58.6 percent) in the sample are almost identical to the actual percentages (41.8 percent and 58.1 percent, respectively). Also extremely close is the average age of our respondents (a mean of 50.1 years for our sample as compared to 49.7 years for the House's total membership); tenure in Congress (a sample mean of 8.25 years as compared to 8.38), percent African American (5.7 percent versus 4.6 percent), and comparisons of

Table A.4

Comparison of Characteristics of the Congressional Sample with
Actual Membership of the House of Representatives, 1986

	Weighted sample (N = 58)	Actual membership (N = 435)
Party		
Republican	41.3	41.8
Democrat	58.6	58.1
Region		
East	23.4	23.9
Midwest	30.0	26.0
West	16.2	19.5
South	30.4	30.6
Education		
College degree or less	35.7	32.7
M.A./Ph.D.	10.0	24.1
Law degree	54.3	43.7
Mean Age	50.1	49.7
Percent Female	2.7	5.1
Percent Minority		
Black	5.7	4.6
Hispanic	.6	2.8
Mean Years in Congress (Tenure)	8.3	8.4
Ratings by Organizations		
Children's Defense Fund (1985)	54.4	56.3
National Council of Senior Citizens (1985)	61.4	56.3
Americans for Democratic Action (1983 and 1984)	51.8	49.1
Americans for Constitutional Action (1983 and 1984)	45.1	46.7
National Journal—Social Issues (1985)	50.0	50.0
National Journal—Economic Issues (1985)	46.4	50.0
National Journal—Foreign Issues (1985)	48.5	50.0

rating scores developed by the Children's Defense Fund, the National
Council of Senior Citizens, Americans for Democratic Action, Americans for Constitutional Action, and the National Journal.

The regional representation of our sample is very close to the
distribution in the entire Congress, especially with regard to the east-
ern and southern portions of the United States. Our sample has a
slight overrepresentation of midwestern Congress members and a slight
underrepresentation of western Congress members. The educational
background of our respondents differs slightly from the full Congress.
Our sample has more lawyers and fewer members with masters and
doctoral degrees. Taking into account the comparisons of all these

Table A.5
Congressional Weighting Procedure

	Probability	Weight formula	Weight
Republicans in purposive sample	$\dfrac{10}{17}$	$\dfrac{17}{10} \times \dfrac{58}{435}$ =	0.2267
Republicans in random sample	$\dfrac{14}{165}$	$\dfrac{165}{14} \times \dfrac{58}{435}$ =	1.5714
Democrats in purposive sample	$\dfrac{14}{17}$	$\dfrac{17}{14} \times \dfrac{58}{435}$ =	0.1619
Democrats in random sample	$\dfrac{20}{236}$	$\dfrac{236}{20} \times \dfrac{58}{435}$ =	1.5733

sociodemographic and political characteristics, however, it is fair to conclude that, overall, our sample achieves a good resemblance of the U.S. House of Representatives in the 99th Congress.

Weighting procedures. In order to speak of the views of the entire membership of the House of Representatives, we must weight the sample of fifty-eight Congress members such that the committee leadership represents its true proportion within the House. Thus, we have calculated weights for each of the four groups, or strata, comprising the total sample: Republican ranking minority members of social welfare committees or subcommittees, Republican nonranking minority members, Democratic chairs of social welfare committees or subcommittees, and Democratic nonchairs. The weights are proportional to the reciprocals of the probabilities of being in the four strata (Cochran 1977:519). These probabilities are simply the ratios of stratum sample size over stratum population size. To return the working sample size back to fifty-eight, the weights have been deflated by 58/435 (the ratio of the total sample size to the total number in the House of Representatives). Table A.5 provides the weights applied to responses from each of the four groups.

The Measures

We developed two questionnaires for each of the respondent groups. Although many of the questions were the same, we also included questions tailored specifically to probe the unique perspectives of the particular type of respondent. The actual questionnaires are provided in appendix B for the public version and appendix C for the congressional version.

Support for Social Welfare Programs

The two questionnaires both began with a question designed to determine respondent support for seven major programs within the U.S. social welfare system: the social insurance programs of Social Security, Medicare, and Unemployment Insurance; and the public assistance programs of Medicaid, Supplemental Security Income (SSI), Aid to Families with Dependent Children (AFDC), and Food Stamps. For each program, we asked respondents whether they believed benefits for individuals should be increased, decreased, or maintained. In addition, at the end of the question about the seven programs, we asked Congress members whether there were other programs they considered important and relevant. Forty-six percent (32 percent of Republicans and 56 percent of Democrats) mention at least one other program they feel is important to include, while the other 54 percent of Congress members say they think these seven programs are the key ones in the social welfare domain. Because of the time limitations of a telephone survey, members of the public answered these support questions quite succinctly as "increase," "decrease," or "maintain." Congress members, on the other hand, were encouraged to go into detail to explain their responses and to elaborate their perspective on each program. These detailed responses provide a rich qualitative overview of the policymakers' analyses of the successes and failures, problems and promises of U.S. social welfare policy.

To gain additional information on program support by members of the general public, we selected three contrasting programs to explore in greater detail: Social Security, Medicaid, and AFDC. These programs were chosen for two primary reasons. First, they represent three different types of programs: Social Security is a social insurance programs, AFDC provides cash public assistance, and Medicaid is an in-kind public assistance program. Second, each represents a program that some commentators claim are in real political trouble: Social Security because of what is portrayed as a growing intergenerational conflict and resistance on the part of the young to pay for programs for the elderly (e.g., Preston 1984; Longman 1982), AFDC because some claim it makes recipients dependent on aid and unwilling to be self-sufficient (e.g., Murray 1984), and Medicaid because its costs have continued to skyrocket dramatically since its inception in 1965 (Marmor, Mashaw, and Harvey 1990).

Support for these programs was conceptualized in three ways.

1. As *satisfaction:* "In general, how satisfied are you with the fact that our tax dollars go to support AFDC? Would you say you are satisfied, somewhat satisfied, not very satisfied, or not at all satisfied?" If the respondent expressed satisfaction, *strength of satisfaction* was measured by the answer to the question: "If you were told that federal spending for AFDC was going to be cut back, would you be strongly opposed, somewhat opposed, or indifferent?" *Strength of dissatisfaction* was measured by the answer to the question: "If you were told that federal spending was going to be expanded, would you be strongly opposed, somewhat opposed, or indifferent?"

2. As *willingness to take action:* "Would you sign a petition or write a letter to your congressman expressing your feelings about the cutback [about the increase in AFDC]?"

3. As *willingness to make a monetary commitment:* "In order to prevent the AFDC program from being cut back, would you be willing to pay no more taxes, $0.50 more for every $100 in taxes you already pay, $1.00 more for every $100 in taxes you already pay, or $2.00 more for every $100 in taxes?" [or "To show your disapproval of AFDC, would you like the program to be maintained at its current funding, be cut back by $.50 for every $100 spent on it, be cut back $1.00 for every $100 spent, or be cut back $2.00 for every $100 spent?"]

An overall measure of public support was constructed by adding these three individual measures together and creating a score that ranged from -10 to $+10$. These measures fit well together as a scale (Cronbach's alpha 0.92 for AFDC, 0.92 for the Medicaid scale, and 0.88 for the Social Security scale).

Helping groups through services. The second set of questions that was common to both questionnaires was four questions that examined prioritized support for targeted groups for specific programs. The program areas included food and nutrition, education, catastrophic health, and the general area of "additional help" implying additional monetary assistance. Potential groups to receive help included the poor and the physically disabled divided into age categories. Thus, the six principal groups were: physically disabled children, poor children, physically disabled adults under 65, poor adults under 65, physically disabled elderly, and poor elderly. In addition, when respondents were asked to prioritize support for additional financial assistance, we also included as potential recipients female heads of household and able-bodied unemployed men. When considering the school lunch program as a food and nutrition service, respondents were allowed to prefer including all children and not just the poor or disabled. And when asked about catastrophic health insurance, respondents could choose to help all within a particular age group (i.e., all elderly, all children, and all adults under 65). These selections were added to make the question more realistic to the actual policy options on that particular issue.

Discovering the preferences of Congress members was relatively easy because of the personal interview setting. Each Congress member was given a set of cards listing the potential service and the recipient group. The respondent was then asked to organize the cards according to his/her preference for assistance. Interviews with members of the public were conducted over the telephone thus making it impossible to use any props. Furthermore, the options tended to be rather wordy, making it difficult for the respondent to listen to all options before ranking. Instead we devised a verbal method for discovering priorities. Each member of the public was asked to rate how favorable, on a scale from 1 to 100, they were toward a specific group to receive help through the particular type of service. Then the interviewer read the respondent his/her top choices to verify that the priority list was exactly what the respondent intended. For example, the interviewer said: "Let me make sure that I have this right. Your numbers show that you would give top priority to [GIVE GROUP THAT HAS HIGHEST SCORE]; second priority to [GIVE GROUP THAT HAS SECOND HIGHEST SCORE], and third priority to [GIVE GROUP THAT HAS THIRD HIGHEST SCORE]. Would you like to change this ranking [IF NECESSARY, CHANGE]?" Using this method, there would be a tendency for the respondent to give a particular score to the first option heard then rate the others relative to the first. To avoid this becoming a problem, for each of the four ranking-type questions, we offered three different starting points (or anchors). In one version of the questionnaire, for instance, respondents were asked first to rate the importance of helping poor children with school lunch programs. In another version, however, the respondents were asked to first rate the importance of helping disabled elderly through Meals-on-Wheels. Respondents were randomly selected to receive different versions of the questionnaire. This method of discovering priorities might not be the best, but given the constraints of the telephone, we found it quite useful.

After learning which groups respondents preferred to help, we wanted to know why they made their selections. An earlier study by

Cook (1979) found that the public did not have stereotypical preferences in their prioritization of groups for services, and she theorized
that their judgments rested on (1) whether a group is seen to have
alternative sources of help; (2) whether a program is seen to maximize
individual independence; and (3) whether a program meets the groups'
essential needs. Rather than force Congress members into our list of
reasons, in this current study, we allowed Congress members to describe their reasons to us. We transcribed exactly what they said and
analyzed the major justifications they gave. The reasons fell into the
following six categories. After compiling the list, we then included the
six principal congressional options in the public questionnaire as close-
ended questions.

1. The group is least able to help themselves; *no alternative source*
   of help is available.
2. The program has the potential to *maximize the independence* of
   members of the group (i e , to help people help themselves)
3. Helping the group is an *investment in the future of the society.* Some
   Congress members stressed only general long-term benefits for
   the group members that would in turn produce more capable
   citizens and be good for the country; others stressed economic
   efficiency for the interventions—invest in programs for certain
   groups now and it will save money over the long run.
4. The group is *entitled* to help, a view based solely on the characteristics of the group (e.g., because the elderly have "paid their
   dues" or because the young are innocent and not at fault for
   their situation, some believe they are "entitled" to help as a
   matter of right).
5. The group has the *greatest needs* (Congress members usually
   qualified their reasons for "greatest needs" more specifically as
   one of the above, but on a few occasions, when they failed to
   elaborate further than this, this category was the best fit for their
   responses).
6. The group represents a *problem growing* in size or severity and
   there are *not enough programs* to help them.

Items Unique to the General Public Questionnaire

Members of the general public answered a series of questions concerning their beliefs about social welfare programs (Social Security, AFDC,
and Medicaid) and about the recipients of those programs. Each item
tapped into a different attitudinal dimension. Four statements probed

respondents' views about the quality of the program (e.g., it leads to independence, it benefits society, it makes recipients dependent on the system, or there is a lot of cheating within the program), and five statements probed their views about the recipients (e.g., they really need the benefits, they have no other sources, they want independence, they spend their benefits wisely, and they are to blame for their dependence on benefits).

Items Unique to the Congressional Questionnaire

Congress members were asked how much they heard from their constituents and from interest groups about social welfare issues. They were also asked how they made their decisions about two particular votes having to do with AFDC and Social Security.

APPENDIX B
Public Questionnaire

Intro/Selection Sheet: Social Welfare Policy Survey

Hello, is this _____? [VERIFY NUMBER]

My name is _____, and I'm calling from the Northwestern University Survey Laboratory in Evanston, Illinois. We are conducting a national public opinion survey about social welfare programs.

* *

For this survey, I need to speak with the person in your household—18 years of age or older—who had the last birthday. Is that you?

    YES .... [CONTINUE WITH INTRO BELOW.]

    NO .... Could I please speak with that person?

[WHEN CORRECT ADULT COMES TO PHONE REPEAT 1ST PARAGRAPH AND THEN CONTINUE WITH PARAGRAPH BELOW.]

[IF ADULT WITH LAST BIRTHDAY IS UNAVAILABLE, DETERMINE WHEN TO CALL BACK AND RECORD ON CALL-SHEET. ALSO, DETERMINE WHICH ADULT HAD LAST BIRTHDAY, SO NEXT INTERVIEWER WILL KNOW WHO TO ASK FOR.]

* *

President Reagan in his State of the Union Address last February called for an evaluation of social welfare programs in the United States. Professor Fay Cook, here at Northwestern University, is interviewing members of Congress and members of the general public to learn what they think of current social welfare programs. She has already completed interviews with members of Congress, and this is your chance to talk about what you think is important, and·what you think should be done.

[GO RIGHT ON TO Q1]

_____ STARTING TIME   VERSION _____ 1C/

Q1. There are seven major social welfare programs, and I would like to begin by asking you a few questions about your opinion of them.

As I read the list of programs, please tell me whether you feel the benefits for each should be increased, decreased, or maintained at their current levels, keeping up with inflation.

	Increased	Decreased	Maintained (Kept at Current Level)	Other (See Codes Below)	DK	RF
a. Social Security. Do you feel Social Security benefits should be	01	02	03		88	99 11–12/
b. Food Stamps (THEY ARE COUPONS TO BE USED TO BUY GROCERIES)	01	02	03		88	99 13–14/
c. Unemployment Compensation, (WHICH IS INCOME FOR THOSE WHO HAVE WORKED LONG ENOUGH TO QUALITY FOR BENEFITS DURING TIMES WHEN THEY ARE OUT OF WORK)	01	02	03		88	99 15–16/
d. Medicare, which is the federal health insurance program for people who get Social Security benefits, mostly elderly people	01	02	03		88	99 17–18/

e. Medicaid, which is
medical assistance for
people whose
incomes are low enough
to qualify ....01.........02..........03 ......_____...88...99   19–20/

f. Supplemental Se-
curity Income—SSI,
which is income
assistance given to low-
income elderly, blind,
or disabled people .....01.........02..........03 ......_____...88...99   21–22/

g. Aid to Families with
Dependent Children
AFDC, which is income
assistance for low-in-
come mothers, and
sometimes
fathers, who have chil-
dren under 18.........01.........02..........03 ......_____...88...99   23–24/

OTHER CODES:
04. MAINTAIN BUT POLICE THE
SYSTEM BETTER (USE 04)
05. INCREASE BUT POLICE THE
SYSTEM BETTER (USE 05)
06. DECREASE BUT POLICE THE
SYSTEM BETTER (USE 06)
07. GIVE ACCORDING TO IN-
COME (MEANS TEST) (USE 07)
08. REFORM THE SYSTEM
(USE 08)

09. INCREASE THE BENEFITS
BUT REFORM THE SYSTEM
(USE 09)
10. DECREASE THE BENEFITS
AND REFORM THE SYSTEM
(USE 10)
11. DO AWAY WITH THE PRO-
GRAM (USE 11)
12. OTHER (USE 12)

Q2. People have different opinions about the causes of poverty. In your
opinion, which is more often to blame if a person is poor—lack of effort
on his or her own part, or circumstances beyond his or her control?

LACK OF EFFORT............. 1

CIRCUMSTANCES BEYOND HIS
CONTROL ....2 (SKIP TO Q2B)

BOTH ARE EQUALLY TO   3 (IF VOLUNTEERED,
BLAME ....   ASK Q2A and Q2B)

OTHER (SPECIFY) _____

_____ 4 (SKIP TO Q3A)

DON'T KNOW .... 8 (SKIP TO Q3A)

REFUSED .... 9 (SKIP TO Q3A)

25/

Q2a. Does this lack of effort have more to do with laziness, dependence on the welfare system, lack of knowledge about how to help themselves, or with the fact that they've given up trying to raise themselves out of poverty. (PLEASE URGE R TO GIVE ONLY ONE RESPONSE)

LAZINESS................... 1
DEPENDENT ON WELFARE 2
LACK OF KNOWLEDGE 3
INABILITY TO HELP
THEMSELVES 4   (SKIP TO Q3A UNLESS R
GIVEN UP TRYING 5   SAID "BOTH" ON Q2   26/
OTHER (SPECIFY) _____
_____ 6
DON'T KNOW 8
REFUSED 9

Q2b. Are these circumstances more related to the fact that these people have had bad luck, had poor educations in elementary and high schools, came from disadvantaged family backgrounds, or to the fact that they've had poor job opportunities? (PLEASE URGE R TO SAY WHICH ONE IS MOST IMPORTANT)

BAD LUCK 1
POOR EDUCATION 2
DISADVANTAGED FAMILY BACKGROUNDS 3
POOR JOB OPPORTUNITIES 4
OTHER (SPECIFY) _____
_____ 5
DON'T KNOW.................................. 8
REFUSED 9

Q3a. I'm going to read you a list of some of the different groups of poor people, and I'd like you to tell me how important you feel it is that each group gets additional help from the government. Think of a scale from 1 to 100, where 100 means this group should receive top priority in receiving additional help, and 1 means this group should be given low priority for additional help. As I read each group, please give me a number between 1 and 100 that best reflects your feelings about how much additional help the group should receive. Try to avoid giving any two groups the same number. [START AT NUMBER WITH ARROW. IT IS IMPORTANT TO HAVE RANDOM STARTING POINTS FOR METHODOLOGICAL REASONS.

(AFTER YOU READ THE FIRST GROUP, SAY: "On the scale from 1 to 100 where would you place the importance of additional help for this group?")

(NOTE: DO NOT CORRECT R̲ FOR USING SAME NUMBER. BREAK TIES AFTER R̲ HAS RATED ALL GROUPS)

→1. _____ Poor able-bodied men of working age who are
(GIVE NUMBER) unemployed?
                    DK 888   RF 999   28–30/

2. _____ Poor children?
(GIVE NUMBER)   DK 888   RF 999   31–33/

3. _____ Poor female heads of households?
(GIVE NUMBER)   DK 888   RF 999   34–36/

4. _____ The poor elderly?
(GIVE NUMBER)   DK 888   RF 999   37–39/

5. _____ Poor elderly persons who are physically disabled?
(GIVE NUMBER)   DK 888   RF 999   40–42/

6. _____ Poor adults under 65 who are physically disabled?
(GIVE NUMBER)   DK 888   RF 999   43–45/

NOTE: TIE BREAK FOR TOP THREE CHOICES: IF R̲ GIVES THE SAME NUMBER TO TWO OR MORE GROUPS THAT ARE IN HIS/HER TOP 3 CHOICES, HAVE HIM/HER RANK THESE. SAY: "You have given the same number to (LIST ALL GROUPS WITH SAME SCORE). "If you had to choose, which would you give a higher number to?" (CHANGE SCORE OF CHOICE GROUP TO ONE NUMBER HIGHER)

Q3b. Let me make sure that I have this right. Your numbers show that you would give top priority to (GIVE GROUP THAT HAS HIGHEST SCORE), second priority to (GIVE GROUP THAT HAS SECOND HIGHEST SCORE) and third priority to (GIVE GROUP THAT HAS THIRD HIGHEST SCORE). Would you like to change this ranking? (IF NECESSARY, CHANGE SO IT IS CORRECT)

(WRITE GROUP NUMBER,   _____ _____ _____
NOT SCORE)   FIRST   SECOND   THIRD   46–48/

Q3c. Which of the following best describes your major reason for choosing (GIVE FIRST CHOICE HERE)? (GET ONE RESPONSE)

    a. There is no one else to help this
       group, ... 1 (SKIP TO Q4A)
    b. It's an investment in the future of the
       country, ... 2 (SKIP TO Q4A)
    c. There aren't enough programs to help
       this group, ... 3 (SKIP TO Q4A)

d. It will help them to help
themselves, or .... 4 (SKIP TO Q4A)   49/

e. They are entitled to our help? .... 5 (SKIP TO Q4A)

f. OTHER (WRITE VERBATIM. NOTE: IF
R SAY "THEY'RE MOST NEEDY,"
RECORD AND ASK Q3D) _____ 6 (SKIP TO Q4A
_____ UNLESS R SAYS
_____ "NEEDY"

DON'T KNOW .... 8 (SKIP TO Q4A)

REFUSED .... 9 (SKIP TO Q4A)

Q3d. In what way do you think this group's needs are greatest?
Is it because .....

a. There is no one else to help them, ... 1

b. There aren't enough programs to help
them, ... 2

c. They aren't able to help themselves, ... 3

d. They have the most severe
problems, or...................... 4   50/

e. Something else I haven't mentioned?
(RECORD VERBATIM) _____
_____
_____ 5

DON'T KNOW 8

REFUSED 9

Q4a. Now I'd like to ask you about seven very specific programs in the area
of food assistance and nutrition. Again, imagine a scale from 1 to 100,
where 1 means you don't favor it at all and 100 means you favor it very
strongly. For the seven programs I'll read, please tell me how much you
favor each on this scale from 1 to 100. Try not to use the same number
twice. [START AT ARROW.]

(NOTE: DO NOT CORRECT R FOR USING SAME NUMBER. BREAK TIES
AFTER R HAS RATED ALL GROUPS)

→ _____   1. School lunch program for poor children? The   51–53/
(GIVE NUMBER)   idea is that lunches are provided at reduced
DK 888   RF 999   rates for children whose families' income falls
                     below a certain amount.

_____   2. School lunch programs for physically disabled   54–56/
(GIVE NUMBER)   children? (LUNCHES ARE PROVIDED AT RE-
DK 888   RF 999   DUCED RATES TO PHYSICALLY DISABLED
                     CHILDREN, REGARDLESS OF THEIR FAMI-
                     LIES' INCOME)

_____   3. School lunch program for <u>all</u> children?   57–59/
(GIVE NUMBER)   (NOTE: THE FEDERAL GOVERNMENT PAYS
DK 888   RF 999   A SMALL SUBSIDY FOR EVERY CHILD'S
                     LUNCH)

_____   4. Meals on wheels for <u>elderly disabled</u> people?   60–62/
(GIVE NUMBER)   The idea is that hot lunches are delivered to
DK 888   RF 999   people in their homes.

_____   5. Meals on wheels for <u>disabled</u> adults <u>under 65</u>?   63–65/
(GIVE NUMBER)   (HOT LUNCHES ARE DELIVERED TO PEO-
DK 888   RF 999   PLE IN THEIR HOMES)

_____   6. Distribution of staples such as rice, cheese,   66–68/
(GIVE NUMBER)   butter, flour, and so forth to the <u>poor elderly</u>?
DK 888   RF 999

_____   7. Distribution of staples to <u>poor</u> adults <u>under</u>   69–71/
(GIVE NUMBER)   <u>65</u>?
DK 888   RF 999

TIE BREAKER: IF 2 NUMBERS ARE THE SAME, SAY: "You gave (<u>GROUP</u>)
and (<u>GROUP</u>) the same number. If you had to choose, which would you
give the highest number to?" (CHANGE NUMBERS BY RAISING TOP
PRIORITY NUMBER BY ONE)

BEGIN DECK 2

Q4b. I just want to double-check your top choices. You favored the most
(<u>GIVE HIGHEST GROUP</u>) the second most (<u>SECOND HIGHEST</u>), and third
most (<u>THIRD</u>). Would you like to change this order, or are these <u>really</u>
your top priorities? (CHANGE IF NEEDED)

(GIVE NUMBER) _____ _____ _____
                FIRST   SECOND   THIRD
      [_____ _____ _____]
       FOURTH   FIFTH   SIXTH   SEVENTH   5–11/

[WRITE THE NUMBERS OF FIRST 3 CHOICES IN THE PROPER
SPACES. (NOT THE SCORES!) LATER, GO BACK AND FILL IN
NEXT 4]

Q4c. Which of the following statements <u>best</u> describes your reason for
choosing (<u>GIVE GROUP THAT HAS HIGHEST SCORE</u>)? (GET ONE
RESPONSE)

Their needs are greatest, ... 1
They are least able to get help from
other sources . . . . 2 (SKIP TO Q5A)

It's an investment in the future of the
country . . . . 3 (SKIP TO Q5A)

It would increase their chances of being
independent either now or later, or . . . . 4 (SKIP TO Q5A)

They're entitled to our help? . . . . 5 (SKIP TO Q5A)   12/

OTHER? (WRITE VERBATIM. NOTE:
IF <u>R</u> SAYS "THEY'RE MOST NEEDY"
RECORD AND ASK <u>Q4D)</u>_____ 6 (SKIP TO Q5A)

_____ UNLESS <u>R</u> SAYS

_____ "NEEDY")

DON'T KNOW . . . . 8 (SKIP TO Q5A)

REFUSED . . . . 9 (SKIP TO Q5A)

Q4d. In what way do you think the needs are greatest?
Is it because . . . . .

a. They have the fewest other available
sources of help, ... 1

b. They are least able to help
themselves, ... 2

c. They have the most severe
problems, or 3   13/

d. Something I haven't mentioned? (GIVE
VERBATIM)

_____

_____ 4

DON'T KNOW 8

REFUSED 9

Q5a. Now let's look at a list of current or proposed education-type programs
for different groups of people. Once more thinking in terms of a scale
from 1 to 100, where <u>100</u> means you <u>favor the program strongly</u> and <u>1</u>
means you <u>don't favor it at all</u>, please tell me how much you favor the
following education-type programs. As you do so, try not to use the
same number twice.

> NOTE: DON'T CORRECT <u>R</u> FOR USING SAME NUMBER TWICE. WAIT
> UNTIL <u>R</u> HAS RATED ALL GROUPS)

→ _____ 1. Information and referral services for <u>people</u>   14–16/
(GIVE NUMBER)   <u>over 65 who are physically disabled</u> to inform
DK 888   RF 999   them of programs of which they are eligible
                    and to help them apply for benefits.

_____ 2. Information and referral services for <u>poor peo-</u>   17–19/
(GIVE NUMBER)   <u>ple over 65</u> to inform them of services for
DK 888   RF 999

which they are eligible, and to show them
how to apply for benefits?

_____ 3. Rehabilitation and job training programs for   20–22/
(GIVE NUMBER)   physically disabled people under 65 to train
DK 888   RF 999   them so they can get jobs?

_____ 4. Job training programs for poor people under   23–25/
(GIVE NUMBER)   65 to train them so they can get jobs?
DK 888   RF 999

_____ 5. Preschool programs for poor children to give   26–28/
(GIVE NUMBER)   them special attention before they start
DK 888   RF 999   school so that they will not have so much
                    trouble later?

_____ 6. Special education programs for physically dis- 29–31/
(GIVE NUMBER)   abled children to help them cope with their
DK 888   RF 999   handicaps and receive the education matched
                    to their skills?

TIE BREAKER: IF R GIVES THE SAME NUMBER TO TWO OR MORE
GROUPS, HAVE HIM/HER RANK THESE GROUPS IN IMPORTANCE.
PROBE: "You have told me that you favor (LIST ALL GROUPS THAT
SHARE THE SAME NUMBER) with a (GIVE NUMBER) priority. If you had
to choose one group to get a high number, which would you choose?"
(WRITE NEW SCORE AS BEING ONE NUMBER HIGHER)

Q5b. Double-checking, you favored the most (GIVE HIGHEST), the second
most (SECOND GROUP), and third (THIRD GROUP). Is this right?

(GIVE NUMBER) _____ _____ _____
                 FIRST   SECOND   THIRD
      [_____ _____ _____]
        FOURTH   FIFTH   SIXTH   32–37

(NOTE: WRITE THE NUMBERS OF FIRST 3 CHOICES IN THE
PROPER SPACES. BACK AND LATER, GO ADD THE NEXT 3)

Q5c. Which of the following statements best describes why you support
      (GIVE FIRST CHOICE HERE—GIVE PROGRAM AND GROUP) the most?

         Their needs are greatest, ... 1
         They are least able to get help from
         other sources, ... 2 (SKIP TO Q6A)
         It is an investment in the future of the
         country, ... 3 (SKIP TO Q6A)
         It will help them help themselves, or .. 4 (SKIP TO Q6A)   38/
         They are entitled to our help?. . . . . 5 (SKIP TO Q6A)

OTHER? (WRITE VERBATIM. NOTE:
IF <u>R</u> SAYS "THEY'RE MOST "NEEDY"
RECORD AND ASK Q5D) —————— 6 (SKIP TO Q6A
————————————————— UNLESS <u>R</u> SAID
————————————————— "NEEDY"

DON'T KNOW . . . . 8 (SKIP TO Q6A)

REFUSED . . . . 9 (SKIP TO Q6A)

Q5d. In what way do you think the needs are greatest?
Is it because . . . . .

   a. They have the fewest other available
       sources of help, ... 1   39/

   b. They are least able to help
       themselves, ... 2

   c. They have the most severe
       problems, or 3

   d. Something I haven't mentioned? (GIVE
       VERBATIM)

       ————————————————————————
       ———————————————————————— 4

       DON'T KNOW 8
       REFUSED 9

Q6a. There have been recent discussions about the federal government setting up programs to provide aid against catastrophic illnesses or acci-
dents that could wipe out a family's savings. I'd like you to tell me
which <u>three</u> groups that I'll read should have highest priority for receiving help from the federal government with catastrophic health coverage. The groups are. . . . .

   01. <u>Elderly in general</u>,
   02. <u>poor</u> elderly,
   03. <u>disabled</u> elderly,
   04. <u>Adults under 65 in general</u>,
   05. <u>poor</u> adults under 65,
   06. <u>disabled</u> adults under 65,
   07. <u>Children in general</u>
   08. <u>poor</u> children,
   09. <u>disabled</u> children.

Which of these groups should receive first priority, second priority, and
third priority?

(GIVE NUMBER)   FIRST——————————

                SECOND—————————— DK 88   RF 99   40–45.

THIRD_____ DK 88   RF 99

NOT THE ROLE OF
THE FEDERAL
GOVERNMENT........ 555555 (SKIP TO Q7)

GIVE BENEFITS TO
ALL EQUALLY .... 666666 (SKIP TO Q7)

GIVE BENEFITS TO
NONE .... 777777 (SKIP TO Q7)

OTHER_____ 444444 (SKIP TO Q7)

DON'T KNOW........ 888888 (SKIP TO Q7)

REFUSED .... 999999 (SKIP TO Q7)

Q6b. Which of the following statements <u>best</u> explains why you favor (GIVE
FIRST CHOICE HERE) the most? (GET ONE RESPONSE)

a. Their needs are greatest, ... 1
b. They are least able to get help from
   other sources,...................... 2 (SKIP TO Q7)
c. It's an investment in the future of the
   country, ... 3 (SKIP TO Q7)   46/
d. It will help them help themselves, or... 4 (SKIP TO Q7)
e. They are entitled to our help?......... 5 (SKIP TO Q7)
   OTHER (WRITE VERBATIM. NOTE: IF
   <u>R</u> SAYS "THEY'RE MOST NEEDY," RE-
   CORD AND ASK Q6C _____ 6 (SKIP TO Q7
   _____   UNLESS <u>R</u> SAID
   _____   "NEEDY"

   DON'T KNOW .... 8 (SKIP TO Q7)
   REFUSED .... 9 (SKIP TO Q7)

Q6c. In what way do you think this group's needs are greatest?
Is it because .....

a. They have the fewest other available
   sources of help..................... 1
b. They are least able to help
   themselves 2
c. They have the most severe
   problems, or....................... 3   47/
d. Something I haven't mentioned? [GIVE
   VERBATIM]

   _____
   _____ 4

   DON'T KNOW 8
   REFUSED 9

Q7. Thinking back to the social welfare programs discussed earlier, I'd like to ask you in more detail about two—AFDC, that is, Aid to Families with Dependent Children, and Medicaid. Let's start with AFDC. As you know, AFDC is the program that provides income assistance to poor mothers, and sometimes fathers, who have children under 18 and whose incomes are low enough to qualify.

In general, how satisfied are you with the fact that our tax dollars go to support AFDC? Would you say you are ....

Very satisfied, ... 1   48/
Somewhat satisfied, ... 2
Not very satisfied, or .... 3 (SKIP TO Q9A)
Not at all satisfied? .... 4 (SKIP TO Q9A)
DON'T KNOW .... 8 (SKIP TO Q10)
REFUSED........................ 9 (SKIP TO Q10)

Q8a. If you were told that federal spending for AFDC was going to be cut back, would you be strongly opposed, somewhat opposed, or indifferent?

STRONGLY OPPOSED 1   49/
SOMEWHAT OPPOSED 2
INDIFFERENT........................... 3 (SKIP TO Q10)
IN FAVOR OF CUT (IF VOLUNTEERED) ...... 4 (SKIP TO Q10)
CHANGE THE SYSTEM (IF VOLUNTEERED) .. 5 (SKIP TO Q10)
DON'T KNOW .... 8 (SKIP TO Q10)
REFUSED .... 9 (SKIP TO Q10)

b. Would you sign a petition or write a letter to your congressman expressing your feelings about the cut back?

YES   "Would you say .. definitely yes, or 1   50/
                        probably yes? 2

NO   "Would you say .. definitely no, or 4
                        probably no? 3

                        DON'T KNOW 8
                        REFUSED 9

c. In order to prevent the AFDC program from being cut back, would you be willing to pay no more taxes, $0.50 more for every $100 in taxes you already pay, $1.00 more for every $100 in taxes you already pay, or $2.00 more for every $100 in taxes?

NO MORE .... 4 (SKIP TO Q10)   51/
$0.50 MORE .... 3 (SKIP TO Q10)
$1.00 MORE .... 2 (SKIP TO Q10)

$2.00 MORE .... 1 (SKIP TO Q10)

OTHER _____ .... 5 (SKIP TO Q10)

DON'T KNOW .... 8 (SKIP TO Q10)

REFUSED .... 9 (SKIP TO Q10)

Q9a. If you were told that federal spending for AFDC was going to be expanded, would you be strongly opposed, somewhat opposed, or indifferent?

STRONGLY OPPOSED 1   52/

SOMEWHAT OPPOSED 2

INDIFFERENT........................... 3 (SKIP TO Q10)

IN FAVOR OF EXPANSION (IF
VOLUNTEERED) .... 4 (SKIP TO Q10)

CHANGE THE SYSTEM.................... 5 (SKIP TO Q10)

DON'T KNOW .... 8 (SKIP TO Q10)

REFUSED .... 9 (SKIP TO Q10)

b. Would you sign a petition or write a letter to your congressman expressing your disapproval about the increase in AFDC?

YES "Would you say .. definitely yes, or 1   53/
                          probably yes? 2

NO   "Would you say .. definitely no, or..... 4
                          probably no?........ 3

                          DON'T KNOW 8
                          REFUSED 9

c. To show your disapproval of AFDC, would you like the program to be maintained at its current funding, be cut back by $0.50 for $100 dollars spent on it, be cut back by $1.00 for every $100 spent, or be cut back by $2.00 for every $100 spent?

MAINTAIN 4   54/

$0.50 LESS 3

$1.00 LESS 2

$2.00 LESS 1

OTHER _____ 5

DON'T KNOW 8

REFUSED 9

Q10. I'm going to read you a few statements about the people who receive AFDC benefits. For each, please tell me whether you agree, somewhat agree, somewhat disagree, or disagree.

		Somewhat			Somewhat			
	Agree, or	Agree?	Disagree, or	Disagree?	DK	RF	

Most people now re-
ceiving AFDC really
need the money
provided. Do you .... 1 ....2 ....3 ....4 .....8 ..9 55/

Q11. Most people who
get AFDC have <u>no</u>
sources of income
other than govern-
ment benefits .... 1 ....2 ....3 ....4 .....8 ..9 56/

Q12. AFDC helps most
people who get it
become more inde-
pendent and better
able to help them-
selves .... 1 ....2 ....3 ....4 .....8 ..9 57/

Q13. It's their own fault
that most AFDC re-
cipients are on AFDC   1 ....2 ....3 ....4 .....8 ..9 58/

Q14. Most people who
get AFDC <u>want</u> to be
independent and
self-reliant .... 1 ....2 ....3 ....4 ....8 ...9 59/

Q15. AFDC makes possible
an adequate standard
of living for those
who get it .... 1 ....2 ....3 ....4 .....8 ..9 60/

Q16. Society as a whole
benefits because we
have AFDC .... 1 ....2 ....3 ....4 .....8 ..9 61/

Q17. AFDC makes most
people who get it
dependent and
makes it harder for
them to make it on
their own .... 1 ....2 ....3 ....4 .....8 ..9 62/

Q18. Most people who
get AFDC spend their
money wisely .... 1 ....2 ....3 ....4 .....8 ..9 63/

Q19. Different people see the AFDC program as having different purposes. For each statement, please tell me whether or not you believe it <u>should be</u> a purpose of the AFDC program.

	YES	NO	DK	RF	
a. <u>Need</u>: that is, AFDC should provide money to those poor families who <u>really</u> need it	1	2	8	9	64/
b. <u>Earnings Based</u>: that is, AFDC should provide money to those who have <u>worked</u> in the past	1	2	8	9	65/
c. <u>Equal Opportunity</u>: that is, AFDC should provide money to people in a way that increases their chances for more equal opportunities to make the most of their lives	1	2	8	9	66/
d. <u>Reduce Differences</u>: that is, AFDC should provide money in a way that reduces the differences between those people in the population who have a lot of money and those who have very little	1	2	8	9	67/

Q20. Which one of these purposes would you say should be the <u>most important</u> for distributing AFDC? (ONLY LIST CHOICES THAT <u>R</u> RESPONDED <u>YES</u> IN Q19. YOU MAY NEED TO READ THE WHOLE STATEMENTS FROM Q19. USE YOUR JUDGMENT. URGE <u>R</u> TO GIVE ONLY <u>ONE</u> RESPONSE.

a. Need, ... 1   68/
b. Earnings-Based, ... 2
c. Equal opportunity, or 3
d. Reduction of differences? 4
   DON'T KNOW 8
   REFUSED 9

Q21. In the past two questions, I've asked you what you think the purpose of AFDC <u>should</u> be. Now I'd like to ask you what you think AFDC is <u>actually</u> doing.

		SOMEWHAT (IF VOLUN-				
	YES	TEERED)	NO	DK	RF	
a. Is AFDC providing money to those poor families who really need it?	1	2	3	8	9	69/
b. Is AFDC providing money to those who have worked in the past?	1	2	3	8	9	70/
c. Is AFDC providing money so that people who get it have more equal opportunities?	1	2	3	8	9	71/

d. Is AFDC providing money in a way
that reduces the differences between
those people in the population who
have a lot of money and those who
have very little? ....1 ......2 .....3 ..8 ..9   72/

Q22. Of people receiving AFDC benefits, would you say almost all, more
than half, less than half, or only a few are cheating the system—for
example, are collecting more than they are entitled to? (IF R SAYS HE/
SHE DOESN'T KNOW, SAY: "Just give me your best guess.")

ALMOST ALL 1   73/
MORE THAN HALF 2
LESS THAN HALF 3
A FEW 4
DON'T KNOW 8
REFUSED 9

ALTERNATE A for Q23–38

Q23. Now I'd like to focus on the Medicaid program. I'm not asking about
Medicare which is for elderly people. Medicaid is the program that
provides medical care for poor people.

In general, how satisfied are you with the fact that our tax dollars go
to support Medicaid? Would you say you are . . .

Very satisfied, ... 1   74/
Somewhat satisfied, ... 2
Not very satisfied, or .... 3 (SKIP TO Q25a)
Not at all satisfied? .... 4 (SKIP TO Q25a)
DON'T KNOW .... 8 (SKIP TO Q26)
REFUSED .... 9 (SKIP TO Q26)

Q24a. If you were told that federal spending for Medicaid was going to be
cut back, would you be strongly opposed, somewhat opposed, or indifferent to the cutback?

STRONGLY OPPOSED 1   75/
SOMEWHAT OPPOSED 2
INDIFFERENT........................ 3 (SKIP TO Q26)
IN FAVOR OF CUTBACK (IF
VOLUNTEERED) ....4 (SKIP TO Q26)
CHANGE THE SYSTEM
(IF VOLUNTEERED)..................... 5 (SKIP TO Q26)
DK .... 8 (SKIP TO Q26)
RF .... 9 (SKIP TO Q26)

b. Would you sign a petition or write a letter to your congressman expressing your feelings toward the cutback?

YES   "Would you say ...... definitely yes, or 1   76/
                           probably yes? 2

NO   "Would you say ...... definitely no, or 4
                           probably no? 3

                           DON'T KNOW 8
                           REFUSED 9

c. In order to prevent the Medicaid program from being cut back, would you be willing to pay no more taxes, $0.50 more for every $100 in taxes you already pay, $1.00 more for every $100 in taxes you already pay, or $2.00 more for every $100 in taxes?

NO MORE .... 4 (SKIP TO Q26)   77/
$0.50 MORE .... 3 (SKIP TO Q26)
$1.00 MORE .... 2 (SKIP TO Q26)
$2.00 MORE .... 1 (SKIP TO Q26)
OTHER_____ .... 5 (SKIP TO Q26)
DON'T KNOW .... 8 (SKIP TO Q26)
REFUSED .... 9 (SKIP TO Q26)

Q25a. If you were told that federal spending for Medicaid was going to be expanded, would you be strongly opposed, somewhat opposed, or indifferent to the expansion?

STRONGLY OPPOSED.................... 1   78/
SOMEWHAT OPPOSED 2
INDIFFERENT .... 3 (SKIP TO Q26)
IN FAVOR OF EXPANSION
(IF VOLUNTEERED) .... 4 (SKIP TO Q26)
CHANGE THE SYSTEM
(IF VOLUNTEERED) .... 5 (SKIP TO Q26)
DK................................. 8 (SKIP TO Q26)
RF................................. 9 (SKIP TO Q26)/

b. Would you sign a petition or write a letter to your congressman expressing your disapproval about the expansion of Medicaid?

YES   "Would you say .... definitely yes, or 1   79/
                           probably yes? 2

NO   "Would you say .... definitely no, or 4
                           probably no? 3

                           DON'T KNOW 8
                           REFUSED 9

c. To show your disapproval of Medicaid, would you like the program to be maintained at its current funding, be cut back by $0.50 for $100 in taxes spent on it, be cut back by $1.00 for every $100 spent, or be cut back by $2.00 for every $100 spent?

MAINTAIN 4   80/

$0.50 LESS 3

$1.00 LESS 2

$2.00 LESS 1

OTHER _____ 5

DON'T KNOW 8

REFUSED 9

Q26. I'm going to read a few statements about the <u>people</u> who <u>received</u> Medicaid. For each, please tell me whether you agree, somewhat agree, somewhat disagree, or disagree.

> BEGIN DECK 3

	Agree, or	Somewhat Agree?	Disagree, or	Somewhat Disagree?	DK	RF	
Most people now receiving Medicaid <u>really need</u> the assistance provided. Do you	1	2	3	4	8	9	5/
Q27. Without Medicaid, most people who now get it would have <u>no access</u> to doctors and hospitals	1	2	3	4	8	9	6/
Q28. Medicaid helps most people who get it become more independent and better able to care for themselves	1	2	3	4	8	9	7/
Q29. It's their own fault that most Medicaid recipients have Medicaid rather than private health insurance	1	2	3	4	8	9	8/

Q30. Most people who get Medicaid <u>want</u> to be

independent and self-
reliant   1 ....2 ....3 ....4 .....8 ..9   9/

Q31. Medicaid makes pos-
sible an adequate stan-
dard of health care for
those who get it   1 ....2 ....3 ....4 .....8 ..9   10/

Q32. Society as a whole
benefits because we
have Medicaid   1 ....2 ....3 ....4 .....8 ..9   11/

Q33. Medicaid makes most
people who get it de-
pendent and uninter-
ested in paying for
their own health care   1 ....2 ....3 ....4 .....8 ..9   12/

Q34. Most people who get
Medicaid only use it
when they really need
to   1 ....2 ....3 ....4 .....8 ..9   13/

Q35. Different people see the Medicaid program as having different purposes. For each statement, please tell me if you believe it should be a
purpose of Medicaid.

	YES	NO	DK	RF

a. Need: that is, Medicaid should provide
assistance to those low-income people who
really can't afford private health insurance   1 ....2 ....8 9   14/

b. Earnings-Based: that is, Medicaid should
provide assistance to those who worked in
the past   1 ....2 ....8 9   15/

c. Equal Opportunity: that is, Medicaid should
provide assistance so that people have a
more equal opportunity to have medical care   1 ....2 ....8 9   16/

d. Reduce Differences: that is, Medicaid should
provide assistance in a way that reduces the
differences in quality of health care between
those who have a lot of money and those
who have very little   1 ....2 ....8 9   17/

Q36. Which one of these purposes would you say should be the most impor-
tant for distributing Medicaid (ONLY LIST CHOICES THAT R RE-
SPONDED YES IN Q35. YOU MAY NEED TO READ THE WHOLE RE-
SPONSE ABOVE. USE YOUR JUDGMENT. URGE R TO GIVE ONLY ONE
RESPONSE.)

a. Need, ... 1   18/

b. Earnings-Based, ... 2

c. Equal opportunity, or 3

d. Reduction of differences? 4

DON'T KNOW 8

REFUSED 9

Q37. In the past two questions, I've asked you what you think the purpose of Medicaid <u>should</u> be. Now I'd like to ask you what you think Medicaid is <u>actually</u> doing.

	YES	SOMEWHAT (IF VOLUN-TEERED)	NO	DK	RF	
a. Is Medicaid providing assistance to those low-income people who really can't affird private health insurance?	1	2	3	8	9	19/
b. Is Medicaid providing assistance to those who have worked in the past?	1	2	3	8	9	20/
c. Is Medicaid providing assistance so that people have more equal health care opportunities?	1	2	3	8	9	21/
d. Is Medicaid providing assistance in a way that reduces the differences between those in the population who have a lot of money and those who have very little?	1	2	3	8	9	22/

Q38. Of people receiving Medicaid, would you say almost all, more than half, less than half, or only a few are cheating the system—for example, collecting more than they are entitled to? (PROMPT IF NECESSARY: "Just give me your best guess.")

ALMOST ALL 1

MORE THAN HALF 2

LESS THAN HALF 3

A FEW 4

DON'T KNOW 8

REFUSED 9

ALTERNATE B FOR Q23–28

KEYPUNCH: ALTERNATE Q23–Q38 SHOULD BE ON DECK 5. WHEN YOU GET TO Q39, START DECK 3 AND FOLLOW IN ORDER.

BEGIN DECK 5

Q23. Now I'd like to focus on Social Security.

In general, how satisfied are you with the fact that a part of every working person's income goes to support the Social Security program? Would you say you are . . .

Very satisfied,. . . . . 1 (SKIP TO Q24a)   5/
Somewhat satisfied,. . . . . 2 (SKIP TO Q24a)
Not very satisfied, or. 3
Not at all satisfied? 4
DON'T KNOW . . . . 8 (SKIP TO Q26)
REFUSED . . . . 9 (SKIP TO Q26)

Q23a. Are you not satisfied. . . . . (GET ONLY <u>ONE</u> RESPONSE)

because people got more out than they put
in 1   6/
because too many get it who don't really
need it, ... 2
because you could do better to have the
money to invest as you please,. 3
because you don't think it will be there when
you retire, or. 4   (SKIP TO Q25)
because of some other reason? (SPECIFY)

_____

_____ 5
DON'T KNOW 8
REFUSED 9

Q24a. If you were told that spending for Social Security was going to be cut back, would you be strongly opposed, somewhat opposed, or indifferent to the cut back?

STRONGLY OPPOSED. 1   7/
SOMEWHAT OPPOSED 2
INDIFFERENT. . . . . 3 (SKIP TO Q26)
IN FAVOR OF CUT BACK (IF VOLUN-
TEERED) . . . . 4 (SKIP TO Q26)
CHANGE THE SYSTEM (IF VOLUNTEERED) 5 (SKIP TO Q26)
DK . . . . 8 (SKIP TO Q26)
RF . . . . 9 (SKIP TO Q26)

b. Would you sign a petition or write a letter to your congressman expressing your feelings toward the cut back?

YES "Would you say . . . . . . definitely yes, or 1   8/
                            probably yes? 2

NO "Would you say . . . . . . definitely no, or 4
                            probably no? 3

DON'T KNOW 8
REFUSED 9

c. In order to prevent the Social Security program from being cut back, would you be willing to have people pay no more Social Security taxes, $0.50 more for every $100 they already pay, $1.00 more for every $100 they already pay, or $2.00 more for every $100?

NO MORE . . . . 4 (SKIP TO Q26)   9/
$0.50 MORE . . . . 3 (SKIP TO Q26)
$1.00 MORE . . . . 2 (SKIP TO Q26)
$2.00 MORE . . . . 1 (SKIP TO Q26)
OTHER_____ . . . . 5 (SKIP TO Q26)
DON'T KNOW . . . . 8 (SKIP TO Q26)
REFUSED . . . . 9 (SKIP TO Q26)

Q25a. If you were told that spending for Social Security was going to be expanded, would you be strongly opposed, somewhat opposed, or indifferent to the expansion?

STRONGLY OPPOSED 1   10/
SOMEWHAT OPPOSED 2
INDIFFERENT . . . . 3 (SKIP TO Q26)
IN FAVOR OF EXPANSION (IF
VOLUNTEERED) . . . . 4 (SKIP TO Q26)
CHANGE THE SYSTEM (IF VOLUNTEERED) 5 (SKIP TO Q26)
DK . . . . 8 (SKIP TO Q26)
RF . . . . 9 (SKIP TO Q26)

b. Would you sign a petition or write a letter to your congressman expressing your disapproval about the expansion of Social Security?

YES "Would you say . . . . . . definitely yes, or 1   11/
                            probably yes? 2

NO "Would you say . . . . . . definitely no, or 4
                            probably no? 3

DON'T KNOW 8
REFUSED 9

c. To show your disapproval of Social Security, would you like the program to be maintained at its current funding, be cut back by $0.50 for $100 in Social Security taxes spent on it, be cut back by

$1.00 for every $100 spent, or be cut back by $2.00 for every $100 spent?

MAINTAIN 4	12/
$0.50 LESS 3
$1.00 LESS 2
$2.00 LESS 1
OTHER _____ 5
DON'T KNOW 8
REFUSED 9

Q26. I'm going to read you a few questions about the people who receive Social Security. For each, please tell me whether you agree, somewhat agree, somewhat disagree, or disagree.

		Agree, or	Somewhat Agree?	Disagree, or	Somewhat Disagree?	DK	RF	
Most people now receiving Social Security really need the assistance provided. Do you ...		1	2	3	4	8	9	13/
Q27. Most people who get Social Security have no sources of income other than Social Security		1	2	3	4	8	9	14/
Q28. Social Security helps most people who get it become more independent and better able to support themselves		1	2	3	4	8	9	15/
Q29. It's a person's own fault if he gets Social Security instead of private retirement funds		1	2	3	4	8	9	16/
Q30. Most people who get Social Security want to be independent and self-reliant		1	2	3	4	8	9	17/
Q31. Social Security makes possible an adequate standard of living for those who get it		1	2	3	4	8	9	18/

Q32. Society as a whole benefits because we have
Social Security   1 ....2 ....3 ....4 .....8 ..9 19/

Q33. Social Security makes
most people who get it
dependent and not inter-
ested in saving for the
future   1 ....2 ....3 ....4 .....8 ..9 20/

Q34. Most people who get
Social Security spend
their money wisely   1 ....2 ....3 ....4 .....8 ..9 21/

Q35. Different people see the Social Security program as having different
purposes. For each statement, please tell me if you believe it <u>should be</u>
a purpose of Social Security.

	YES	NO	DK	RF	
a. <u>Need:</u> that is, Social Security should provide money to those people who really need it.	1	2	8	9	22/
b. <u>Earnings-Based:</u> that is, Social Security should provide money to those who have <u>worked</u> in the past	1	2	8	9	23/
c. <u>Equal Opportunity:</u> that is, Social Security should provide money so that people have a more equal opportunity to retire	1	2	8	9	24/
d. <u>Reduce Differences:</u> that is, Social Security should provide money in a way that reduces the differences between those retired people who have a lot of money and those who have very little	1	2	8	9	25/

Q36. Which one of these purposes would you say should be the <u>most impor-
tant</u> for distributing Medicaid (<u>ONLY</u> LIST CHOICES THAT <u>R</u> RE-
SPONDED <u>YES</u> IN Q35. YOU MAY NEED TO READ THE WHOLE RE-
SPONSE ABOVE. USE YOUR JUDGMENT. URGE <u>R</u> TO GIVE ONLY ONE
RESPONSE.)

a. Need, ... 1   26/
b. Earnings-Based, ... 2
c. Equal opportunity, or 3
d. Reduction of differences? 4
   DON'T KNOW 8
   REFUSED 9

Q37. In the past two questions, I've asked you what you think the purpose of Medicaid <u>should</u> be. Now I'd like to ask you what you think Medicaid is <u>actually</u> doing.

	YES	SOMEWHAT (IF VOLUN- TEERED)	NO	DK	RF	
a. Is Social Security providing money to those people who really need it?	1	2	3	8	9	27/
b. Is Social Security providing money to those who have worked in the past?	1	2	3	8	9	28/
c. Is Social Security providing money so that people have more equal opportunities to retire?	1	2	3	8	9	28/
d. Is Social Security providing money in a way that reduces the differences between those retired people who have a lot of money and those who have very little?	1	2	3	8	9	30/

Q38. Of people receiving Social Security, would you say almost all, more than half, less than half, or only a few are cheating the system—for example, collecting more than they are entitled to? (PROMPT IF NECESSARY: "Just give me your best guess.")

ALMOST ALL 1   31/

MORE THAN HALF 2

LESS THAN HALF 3

A FEW 4

DON'T KNOW 8

REFUSED.................. 9

VERSION_____   32/

> KEYPUNCH
> END DECK 5

Q39. It would seem that poverty could be eliminated by able-bodied poor adults holding a job. Yet, some people are without jobs for long periods of time. I'm going to read a list of possible reasons. For each reason, tell me how many people you think it applies to.

	Almost all people	More than half	Less than half	Only a few people	NONE (IF VOL.)	DK	RF	
a. Their character, that is, people are lazy and don't want to work	1	2	3	4	5	8	9	24/
b. Their attitudes, that is, people don't know how to act properly and show the right attitudes at work	1	2	3	4	5	8	9	25/
c. Skills, that is, people lack the needed job skills	1	2	3	4	5	8	9	26/
d. Those needing jobs do not live in the same location as the available jobs	1	2	3	4	5	8	9	27/
e. There's discrimination against people	1	2	3	4	5	8	9	28/
f. There aren't enough jobs	1	2	3	4	5	8	9	29/
g. Government programs such as Unemployment Insurance and AFDC make it too easy for people to stay home and not work	1	2	3	4	5	8	9	30/

h. OTHER (IF VOLUNTEERED, RECORD VERBATIM)

_____

_____	1	2	3	4	5	8	9	31/

Q40. Do you think the federal government has a role and a responsibility to see that everyone who wants to work is able to, or do you think that the greatest responsibility should rest within state government, local government, private industry, or the individuals themselves?

FEDERAL GOVERNMENT 1   32/

STATE GOVERNMENT 2

LOCAL GOVERNMENT.................... 3

PRIVATE INDUSTRY..................... 4

INDIVIDUALS 5

DON'T KNOW 8

REFUSED 9

Q41. Very different solutions are now being recommended to attack the problem of poverty. I'm going to read a list of solutions that some people have suggested that Congress should enact. For each solution, I'd like you to tell me whether you favor it or not. Again, please think of a scale from 1 to 100 where <u>100</u> means you <u>favor the solutions very strongly</u> and <u>1</u> means you <u>don't favor it at all</u>. Try not to use the same number twice. [START AT ARROW]

(DO NOT CORRECT <u>R</u> FOR USING SAME NUMBER. WAIT UNTIL END AND BREAK TIE IF IT IS IN TOP 3)

➤ _____ 1. Require <u>work</u> in exchange for benefits from   33–35/
(GIVE NUMBER)   all people who receive public assistance and
DK 888   RF 999   don't have to care for infants?

_____ 2. Expand job training programs?   36–38/
(GIVE NUMBER)
DK 888   RF 999

_____ 3. Improve the public elementary and secondary   39–41/
(GIVE NUMBER)   education systems?
DK 888   RF 999

_____ 4. Stimulate faster economic growth?   42–44/
(GIVE NUMBER)
DK 888   RF 999

_____ 5. Adjust individual tax rate for the working   45–47/
(GIVE NUMBER)   poor so that people working full time make
DK 888   RF 999   enough to keep their incomes above the pov-
                     erty line?

(TIE BREAKER: IF <u>R</u> GIVES SAME NUMBER TO TWO OR THREE GROUPS THAT ARE IN THE TOP 3 CHOICES, HAVE HIM/HER RANK THEM)

Q41b. Let me ask you if these are indeed your top priority solutions. You said you would favor most: (<u>GIVE CHOICE WITH HIGHEST SCORE</u>), second most: (<u>GIVE CHOICE WITH SECOND HIGHEST SCORE</u>) and third most: (<u>GIVE CHOICE WITH THIRD HIGHEST SCORE</u>). Are these your top priorities? (CHANGE IF NECESSARY)

(GIVE NUMBER)   _____   _____   _____   48–50/
                    FIRST   SECOND   THIRD

Q42. Recently, we've been told about female-headed families where the
     mother receives public benefits; her daughters have children, don't get
     married and they, too, receive aid. The cycle continues. How serious a
     problem do you think the generation-to-generation poverty is in fe-
     male-headed households? Do you think it is . . .

> Very serious,............................. 1   51/
> Somewhat serious,........................ 2
> Not too serious, or....................... 3
> Not at all serious? 4
> DON'T KNOW 8
> REFUSED 9

Q43. With what we now know, do you think the problem of generation-to-
     generation poverty in female-headed households can be reduced at all?

> YES 1   52/
> NO 2
> OTHER_____ 3
> DON'T KNOW 8
> REFUSED 9

Q44. There are a number of solutions that the federal government might
     enact to reduce poverty in female-headed households. For each, please
     tell me whether you favor it, favor it and would be willing to pay
     slightly higher taxes, or don't favor it at all.

	FAVOR	FAVOR WITH HIGHER TAXES	DON'T FAVOR	DK	RF	
a. Increase funding for pro- grams in schools that teach young people about family planning (I.E. SEX EDUCATION)?	1	2	3	8	9	53/
b. Increase the funding for the teaching of values and morals in schools?	1	2	3	8	9	54/
c. Provide day care for young mothers and re- quire them to finish their high school educa- tion or to go to work?	1	2	3	8	9	55/

d. Provide job training to
young mothers? ....1 ....2 ....3 .....8 ...9   56/

e. OTHER (IF VOLUNTEERED) (RECORD)

_____

_____....1 ....2 ....3 .....8 ...9   57/

Q45. Now, could you tell me how you feel about the opportunities you have
had in <u>your</u> life to do well and make the most of yourself? Do you feel
that you've had . . .

a lot of good opportunities,............... 1   58/
a good many opportunities, ... 2
just enough opportunities, ... 3
not many opportunities, or 4
hardly any opportunities? 5
DON'T KNOW 8
REFUSED 9

Q46. Compared to you, do you think your children or the children of your
close relatives and friends will have more, about the same, or fewer
opportunities to make the most of their lives?

MORE→ "Would you say a lot more, or..... 1   59/
a bit more?" 2
ABOUT THE SAME 3

FEWER→ "Would you say a bit fewer, or 4
a lot fewer?" 5
DON'T KNOW 8
REFUSED.............................. 9

Q47a. Now, just a few questions about politics. In 1984, Walter Mondale ran
for President on the Democratic ticket against Ronald Reagan for the
Republicans. Did you vote for Mondale or Reagan?

MONDALE............................. 1 SKIP TO Q48)   60/
REAGAN.............................. 2 (SKIP TO Q48)
OTHER CANDIDATE (SPECIFY)_____ 3 (SKIP TO Q48)
DID NOT VOTE 4
INELIGIBLE 5
DON'T REMEMBER 6
DON'T KNOW.......................... 8 (SKIP TO Q48)
REFUSED.............................. 9 (SKIP TO Q48)

Q47b. Who would you have voted for President if you had voted?

MONDALE 1   61/
REAGAN 2

OTHER CANDIDATE (SPECIFY)_____ 3
DON'T KNOW..................... 8
REFUSED 9

I'd like to finish by asking you just a few brief background questions for statistical purposes.

Q48. When it comes to politics would you consider yourself extremely liberal, somewhat liberal, somewhat conservative, or extremely conservative?

EXTREMELY LIBERAL.............. 1   62/
SOMEWHAT LIBERAL............... 2
SOMEWHAT CONSERVATIVE 4
EXTREMELY CONSERVATIVE........ 5
MODERATE .... 3 (IF VOLUNTEERED)
DON'T THINK IN THOSE TERMS..... 6
DON'T KNOW..................... 8
REFUSED 9

Q49. Do you consider yourself, in general, a Republican or Democrat?

REPUBLICAN 1   63/
DEMOCRAT 2
INDEPENDENT 3
VOTE FOR PERSON/CANDIDATE
REGARDLESS OF PARTY 4
OTHER (SPECIFY)_____ 5
DON'T KNOW..................... 8
REFUSED 9

Q50. In what year were you born? _____ REFUSED 9999   64–67/

Q51. Are you currently married, widowed, divorced, separated, or have you never been married?

MARRIED............................ 1   68/
WIDOWED 2
DIVORCED 3
SEPARATED 4
NEVER MARRIED...................... 5
REFUSED............................ 9

Q52. How many people live in your household including yourself?
(INCLUDE NON-FAMILY RESIDENTS)
_____ (IF ONE, SKIP TO Q56)   69–70/

Q53. How many of these are children 17 and under?

(GIVE NUMBER)_____   71/
NONE .... 44 (SKIP TO Q55)

DON'T KNOW .... 88 (SKIP TO Q55)
REFUSED .... 99 (SKIP TO Q55)

Q54. How many of these are your own children or step-children?

_____   72–73/

NONE 44
DON'T KNOW 88
REFUSED 99

Q55. How many of the people in your household are 65 and over?

_____   75–76/

NONE 44
DON'T KNOW 88
REFUSED 99

> BEGIN DECK 4

Q56. What will be your total household income this year from all sources?

$_____ (SKIP TO Q58)   5–10/
DK................................... 888888
RF................................... 999999

Q57. I just need a rough estimate. This is absolutely confidential information. Will your total household income for 1986, from all sources, be (REPEAT UNTIL "NO")

More than $5,000 .... NO .... .01   11–12/
More than $10,000 .... NO .... .02
More than $15,000 .... NO .... .03
More than $20,000 .... NO .... .04
More than $30,000 .... NO .... .05
More than $40,000 .... NO .... .06
More than $50,000 .... NO .... .07
                                YES .... .08
DON'T KNOW .... .88
REFUSED....................................... .99

Q58. We're interested in learning more about the kind of community you live in. I'm going to read some descriptions of communities and you stop me when the description matches where you live. (NOTE: CONTINUE READING UNTIL R STOPS YOU)

In a very large city with a population over 250,000, . . . 1   13/
In a suburb near a large city,..................... 2

In or near a medium-size city with a population be-
tween 50,000–250,000, ... 3
In or near a small city or town with a population under
50,000... 4
On a farm, or.................................. 5
In a rural area? (BUT, NOT A FARM) 6
DON'T KNOW 8
REFUSED...................................... 9

Q59. We have been discussing a number of different government benefits.
As I read down the list, could you tell me for each item whether you or
anyone in your household received it in the past 12 months . . .

	YES	NO	DK	RF	
a. AFDC (THAT IS, AID TO FAMILIES WITH DEPENDENT CHILDEREN)?	1	2	8	9	14/
b. Social Security (OASI)?	1	2	8	9	15/
c. Medicare—that is, the health insurance program for senior citizens? (AND SOME PHYSICALLY DISABLED PEOPLE)	1	2	8	9	16/
d. Medicaid? (FOR LOW-INCOME PEOPLE, OFTEN CALLED THE 'GREEN CARD')	1	2	8	9	17/
e. Food Stamps?	1	2	8	9	18/
f. SSI that is, supplemental security income	1	2	8	9	19/
g. Unemployment Compensation?	1	2	8	9	20/
h. Any other government benefit, like student loan or fellowship, public housing, Head Start or FHA loan? (RECORD) _____	1	2	8	9	21/

Q60. Now I'd like to go through the list again and ask you if you have friends
or family members (not in your household) who received one of these
benefits.

	YES	NO	DK	RF	
a. AFDC? (THAT IS, AID TO FAMILIES WITH DEPENDENT CHILDREN)?	1	2	8	9	22/
b. Social Security (OASI)?	1	2	8	9	23/
c. Medicare? (FOR PEOPLE 65 AND OVER)	1	2	8	9	24/

d. Medicaid? (FOR LOW-INCOME PEOPLE,
   OFTEN CALLED THE 'GREEN CARD') . . . . 1 . . . . 2 . . . . 8 9   25/

e. Food Stamps? . . . . 1 . . . . 2 . . . . 8 9   26/

f. SSI, (SUPPLEMENTAL SECURITY INCOME) . . . . 1 . . . . 2 . . . . 8 9   27/

g. Unemployment Compensation? . . . . 1 . . . . 2 . . . . 8 9   28/

h. Any other government benefit? (RECORD)

   _____. . . . 1 . . . . 2 . . . . 8 9   29/

Q61. What is the highest grade or year of school that you have completed?

NONE. 0   30–31/
ELEMENTARY 01 02 03 04 05 06 07 08
HIGH SCHOOL 09 10 11 12
SOME COLLEGE/VOCATIONAL ED/2-YEAR DEGREE . . . 13
COLLEGE GRADUATE/BACHELORS/4-YEAR DEGREE . . 14
M.A./SOME GRADUATE SCHOOL 15
PhD. 16
MD 17
LAW DEGREE. 18
DON'T KNOW. 88
REFUSED 99

Q62. Are you of Spanish or Hispanic origin or descent?

YES (INCLUDES MIXED) 2   32/
NO 1
REFUSED 9

Q63. What is your racial background? Are you . . .

Asian 1   33/
Black 2
White, or 3
Something else? (SPECIFY)_____ 5

| (NOTE: IF R SAYS: "Mexican" or "Indian", RECORD AND CIRCLE 5) |

DON'T KNOW. 8
REFUSED 9

Thank you so much for answering these questions. Sometime in January, President Reagan is going to address the nation about his recommendations for changes in the social welfare system. To learn your opinions about his proposals, we may want to talk to you again next year. May we call you back then?

NO .... 1 (TRY TO GET THEIR HELP)   34/

YES .... 2 (ASK Q• BELOW)

• And will you give me your name so that we know who to ask for? (TRY TO GET LAST NAME AS WELL AS FIRST)

RECORD NAME 1   35/

(Mr./Mrs./Miss)_____

REFUSED 8

• In case you move between now and then, could you give me the name and number of someone who will know your new phone number so we can be sure to reach you?

RECORD NAME AND NUMBER_____   36/

_____ 1

(WORK NUMBER WOULD BE OK TO GET, AS ALTERNATIVE)

REFUSED.................................. 8

GENDER OF RESPONDENT (ASK IF YOU CAN'T TELL PLEASE!)

MALE 0   37/

FEMALE 1

THANK R AGAIN.

_____ FINISHING TIME

INTERVIEWERS: PLEASE HELP US BY GIVING YOUR IMPRESSIONS OF THE RESPONDENT.

1. How knowledgeable did the respondent seem to be regarding social welfare policies and programs? (Circle one)

not at all   very
knowledgeable 1 .... 2 .... 3 .... 4 .... 5 .... 6 .... 7 knowledgeable 38/

2. How cooperative was the respondent? (Circle one)

not at all   extremely
cooperative   1 .... 2 .... 3 .... 4 .... 5 .... 6 .... 7 cooperative   39/

3. How well do you think the respondent understood the question?

very low   very high
understanding 1 .... 2 .... 3 .... 4 .... 5 .... 6 .... 7 understanding 40/

APPENDIX C
Congressional Questionnaire

INTERVIEW SCHEDULE
MEMBERS OF THE U.S. CONGRESS

INTRODUCTION

I am really pleased to have this opportunity to talk to you. As the letter of introduction from Congressman xxxxxxxxxxx said, I am on the Ford Foundation's Research Advisory Committee on the project "Social Welfare Policy and the American Future." As you know, very fundamental questions have recently been raised about what should be the proper role of government in providing assistance to people. My research in the Ford project is to probe the opinions of the general public and of members of Congress about the social welfare programs and the social groups that should and should not be supported. I'm talking first to members of Congress about these issues and later I'll conduct a nationwide survey of the general public.

One thing I want to emphasize. Your comments today will be kept completely confidential. None of the things you say will ever be attributed directly to you. When you make individual statements that I'd like to quote in a book or scholarly article, no one will be able to identify you from what I write.

SECTION 1

BACKGROUND INFORMATION ON THE RECORD
(The interviewer records this information prior to the interview.)

1a. Respondent _____

1b. Sample
    Random........................1
    Purposive 2

2. Party
    Republican 1
    Democrat 2

3. State _____ [CODE 1 TO 50, alphabetically]

4. Region of Country
    East (ME, NH, VT, MA, RI, CT, NY, NJ, PA, DE, MD, DC).........1
    Midwest (OH, IN, IL, MI, WI, MN, IA, MO, KS, NE, SD, ND) 2
    West (MT, ID, WY, CO, NM, AZ, UT, NV, CA, OR, WA, AK, HI) 3
    South (WV, VA, NC, SC, GA, FL, AL, MS, TN, KY, AR, LA, TX, OK) ..4

5. Age _____

6a. Education
    College 1
    College Graduate..................2
    MA/MS 3
    Law Degree 4
    Ph.D. 5
    Other...........................6
    Less than College 7
    Not Listed 8

6b. Race
    White...........................1
    Black 2
    Hispanic 3
    Other...........................4

6c. Gender
    Male 1
    Female 2

7. Religion
    Jewish 1
    Protestant 2
    Catholic........................3
    None listed 4

8. Length of service in Congress (years) _____

9. Liberalism-Conservatism [Both are averages over two years]

    A. Voting record score assigned by
       Americans for Democratic Action _____

    B. Voting record score assigned by
       Americans for Constitutional Action _____

10. Committees on which Congressperson serves (House 2; Senate 3)

    A. _____ (Subcommittees _____)

    B. _____ (Subcommittees _____)

    C. _____ (Subcommittees _____)

    D. _____ (Subcommittees _____)

    [Code of degree of social welfare relevance   Hi   Med   Lo]
                                                   5   4   3   2   1

    E. Chair of   No 1
       Committee: Comm. Chair re. social welfare 2
                  Comm. Chair not re. social welfare 3

    F. Chair of   No 1
       Subcommittee: Subcomm. Chair re. social welfare. 2
                  Subcomm. Chair not re. social welfare 3

11. Recognized area of expertise _____

12. Safety of seat (percent margin of victory in last election) _____

13. Voting record rating by the Children's Defense Fund _____

14. Voting record rating by the National Council of Senior Citizens _____

15. Voting record rating by the *National Journal*

    Social issues   _____

    Economic issues   _____

    Foreign policy issues   _____

16. Any legislation sponsored in relation to social welfare policy:

    No 1
    Yes 2

17. District's racial composition (%)   Black   _____
                                        Spanish   _____
                                          Asian   _____
                                          Am. Indian   _____

18. Median house value ($) _____

19. Median Rent ($/mo) _____

20. Family Composition (%):   Families   _____
                               Families with children   _____
                               Married couples   _____

21. Number of Districts in State   _____

22. Median Family Income ($)   _____

23. Median School Years   _____

24. Percentage Urban   _____

25. Unemployment Rate   _____

26. Community Type   _____

27. Age Composition of District

    Under 18 (1,000s)   _____
    Over 18 (1,000s)   _____
    Children (%)   _____
    Elderly (%)   _____

SECTION 2
(Interviewer's questions to respondent begin here.)

1. Recently there has been much debate in academic and policy circles
   about the major programs that make up our social welfare system. I'd like
   to begin by asking you a few questions about your opinions of these
   programs. [HAND CARD A] Let's begin with Social Security. Some people want to increase benefits for individuals in real dollar terms, others to
   decrease them, and others to maintain them. What do you support?
   [RECORD ON CHART]

   A. How strongly do you feel about that?

          Very 1
          Not very 2

   [CONTINUE THROUGH EACH PROGRAM, ASKING BOTH ABOUT THE
   PROGRAM (How about . . . ? AND ABOUT INTENSITY OF FEELING
   (How strongly . . . ?) AT END, ASK: Are there any other social welfare
   programs that you consider major?]

CARD A
Some of the Major Social Welfare Programs

	Increase Benefits	Decrease Benefits	Maintain Current Levels
Social Security (OASI)			
Unemployment Compensation			
Medicare (elderly)			
Medicaid (low income)			
Supplemental Security Income (SSI)			
Aid to Families with Dependent Children (AFDC)			
Food Stamps			
Other programs . . .			

    A. Why do you support increased benefits for people receiving _____ ?

    _____

    _____

    B. Why do you support decreased benefits for people receiving _____ ?

    _____

    _____

2. I know you have to deal with a lot of very different issues—from tax reform to foreign policy. In comparison to all the other issues you deal with, how much do you hear from your constituency and other interested groups and organizations about social welfare issues—the programs we've just looked at and others of similar ilk?

    • PROBES RE: FREQUENCY AND INTENSITY:

    In comparison to other issues? _____
    _____ , how frequently do you hear about these issues? _____.

    How intense are opinions in comparison to other issues? _____
    _____ _____ .

    • PROBES RE: TYPES OF PEOPLE/GROUPS HEARD FROM:

    What types of people do you hear from?

Types of groups? —how powerful in terms of money and votes they
control
—how articulate, politically
—how similar to Congress members' own background

A. How are the points of view you hear about Social Security different
from those you hear about AFDC?

_____

_____

• PROBES: Amount?
Intensity?
Types of people/groups?
—how powerful in terms of money and votes they
control
—how articulate, politically
—how similar to Congress member's own background

3. Given the national deficit, most commentators anticipate limited future
funds for social welfare programs. Here are some of the different poor
groups now getting attention in the press, academic, and Washington
circles. [HAND CARD B] I know the groups overlap somewhat but could
you rank the groups that you think should have additional federal financial support, if any?

[RECORD] _____

A. Which definitely do not need additional help or might be cut back?

[RECORD] _____

CARD B

Priority for
additional
financial support

1. _____ Poor people in small towns and rural areas.
2. _____ Members of the so-called urban underclass.
3. _____ Poor able-bodied men of working age who are unemployed.
4. _____ Poor children.
5. _____ Poor female heads of households with children.
6. _____ The poor elderly.
7. _____ Poor elderly persons who are physically disabled.
8. _____ Poor adults under 65 who are physically disabled.
9. _____ Other: _____

B. Why do you think (_____ top priority _____) should receive additional support?

_____

_____

[PROBES, IF CONVICTION THEORY REASONS AREN'T GIVEN:

a. To what extent do you think help exists for this group other than through the federal government?

b. To what extent do you think most _____ are responsible for the difficult situation they are in?

c. What do you think are the most basic needs of _____ with which the federal government can help?]

[PROBES, IF POLITICAL REASONS AREN'T GIVEN:

a. To what extent do you think targetting aid at _____ will be politically acceptable? [for example, to your constituency? general public? powerful interest groups? the party and party leadership? to legislators and bureaucrats concerned with budgets? to PACs that support you?]

[PROBES, INFORMATION/DELIBERATION:

In regard to _____ , have you changed your mind or your view in the last year or so that they should be targetted for more help?]

Yes—[ASK b]

No—[ASK a]

a. Has any information or new way of thinking come along that strengthened the opinion you already had?

Yes—[ASK b]

No—[GO TO NEXT QUESTION c.]

b. What kinds of things influenced you?

[PROBES: 1) any particular persons you talked with?
2) any other Congressperson?
3) any staff person?
4) any representative of an interest group?
5) any agency people?
6) any TV story or newspaper article?
7) any person from your constituency?
8) any researcher and/or academic?
9) anything in your own personal experience?

c. Going back to the groups you said needed additional help, you said
_____(low priority)_____ didn't need additional help [should
be a lower priority for additional help.] Why is that?

_____

_____

d. Which of the groups do you think the general public is most likely to
believe should receive high priority for federal support? _____

Least support? _____

4. In the debate on social welfare reform, radically different strategies are
now being advocated to attack the problem of poverty. Here are some of
the major points of attack being advocated. [HAND CARD C] As you can
see, the first three focus on altering parts of the social welfare system, the
fourth on the education system, the fifth on macroeconomic policy, the
sixth on tax reform, the seventh on public service, and the eighth on
enterprise zones. On which do you think the Congress should focus most
of all?

CARD C
Different Strategies Advocated to Reduce Poverty

1. _____ Modify the social welfare system (cut or expand)

2. _____ Require work in exchange for benefits from all able-bodied public assistance recipients without infants

3. _____ Expand job training programs

4. _____ Improve the education system

5. _____ Stimulate faster economic growth

6. _____ Adjust individual tax rates for the working poor

7. _____ Require two years of public service obligation of citizens
in their late teens or early twenties

8. _____ Create economic enterprise zones

9. _____ Other strategy you prefer?

[PROBE: Try to learn their top 1, 2, or 3 priorities and the 1, 2, 3
strategies they least favor.]

a. Why do you think Congress should focus most of all on _____ ?

_____

_____

B. Why do you think Congress should not focus on _____ ?

_____

_____

5. Now I'd like to ask you about some <u>specific</u> and highly targetted programs so that I can better understand which programs and groups you are most willing to support and why. Let's start with the food and nutrition programs on this card. [HAND CARD D]

Could you rank the programs in terms of the degree to which you support them, with 1 indicating most support and 7 indicating least support?

CARD D

1. _____ School lunch program for poor children.

2. _____ School lunch program for physically disabled children.

3. _____ School lunch subsidies for all school children.

4. _____ Meals on Wheels for elderly disabled people.

5. _____ Meals on Wheels for disabled adults under 65.

6. _____ Commodities distributions of such staples as rice, cheese, butter, flour, etc., to the poor elderly.

7. _____ Commodities distributions for poor adults under 65.

A. You particularly support (____high priority____). Why?

  • PROBE CONVICTION REASONS (Need. Not responsible for plight. No alternative source of help. Maximize self-sufficiency.)

_____

  • PROBE POLITICAL REASONS (To what extent do you think _____ is politically acceptable? (to constituency? general public? powerful interest groups? party and party leaders? to other legislators? to PACS that support you?)

  • PROBE INFORMATION/DELIBERATION (Have you changed your view about _____ in the last year or so? Has any information or different perceptions come along that strengthened the view you already had? What?)

_____

B. You don't seem to support _____ a lot. Why?

[PROBES]

C. How do you think members of the general public would rank these programs?

[RECORD] _____

6. There have been recent discussions of the need for programs providing coverage against catastrophic illnesses that could wipe out a family's assets. Given the deficit, we may have to phase in federal funding for catastrophic coverage. If that happens, which of the following groups should have highest priority for federal benefits? [HAND CARD E]

CARD E	Priority (1–?)
1. Elderly in general	_____
2. Children in general	_____
3. Adults under 65 in general	_____
4. Poor elderly	_____
5. Disabled elderly.................	_____
6. Poor children	_____
7. Disabled children................	_____
8. Poor adults under 65	_____
9. Disabled adults under 65	_____

A. Would you explain how you made your decisions?

_____

_____

_____

_____

7. Now let's look at a list of actual or proposed education-type programs. Could you rank the programs in terms of the degree to which you support them with 1 indicating most support and 7 indicating least support. [HAND CARD F]

CARD F

(1) _____ Information and Referral Services for People over 65 Who Are Physically Disabled to inform them about programs for which they are eligible and to help them apply for benefits.

(2) _____ Information and Referral Services for Poor People over 65 to inform them about services for which they are eligible, and to show them how to apply for benefits.

(3) _____ Rehabilitation and Job Training Programs for Physically Disabled People under 65 to help them get and keep jobs.

(4) _____ Job Training Programs for poor people under 65 to train them so that they can get jobs.

(5) _____ Preschool Intervention Programs for Poor Children to give them special attention before they start school so that they will not have so much trouble later.

(6) _____ Special Education Programs for Physically Disabled Children to help them cope with their handicaps and receive an education commensurate with their skills.

A. Why do you particularly support _____ ?

_____

_____

B. Why do you not support _____ _____ so much?

_____

_____

8. One crucial problem that almost everyone in the social welfare field from the right and left has puzzled about is the issue of jobs. For the able-bodied, non-elderly who are poor, it would <u>seem</u> that poverty could be eliminated by holding a job. Why do you think it is that this job solution has not worked very well in that some people are without a job for a long period of time?

[OPEN-ENDED. PROBE FOR <u>MAJOR</u> REASONS. POSSIBLE RESPONSES]

—Character—lazy, don't want to work.
—Skills—don't have job skills.
—Poor mesh between location of jobs and people who need them.
—Economy can't produce enough jobs.
—Minimum wage is too high so some employers won't hire workers.
—Minimum wage is too low so job doesn't bring a way out of poverty.
—Other: _____

A. What do you think the Federal government's role and responsibility, if any, should be in the job areas?

_____

_____

9. There's been much recent focus on the problem of female-headed families and the transmission of poverty from one generation to the next.

We're told about families where the mother is on AFDC; her daughters have children, don't get married and go on AFDC; and this pattern continues.

A. How serious a problem do you think multi-generational poverty is in female-headed households?

> Very serious 4
> Somewhat 3
> Not too 2
> Not at all 1

Why? [OPEN] _____

> numbers involved . . . .
> erodes national character . . . . . .
> effect on children . . . .
> other . . . .

B. Many people of all political persuasions are struggling with what causes this pattern of female-headed families needing public assistance from one generation to the next. What do you think are the major causes?

_____

_____

C. With what we now know, do you think the problem of multi-generational poverty in female-headed families can be reduced at all?

> Yes . . . . [ASK D]
> No . . . . [GO TO QUESTION 10]

D. What do you think should be done?

_____

_____

[IF HE/SHE DOESN'T MENTION A RESPONSIBILITY FOR THE FEDERAL GOVERNMENT, ASK: And should the government have a role?]

10. As you know, 26 states offer AFDC to one parent families only [unless the second parent is incapacitated]. In last year's Deficit Reduction Amendments there was a provision which would have required all states to offer AFDC to needy and financially eligible two-parent families in which the principal earner was unemployed. On October 31, 1985 you voted [for, against] the deficit reduction bill in general. Can your vote for the omnibus bill be interpreted to mean that you [favor, oppose] the specific policy requiring all states to offer AFDC to financially eligible two-parent families?

Favor: Yes _____ (ASK B)
       No _____ (ASK A)

Oppose: Yes _____ (ASK B)
        No _____ (ASK A)

A. How should your vote be interpreted then? _____

[FIND OUT IF HE/SHE FAVORS OR OPPOSES STANDARDIZATION
OF STATE TREATMENT OF AFDC families [favor, oppose].

B. Could you tell me how you arrived at that decision [opinion]?

[PROBE CONVICTION THEORY—I.E., NEED/ALTERNATIVE
SOURCE OF HELP/MAXIMIZATION OF INDEPENDENCE]

[ALSO PROBE POLITICAL THEORY OF INTERESTS/PARTY LEAD-
ERSHIP/CONSTITUENCY. PROBE ROLE OF INFORMATION IN
DECISION AND DELIBERATION QUESTION.]

How much information do they cite? Where do they get information—committee, colleagues, researchers, interest group? Our experience and knowledge? Interests of District?

11. Last year, Representative Leath offered an amendment to the first budget resolution for FY86 to freeze 1986 COLAs for Social Security, Federal retirement, and veterans compensation while adding 20% of the
anticipated savings back to programs that aid the poor elderly and the
disabled. You voted [for, against] the amendment. Could you tell me a
bit about how you made that decision?

[PROBE CONVICTION THEORY—I.E. NEED/ALTERNATIVE
SOURCE OF HELP/MAXIMIZATION OF INDEPENDENCE]

[ALSO PROBE POLITICAL THEORY OF INTERESTS/PARTY LEADER-
SHIP/CONSTITUENCY. PROBE ROLE OF INFORMATION IN DECI-
SION AND MANSBRIDGE DELIBERATION QUESTION.]

How much information do they cite? Where do they get information—
committee, colleagues, researchers, interest group? Our experience
and knowledge? Interests of district?

12. How do you think your position on _____ committee has influenced your thinking about social welfare issues?

13. What questions would you like to see me ask the general public that I
haven't asked you?

References

Abramson, Paul R. 1983. *Political Attitudes in America: Formation and Change.* San Francisco: W. H. Freeman.

Abramson, Paul R. 1975. *Generational Change in American Government.* Lexington, Mass.: Heath.

American Enterprise Institute. 1987. *A Community of Self-Reliance: The New Consensus on Family and Welfare.* Report of the Working Seminar on Family and American Welfare Policy. Washington, D.C.: American Enterprise Institute.

American Public Welfare Association. 1986. *One Child in Four.* Part 1 of *Investing in Poor Families and Their Children: A Matter of Commitment.* Washington, D.C.: APWA.

Arrington, T. S. 1976. "Communication." *American Political Science Review* 70:1227–1231.

AuClaire, Philip Arthur. 1984. "Public Attitudes toward Social Welfare Expenditures." *Social Work* 29:139–144.

Axinn, June, and Herman Levin. 1975. *Social Welfare: A History of the American Response to Need.* New York: Harper & Row.

Axinn, June, and Mark J. Stern. 1985. "Age and Dependency: Children and the Aged in American Social Policy." *Milbank Memorial Fund Quarterly* 63:648–670.

Backstrom, Charles H. 1977. "Congress and the Public: How Representative is the One of the Other?" *American Politics Quarterly* 5:411–435.

Bane, Mary Jo. 1986. "Household Composition and Poverty." In *Fighting Poverty: What Works and What Doesn't,* edited by Sheldon H. Danziger and

Daniel H. Weinberg, pp. 209–231. Cambridge, Mass.: Harvard University Press.

Barrett, Edith J. and Fay L. Cook. 1991. "Congressional Attitudes and Voting Behavior: An Examination of Support for Social Welfare." *Legislative Studies Quarterly* 16:375–392.

Bauer, Wilhelm A. 1934. "Public Opinion." In *Encyclopeadia of the Social Sciences*, vol. 12, pp. 669–674. New York: Macmillian.

Becker, Gary S. 1976. *The Economic Approach to Human Behavior.* Chicago: University of Chicago Press.

Berkowitz, L., and D. H. Connor. 1966. "Success, Failure, and Social Responsibility." *Journal of Personality and Social Psychology* 31:664–669.

Bremner, Robert II. 1956. *From the Depths: The Discovery of Poverty in the United States.* New York: New York University Press.

Buchanan, James M., and Gordon Tullock. 1962. *The Calculus of Consent: Logical Foundations of Constitutional Democracy.* Ann Arbor: University of Michigan Press.

Bullock, Charles S., III, and David W. Brady. 1983. "Party, Constituency, and Roll-Call Voting in the U.S. Senate." *Legislative Studies Quarterly* 8:29–43.

Burnstein, Paul, and William Freudenburg. 1978. "Changing Public Policy: The Impact of Public Opinion, Antiwar Demonstrations, and War Costs on Senate Voting on Vietnam War Motions." *American Journal of Sociology* 84:99–122.

Butler, Stuart M. 1987. "A Conservative Vision of Welfare." *Policy Review* 40:3–8.

Butler, Stuart, and Anna Kondratas. 1987. *Out of the Poverty Trap: A Conservative Strategy for Welfare Reform.* New York: Free Press.

California Department of Social Services. 1986. "Greater Avenues for Independence Program."

Campbell, Angus, Philip E. Converse, W. E. Miller, and D. E. Stokes. 1960. *The American Voter.* New York: Wiley.

Cantril, Hanley. 1944. *Gauging Public Opinion.* Princeton: Princeton University Press.

Carmines, Edward G., and James A. Stimson. 1989. *Issue Evolution: Race and the Transformation of American Politics.* Princeton: Princeton University Press.

Carter, G. W., L. H. Fifield, and H. Shields. 1973. *Public Attitudes Toward Welfare—An Opinion Poll.* Los Angeles: University of Southern California Regional Institute in Social Welfare.

Cavanaugh, Thomas E., and James L. Sundquist. 1985. "The New Two-Party System." In *The New Direction in American Politics*, edited by John E. Chubb and Paul E. Petersen, pp. 33–68. Washington, D.C.: Brookings Institution.

Chisman, Forrest, and Alan Pifer. 1987. *Government for the People.* New York: W. W. Norton.

Clausen, Aage. 1973. *How Congressmen Decide: A Policy Focus.* New York: St. Martin's Press.

Cochran, W. G. 1977. *Sampling Techniques*. New York: Wiley.

Converse, Philip E. 1964. "The Nature of Belief Systems in Mass Publics." In *Ideology and Discontent*, edited by David E. Apter, pp. 219–227. New York: Free Press.

Cook, Fay Lomax. 1986. "Survey of Surveys on Public Attitudes about Social Welfare Beneficiaries, Programs, and Policies." Report to the Executive Office of the White House. Evanston, Ill.: Center for Urban Affairs and Policy Research and School of Education and Social Policy, Northwestern University.

Cook, Fay Lomax. 1979. *Who Should Be Helped? Public Support for Social Services*. Beverly Hills, Calif.: Sage.

Coughlin, Richard M. 1989. "Welfare Myths and Stereotypes." In *Lessons, Limits, and Choices*, edited by Richard M. Coughlin, pp. 79–106. Albuquerque: University of New Mexico Press.

Coughlin, Richard M. 1980. *Ideology, Public Opinion, and Welfare Policy: Attitudes Toward Taxes and Spending in Industrialized Societies*. Berkeley: International Studies, University of California.

Coyle, D., and Aaron Wildavsky. 1986. "Requisites of Radical Change: Income Maintenace Versus Tax Reform." Paper presented at a conference on "The Income Maintenance Experiments: Lessons for Welfare Reform," sponsored by the Federal Research Bank of Boston and the Brookings Institution, Bald Peak Colony Club, Melvin Village, N.H.

Czaja, Ronald, John Blair, and Jutta P. Sebestik. 1982. "Respondent Selection in Telephone Survey: A Comparison of Three Techniques." *Journal of Marketing Research* 19:381–385.

Daeley, John A. 1989. "Up from Dependency: The President's National Welfare Strategy." In *Reforming Welfare: Lessons, Limits, and Choices*, edited by Richard M. Coughlin, pp. 179–199. Albuquerque: University of New Mexico.

Dahl, Robert A. 1956. *A Preface to Democratic Theory*. Chicago: University of Chicago Press.

Darcy, R., Susan Welch, and Janet Clark. 1987. *Women, Elections, and Representation*. New York: Longman.

Dawson, Richard E., Kenneth Prewitt, and Karen S. Dawson. 1977. *Political Socialization*, 2d ed. Boston: Little, Brown.

Davidson, Roger H., and Walter J. Oleszek. 1985. *Congress and Its Members*, 2d ed. Washington, D.C.: Congressional Quarterly.

Day, Christine L. 1990. *What Older Americans Think: Interest Groups and Aging Policy*. Princeton: Princeton University Press.

DeMaio, Theresa J. 1984. "Social Desirability and Survey Measurement: A Review." In *Surveying Subjective Phenomena*, edited by Charles F. Turner and Elizabeth Martin, vol. 2, pp. 257–282. New York: Russell Sage Foundation.

Derthick, M. 1975. *Uncontrollable Spending for Social Service Grants*. Washington, D.C.: Brookings Institution.

Dodd, Lawrence C. 1977. "Congress and the Quest for Power." In *Congress*

Reconsidered, edited by Lawrence C. Dodd and Bruce I. Oppenheimer, pp. 269–307. New York: Praeger.

Downs, Anthony. 1957. *An Economic Theory of Democracy.* New York: Harper.

Duncan, Greg. 1984. *Years of Poverty, Years of Plenty: The Changing Economic Fortunes of American Workers and Their Families.* Ann Arbor: Survey Research Center, Institute for Social Research, University of Michigan.

Easton, David, and Jack Dennis. 1969. *Children in the Political System: Origins of Political Legitimacy.* New York: McGraw-Hill.

Ehrenreich, Barbara, and Frances Fox Piven. 1984. "The Feminization of Poverty." *Dissent* 31:162–170.

Ellwood, David T. 1988. *Poor Support: Poverty in the American Family.* New York: Basic Books.

Esping-Anderson, Gosta. 1983. "After the Welfare State." *Public Welfare* 44:28–34.

Farkas, Steve, Robert Y. Shapiro, and Benjamin Page. 1990. "The Dynamics of Public Opinion and Policy." Paper presented at the Annual Meeting of the American Public Opinion Research Organization, Lancaster, Pa.

Feagin, J. R. 1972. "America's Welfare Stereotype." *Social Science Quarterly* 52:920–933.

Ferejohn, John A. 1977. "On the Decline of Competition in Congressional Elections." *American Political Science Review* 71:166–176.

Ferguson, Thomas, and Joel Rogers. 1986. "The Myth of America's Turn to the Right." *Atlantic Monthly* May:43–53.

Fiorina, Morris P. 1977. *Congress: Keystone of the Washington Establishment.* New Haven: Yale University Press.

Fishbein, Martin, and Icek Ajzen. 1975. *Beliefs, Attitudes, Intentions and Behavior: An Introduction to Theory and Research.* Reading, Mass.: Addison-Wesley.

Flora, Peter. 1985. "On the History and the Current Problems of the Welfare State." In *The Welfare State and Its Aftermath,* edited by S. N. Eisenstadt and Ora Ahimeir, pp. 11–28. Totowa, N.J.: Barnes and Noble.

Ford Foundation. 1989. *The Common Good: Social Welfare and the American Future.* Policy Recommendations of the Executive Panel, Ford Foundation Project on Social Welfare and the American Future. New York: Ford Foundation.

GAO. 1983. *Improving Medicare and Medicaid Systems to Control Payments for Unnecessary Physicians' Services.* Washington, D.C.: U.S. Government Printing Office.

GAO. 1976. *Tighter Controls Needed . . . Overpayment for Laboratory Services under Medicare and Medicaid.* Washington, D.C.: U.S. Government Printing Office.

Goodwin, Leonard, and J. Tu. 1975. "The Social Psychological Basis for Public Acceptance of the Social Security System: The Role for Social Research in Public Policy Formation." *American Psychologist* 30:875–883.

Grace, J. P. 1984. *War on Waste: President's Private Sector Survey on Cost Control.* New York: Macmillan.

Green, Donald Philip, and Ann Elizabeth Gerken. 1989. "Self-Interest and Public Opinion toward Smoking Restrictions and Cigarette Taxes." *Public Opinion Quarterly* 53:1–16.

Greenstein, Robert. 1991. "Universal and Targeted Approaches to Relieving Poverty: An Alternative View." In *The Urban Underclass*, edited by Christopher Jencks and Paul E. Petersen, pp. 437–459. Washington, D.C.: Brookings Institution.

Groves, Robert M. and Robert L. Kahn. 1979. *Surveys by Telephone: A National Comparison with Personal Interviews*. New York: Academic.

Gutman, Amy, ed. 1988. *Democracy and the Welfare State*. Princeton: Princeton Unviersity Press.

Harpham, Edward J., and Richard K. Scotch. 1989. "Ideology and Welfare Reform in the 1980s." In *Reforming Welfare: Lessons, Limits, and Choices*, edited by Richard M. Coughlin, pp. 43–60. Albuquerque: University of New Mexico.

Hasenfeld, Yeheskel, and Jane A. Rafferty. 1989. "The Determinants of Public Attitudes toward the Welfare State." *Social Forces* 67:1027–1048.

Haveman, Robert H., ed. 1987. *Poverty Policy and Poverty Research: The Great Society and the Social Sciences*. Madison: University of Wisconsin Press.

Heclo, Hugh. 1986. "General Welfare and Two American Political Traditions." *Political Science Quarterly* 101:179–196.

Heclo, Hugh. 1974. *Modern Social Politics in Britain and Sweden*. New Haven: Yale University Press.

Hewlett, Sylvia Ann. 1991. *When The Bough Breaks*. New York: Basic Books.

Hunter, Robert. 1904. *Poverty*. New York: Harper & Row.

Hurley, Patricia A. 1982. "Collective Representation Reappraised." *Legislative Studies Quarterly* 7:119–136.

Jackson, John E. 1974. *Constituency and Leaders in Congress*. Cambridge, Mass.: Harvard University Press.

Jacob, Bruce. 1990. "Aging and Politics." In *Handbook of Aging and the Social Sciences*, edited by Linda George and Robert Binstock, pp. 350–361. San Diego: Academic Press.

Janda, Kenneth, Jeffrey M. Berry, and Jerry Goldman. 1989. *The Challenge of Democracy: Government in America*, 2d ed. Boston: Houghton-Mifflin.

Janda, Kenneth, Jeffrey M. Berry, and Jerry Goldman. 1987. *The Challenge of Democracy: Government in America*. Boston: Houghton-Mifflin.

Jennings, M. K., and R. G. Niemi. 1974. *The Political Character of Adolescence: The Influence of Families and Schools*. Princeton: Princeton University Press.

Jerome, Robert W. 1990. *U.S. Senate Decision-Making: The Trade Agreements Act of 1979*. Westport, Conn.: Greenwood Press.

Jöreskog, Karl G., and Dag Sörbom. 1989. *LISREL 7 User's Reference Guide*, 1st ed. Mooresville, Ind.: Scientific Software.

Judd, Charles M., and Michael M. Milburn. 1980. "The Structure of Attitude Systems in the General Public: Comparisons of a Structural Equation Model." *American Sociological Review* 45:627–643.

Kallman, Ann. 1991. "Public Social Welfare Expenditures, Fiscal Year 1988." *Social Security Bulletin* 54:7–10.

Katz, Michael B. 1986. *In the Shadow of the Poorhouse: A Social History of Welfare in America*. New York: Basic Books.

Keefe, William J. 1984. *Congress and the American People*, 2d ed. Englewood Cliffs, N.J.: Prentice-Hall.

Kelman, Steven. 1987. *Making Public Policy: A Hopeful View of American Government*. New York: Basic Books.

Kelman, Steven. 1986. " 'Public Choice' and Public Spirit." *The Public Interest* 87:80–94.

Kinder, Donald R. 1981. "Presidents, Prosperity, and Public Opinion." *Public Opinion Quarterly* 45:1–21.

Kingdon, John. 1981. *Congressmen's Voting Decisions*, 2d ed. New York: Harper & Row.

Kirkpatrick, Evron M. 1971. "Toward a More Responsible Two-Party System: Political Science, Policy Science, or Pseudo-Science?" *American Political Science Review* 65:965–990.

Kluegel, James R., and Eliot R. Smith. 1986. *Beliefs About Inequality: American Views of What is and What Ought to Be*. New York: Aldine de Gruyter.

Kothandapani, V. 1971. "Validation of Feeling, Belief, and Intention to Act as Three Components of Attitudes and Their Contribution to Prediction of Contraceptive Behavior." *Journal of Personality and Social Psychology* 19: 321–333.

Krebs, D. L. 1970. "Altruism: An Examination of the Concept and a Review of the Literature." *Psychological Bulletin* 73:258–302.

Kritzer, Herbert M., and Robert E. Eubank. 1979. "Presidential Coattails Revisited: Partisanship and Incumbency Effects." *American Journal of Political Science* 23:615–626.

Ladd, Everett C. 1985. *The American Polity: The People and Their Government*. New York: W. W. Norton.

Ladd, Everett C. 1984. "The Reagan Phenomenon and Public Attitudes toward Government." In *The Reagan Presidency and the Governing of America*, edited by Lester M. Salamon and Michael S. Lund. Washington, D.C.: Urban Institute Press.

Lane, Robert, and David O. Sears. 1964. *Public Opinion*. Englewood Cliffs, N.J.: Prentice-Hall.

Lau, Richard, T.A. Brown, and David O. Sears. 1978. "Self-Interest and Civilians' Attitudes toward the Vietnam War." *Public Opinion Quarterly* 42:464–483.

Lehmann, Nicholas. 1989. "The Unfinished War," part II. *Atlantic Monthly* 263:53–68.

Lehmann, Nicholas. 1988. "The Unfinished War," part I. *Atlantic Monthly* 262:37–56.

Leiby, James. 1978. *A History of Social Welfare and Social Work in the United States*. New York: Columbia University Press.

Levitan, Sar A. 1990. *Programs in Aid of the Poor*, 6th ed. Baltimore: Johns Hopkins University Press.

Levy, Frank. 1989. "Paying for College: A New Look at Family Income Trends." *College Board Review* Summer:18–21, 32–33.

Lewis, I. A., and William Schneider. 1985. "Hard Times: The Public on Poverty." *Public Opinion* June/July:2–3, 57–60.

Lipset, Seymour Martin, and William Schneider. 1987. *The Confidence Gap: Business, Labor, and Government in the Public Mind*, rev. ed. Baltimore: Johns Hopkins University Press.

Longman, Phillip. 1982. "Taking America to the Cleaners." *Washington Monthly* November:24–30.

Lynn, Lawrence, Jr. 1977. "A Decade of Policy Developments in the Income Maintenance System." In *A Decade of Federal Antipoverty Programs: Achievements, Failures, and Lessons*, edited by Robert H. Haveman. New York: Academic Press.

Maass, Arthur. 1983. *Congress and the Common Good*. New York: Basic Books.

Macarov, David. 1978. *The Design of Social Welfare*. New York: Holt, Rinehart, and Winston.

Mackie, J. L. 1980. *The Cement of the Universe: A Study of Causation*. Oxford: Clarendon Press.

MacRae, D., Jr. 1958. *Dimensions of Congressional Voting*. Berkeley: University of California Press.

Mansbridge, Jane J., ed. 1990. *Beyond Self-Interest*. Chicago: University of Chicago Press.

Marmor, Theodore R., and Fay Lomax Cook. 1988. "Social Security Crisis-Mongering." *Chicago Tribune*, May 10, sec. 1, p. 13.

Marmor, Theodore R., Jerry L. Mashaw, and Philip L. Harvey. 1990. *America's Misunderstood Welfare State: Persistent Myths, Enduring Realities*. New York: Basic Books.

Marshall, T. H. 1950. *Class, Citizenship, and Social Development*. Garden City, N.Y.: Doubleday.

Matt, Georg E., and Thomas D. Cook. 1991. "The War on Fraud and Error in the Food Stamp Program. What Did the Carter and Reagan Years Achieve?" Working paper, Center for Urban Affairs and Policy Research, Northwestern University.

Matthews, Donald R., and James A. Stimson. 1970. "Decision-Making by U.S. Representatives: A Preliminary Model." In *Political Decision Making*, edited by S. Sidney Ulmer. New York: Van Nostrand Reinhold.

Mayhew, D. R. 1974. *Congress: The Electoral Connection*. New Haven: Yale University Press.

Mayhew, D. R. 1966. *Party Loyalty Among Congressmen: The Differences Between Democrats and Republicans, 1947–1962*. Cambridge, Mass.: Harvard University Press.

Mead, Lawrence. 1986. *Beyond Entitlement: The Social Obligations of Citizenship*. New York: Free Press.

Miller, Warren E., and Donald E. Stokes. 1963. "Constituency Influence in Congress." *American Political Science Review* 57:45–56.

Mitchell, William C. 1970. *Public Choice in America: An Introduction to American Government*. Chicago: Markham.

Monroe, Alan D. 1979. "Consistency between Public Preferences and National Policy Decisions." *American Politics Quarterly* 7:3–19.

Murray, Charles. 1984. *Losing Ground*. New York: Basic Books.

Myles, John. 1989. *Old Age in the Welfare State: The Political Economy of Public Pensions*, rev. ed. Lawrence: University Press of Kansas.

National Governors' Association. 1987. *NGA Welfare Reform Policy*. Washington, D.C.: National Governors' Association.

Noelle-Neumann, Elisabeth. 1984. *The Spiral of Silence: Public Opinion—Our Social Skin*. Chicago: University of Chicago Press.

Norpoth, Helmut. 1976. "Explaining Party Cohesion in Congress: The Case of Shared Policy Attitudes." *American Political Science Review* 70:1156–1171.

OECD. 1981. *The Welfare State in Crisis: An Account of the Conference on Social Policies in the 1980s*. Paris: Organization for Economic Cooperation and Development.

Opinion Roundup. 1985. *Public Opinion* 7:27.

Ornstein, Norman J., Thomas E. Mann, Michael J. Malbin, and John F. Bibby. 1982. *Vital Statistics on Congress, 1982*. Washington, D.C.: American Enterprise Institute.

Page, Benjamin I. 1978. *Choices and Echoes in Presidential Elections: Rational Man and Electoral Democracy*. Chicago: University of Chicago Press.

Page, Benjamin I., and Shapiro, Robert Y. 1983. "Effects of Public Opinion on Policy." *American Political Science Review* 77:175–190.

Page, Benjamin I., Robert Y. Shapiro, Paul W. Gronke, and Robert M. Rosenberg. 1984. "Constitutency, Party, and Representation in Congress." *Public Opinion Quarterly* 48:741–756.

Palmer, John L., and Isabel Sawhill, eds. 1984. *The Reagan Record*. Washington, D.C.: Urban Institute.

Palmer, John L., and Isabel Sawhill. 1982. *The Reagan Experiment*. Washington, D.C.: Urban Institute.

Parker, Glenn R. 1986. *Homeward Bound: Explaining Changes in Congressional Behavior*. Pittsburgh: University of Pittsburgh Press.

Parker, Glenn R. 1985. "Determinants of Floor Voting." In *Studies of Congress*, edited by Glenn R. Parker, pp. 387–393. Washington, D.C.: Congressional Quarterly.

Patterson, James. 1981. *America's Struggle Against Poverty, 1900–1980*. Cambridge, Mass.: Harvard University Press.

Pear, Robert. 1981. "Welfare Trims Hit Working Mothers." *New York Times*, September 29, sec. 2, p. 1.

Pereira, Joseph A., and Peter H. Rossi. 1985. "Who Should be Supported? New Yorkers' Normative Views on Welfare Entitlement." Report to the Community Service Society on pilot study of Popular Views of What

Justifies Support Payments from Public Funds. Amherst, Mass.: Social and Democraphic Research Institute.

Peterson, Paul E., and Mark Rom. 1988. "Lower Taxes, More Spending and Budget Deficits." In *The Reagan Legacy: Promise and Performance*, edited by Charles O. Jones. Chatham, N.J.: Chatham House.

Pierce, J. C., and D. D. Rose. 1974. "Non-Attitudes and American Public Opinion." *American Political Science Review* 68:626–649.

Piven, Frances Fox, and Richard A. Cloward. 1988. "Popular Power and the Welfare State." In *Remaking the Welfare State: Retrenchment and Social Policy in America and Europe*, edited by Michael K. Brown. Philadelphia: Temple University Press.

Piven, Frances Fox, and Richard A. Cloward. 1982. *The New Class War: Reagan's Attack on the Welfare State and Its Consequences*. New York: Pantheon.

Pomper, Gerald. 1972. "From Confusion to Clarity: Issues and the American Voters, 1956–1968." *American Political Science Review* 66:415–428.

Ponza, Michael, Greg J. Duncan, Mary Corcoran, and Fred Groskind. 1988. "The Guns of Autumn? Age Differences in Support for Income Transfers to the Young and Old." *Public Opinion Quarterly* 52:441–466.

Poole, Keith T. 1988. "Recent Developments in Analytical Models of Voting in the U.S. Congress." *Legislative Studies Quarterly* 13:117–133.

Popkin, Susan J. 1985. "Something for Nothing: Understanding Public Attitudes Toward Welfare." Master's thesis, Department of Human Development and Social Policy, Northwestern University.

Preston, Samuel H. 1984. "Children and the Elderly: Divergent Paths for America's Dependents." *Demography* 21:435–457.

Quirk, Paul J. 1988. "In Defense of the Politics of Ideas." *Journal of Politics* 50:31–41.

Reagan, Ronald. 1983. "State of the Union Address." *Washington Post*, January 26, p. A12.

Reagan, Ronald. 1981. "State of the Union Address." *New York Times*, February 19, p. B8.

Reich, Robert B., ed. 1988. *The Power of Public Ideas*. Cambridge, Mass.: Ballinger.

Riis, Jacob. 1970 [1892]. *The Children of the Poor*. New York: Johnson Reprints.

Rochefort, David A. 1986. *American Social Welfare Policy: Dynamics of Formulation and Change*. Boulder, Colo.: Westview Press.

Rose, Nancy E. 1989. "The Political Economy of Welfare." *Journal of Sociology and Social Welfare* 16(2):87–108.

Ryan, William. 1971. *Blaming the Victim*. New York: Vintage.

Salmon, Charles T., and John Spicer Nichols. 1983. "The Next Birthday Method of Respondent Selection." *Public Opinion Quarterly* 47:270–276.

Sanders, Arthur. 1988. "Rationality, Self-Interest, and Public Attitudes on Public Spending." *Social Science Quarterly* 69:311–324.

Schattschneider, E. E. 1942. *Party Government*. New York: Holt, Rinehart, and Winston.

Schlozman, Kay Lehman, and Sidney Verba. 1979. *Injury to Insult: Unemployment, Class, and Political Response*. Cambridge, Mass.: Harvard University Press.

Schwartz, S. 1975. "The Justice of Need and Activism of Humanitarian Norms." *Journal of Social Issues* 31:111–136.

Schwarz, John E. 1988. *America's Hidden Success: A Reassessment of Public Policy from Kennedy to Reagan*, rev. ed. New York: W. W. Norton.

Searing, Donald, Gerald Wright, and George Rabinowitz. 1976. "The Primacy Principle: Attitude Change and Political Socialization." *British Journal of Political Science* 6:83–113.

Sears, David O. 1983. "The Persistence of Early Political Predispositions: The Roles of Attitude Object and Life Stage." In *Review of Personality and Social Psychology*, edited by L. Wheeler and P. Shaver, vol. 4, pp. 79–116. Beverly Hills, Calif.: Sage.

Sears, David O. 1975. "Political Socialization." In *Handbook of Political Science*, edited by F. I. Greenstein and N. W. Polsby, vol. 2, pp 93–153. Reading, Mass.: Addison Wesley.

Sears, David O., and Jack Citrin. 1982. *Tax Revolt: Something for Nothing in California*. Cambridge, Mass.: Harvard University Press.

Sears, David O., and Carolyn L. Funk. 1990. "Self-Interest in Americans' Political Opinions." In *Beyond Self-Interest*, edited by Jane J. Mansbridge, pp. 147–170. Chicago: University of Chicago.

Sears, David O., C. P. Hensler, and L. K. Speer. 1979. "Whites' Opposition to 'Busing': Self-Interest or Symbolic Politics." *American Political Science Review* 73:369–384.

Sears, David O., Richard R. Lau, Tom R. Tyler, and Harris M. Allen, Jr. 1980. "Self-Interest and Symbolic Politics in Policy Attitudes and Presidential Voting." *American Political Science Review* 74:670–684.

Sen, Amartya K. 1977. "Rational Fools: A Critique of the Behavioral Foundations of Economic Theory." *Philosophy and Public Affairs* 6:317–344.

Shadish, William R., Thomas D. Cook, and Laura C. Leviton. 1991. *Foundations of Program Evaluation: Theories of Practice*. Newbury Park, Calif.: Sage.

Shapiro, Robert Y., and Lawrence R. Jacobs. 1989. "The Relationship between Public Opinion and Public Policy." In *Political Behavior Annual*, edited by Samuel Long. Boulder, Colo.: Westview Press.

Shapiro, Robert Y., and Kelly D. Patterson. 1986. "The Dynamics of Public Opinion toward Social Welfare Policy." Paper presented at the annual meeting of the American Political Science Association, Washington, D.C.

Shapiro, Robert Y., Kelly D. Patterson, J. Russell, and John T. Young. 1987. "The Polls: Public Assistance." *Public Opinion Quarterly* 57:120–130.

Shapiro, Robert Y., and John T. Young. 1988. "Public Opinion toward Social Welfare Policies: The United States in Comparative Perspective." In *Re-*

search in Micropolitics, edited by Samuel Long. Greenwich, Conn.: JAI Press.

Sheehan, Susan. 1977. *A Welfare Mother*. New York: New American Library.

Siegel, Jacob S., and Cynthia M. Taeuber. 1986. "Demographic Dimensions of an Aging Population." In *Our Aging Society: Paradox and Promise*, edited by Alan Pifer and Lydia Bronte. New York: W. W. Norton.

Skocpol, Theda. 1991. "Targeting within Universalism: Politically Viable Policies to Combat Poverty in the United States." In *The Urban Underclass*, edited by Christopher Jencks and Paul E. Petersen, pp. 411–436. Washington, D.C.: Brookings Institution.

Skocpol, Theda. 1990. "Sustainable Social Policy: Fighting Poverty without Poverty Programs." *American Prospect* 2:58–70.

Smith, Adam. 1799 [1776]. *An Inquiry into the Nature and Causes of the Wealth of Nations*, 9th ed. London: Printed for A. Strahan, T. Cadell, and W. Davies.

Smith, Steven Rathgeb, and Deborah A. Stone. 1988. "The Unexpected Consequences of Privatization." In *Remaking the Welfare State: Retrenchment and Social Policy in America and Europe*. Philadelphia: Temple University Press.

Smith, Steven S. 1989. *Call to Order: Floor Politics in the House and Senate*. Washington, D.C.: Brookings Institution.

Smith, Steven S., and Christopher J. Deering. 1984. *Committees in Congress*. Washington, D.C.: Congressional Quarterly.

Smith, Tom. 1987a. "The Polls—A Report: The Welfare State in Cross-National Perspective." *Public Opinion Quarterly* 51:404–421.

Smith, Tom. 1987b. "That which We Call Welfare by any Other Name would Smell Sweeter: An Analysis of the Impact of Question Wording on Response Patterns." *Public Opinion Quarterly* 51:75–83.

Smith, Tom. 1984. "Nonattitudes: A Review and Evaluation." In *Surveying Subjective Phenomena*, edited by Charles F. Turner and Elizabeth Martin, vol. 2, pp. 215–255. New York: Russell Sage Foundation.

Social Security Bulletin. 1987a. *Annual Statistical Supplement*. Washington, D.C.: U.S. Department of Health and Human Services, Social Security Administration.

Social Security Bulletin. 1987b. *Fast Facts and Figures about Social Security*, vol. 50(5), pp. 5–22. Washington, D.C.: U.S. Department of Health and Human Services, Social Security Administration.

Stein, Bruno. 1971. *On Relief: The Economics of Poverty and Public Welfare*. New York: Basic Books.

Stigler, George J. 1971. "The Theory of Economic Regulation." *Bell Journal of Economics and Management* 2:3–21.

Stockman, David A. 1986. *The Triumph of Politics: How the Reagan Revolution Failed*. New York: Harper & Row.

Stoesz, David, and Howard Jacob Karger. 1992. *Reconstructing the American Welfare State*. Lanham, Md.: Rowman and Littlefield.

Taylor-Gooby, Peter. 1985. *Public Opinion, Ideology, and State Welfare*. Boston: Routledge and Kegan Paul.

Tocqueville, Alexis. 1969 [1848]. *Democracy in America*, translated by G. Lawrence. Garden City, N.Y.: Doubleday.

Trattner, Walter I. 1989. *From Poor Law to Welfare State: A History of Social Welfare in America*, 4th ed. New York: Free Press.

Truman, D. B. 1959. *The Congressional Party*. New York: Wiley.

Tufte, E. R. 1978. *Political Control of the Economy*. Princeton: Princeton University.

Tyler, Tom R., and Renee Weber. 1982. "Support for the Death Penalty: Instumental Response to Crime or Symbolic Attitude?" *Law and Society Review* 17:21–45.

U.S. Arms Control and Disarmament Agency. 1990. *World Military Expenditures and Arms Transfers: 1989*. Washington, D.C.: U.S. Government Printing Office.

U.S. Bureau of the Census. 1991a. "Facts from the Summary Tape, File 1A." *The Census and You* 26 (7):5–7.

U.S. Bureau of the Census. 1991b. "Marital Status and Living Arrangements: March 1990." *Current Population Reports*, Series P-60, No. 450. Washington, D.C.: U.S. Government Printing Office.

U.S. Bureau of the Census. 1991c. "Poverty in the United States: 1990." *Current Population Reports*, Series P-60, No. 175. Washington, D.C.: U.S. Government Printing Office.

U.S. Bureau of the Census. 1991d. *Statistical Abstract of the U.S.* Washington, D.C.: U.S. Government Printing Office.

U.S. Bureau of the Census. 1990. "Money and Poverty Status in the United States: 1989." *Current Population Reports*, Series P-60, No. 168, Table C. Washington, D.C.: U.S. Government Printing Office.

U.S. Bureau of the Census. 1989. "Projections of the Population of the United States by Age, Sex, and Race: 1988 to 2080." *Current Population Reports*, Series P-25, No. 1018. Washington, D.C.: U.S. Government Printing Office.

U.S. Bureau of the Census. 1983. *Congressional Districts of the 98th Congress*. Washington, D.C.: U.S. Government Printing Office.

U.S. Department of Health and Human Services. 1991. *Characteristics and Financial Circumstances of AFDC Recipients: FY 1989*. Washington, D.C.: U.S. Government Printing Office.

U.S. Department of Health and Human Services. 1990. *Fast Facts and Figures about Social Security*. Washington, D.C.: U.S. Government Printing Office.

U.S. House of Representatives, Committee on Ways and Means. 1991. *Overview of Entitlement Programs. 1991 Green Book. Background Material and Data on Programs Within the Jurisdiction of the Committee on Ways and Means*. Washington, D.C.: U.S. Government Printing Office.

Verba, Sidney, and Gary R. Orren. 1985. *Equality in America: The Views from the Top*. Cambridge, Mass.: Harvard University Press.

Wald, Matthew L. 1981. "Connecticut's Welfare Recipients are Given Jobs to Pay Back Cities." *New York Times*, sec. 2, p. 1, May 20.

Washington State Department of Social and Health Services and the Employment Service Department. 1986. "The Family Independence Program."

Weaver, R. Kent. 1986. "The Politics of Blame Avoidance." *Journal of Public Policy* 6:371–396.

Weir, Margaret, Ann Orloff, and Theda Skocpol, eds. 1988. *The Politics of Social Policy in the United States*. Princeton: Princeton University Press.

Weiss, Carol H. 1983. "Ideology, Interests, and Information: The Basis of Policy Positions." In *Ethics, the Social Sciences, and Policy Analysis*, edited by Daniel Callahan and Bruce Jennings, pp. 213–245. New York: Plenum.

Weissberg, Robert. 1979. "Assessing Legislator-Constituency Policy Agreement." *Legislative Studies Quarterly* 4:605–622.

Weissberg, Robert. 1978. "Collective vs. Dyadic Representation in Congress." *American Political Science Review* 72:535–547.

Weissberg, Robert. 1976. *Public Opinion and Popular Government*. Englewood Cliffs, N.J.: Prentice-Hall.

Weissberg, Robert. 1974. *Political Learning, Political Choice, and Democratic Citizenship*. Englewood Cliffs, N.J.: Prentice-Hall.

West, Darrell M. 1988. "Activism and Economic Policymaking in Congress." *American Journal of Political Science* 32(3):662–680.

White House Domestic Policy Council. 1986. "Up From Dependency: A New National Public Assistance Strategy." A Report to President Reagan by the Low-Income Opportunity Working Group of the White House Domestic Policy Council, Charles Hobbs, Chair.

Wilson, Glenn D., and Florence Caldwell. 1988. "Social Attitudes and Voting Intentions of Members of the European Parliament." *Individual Differences* 9:147–153.

Wilson, James Q., and E. C. Banfield. 1964. "Public Regardingness as a Value Premise in Voting Behavior." *American Political Science Review* 58: 876–887.

Wilson, William Julius. 1987. *The Truly Disadvantaged: The Inner City, The Underclass, and Public Policy*. Chicago: University of Chicago Press.

Wittkopf, Eugene R. 1990. *Faces of Internationalism: Public Opinion and American Foreign Policy*. Durham, N.C.: Duke University Press.

Woodroofe, K. 1962. *From Charity to Social Work in England and the United States*. Toronto: University of Toronto Press.

Yankelovich, Daniel. 1991. *Coming to Public Judgment: Making Democracy Work in a Complex World*. Syracuse: Syracure University Press.

Author Index

Subject Index

Aid to Families with Dependent Children (AFDC): history and characteristics of, 4, 5, 6n, 10, 12–14, 16, 19, 61; level of support for, 254–255; support of Congress in general, 76–78, 80, 88; support of congressional leaders for, 78, 85, 86, 88; support among public for, 61–70, 215–217; support of public and Congress compared for, 89–93, 228–229; see also Deservingness; Disposition-attribution model; Political predisposition; Program effectiveness; Self-interest

American Association of Retired Persons (AARP), 169

Americans for Constitutional Action (ACA), 172, 252

Americans for Democratic Action (ADA), 172, 252

Blind, see Disabled and blind

Carter, Jimmy, 16–17, 236

Catastrophic Health Insurance: explanation and level of support for, in Congress, 77, 79, 82–83, 86–89, 92, 115–117, 137–138, 255–256; explanation and level of support for, among public, 71, 72, 75–76, 92, 106–108, 124–126, 217, 221, 255–256

Children, 12, 13–14; and demographic crisis, 21–23; explanation of support for, 37, 41, 49, 52, 144, 144n; explanation of support in Congress for, 110–111, 115–117, 129–133, 164, 167–168, 178–182, 186–187, 207, 229–230; explanation of support among public for, 101, 104, 106–108, 113, 124–127, 137–138, 149, 156, 156n, 160, 229–230; history of support for, 8, 9–10, 15, 16; level of support by Congress for, 79–83, 88–89, 252, 255–256; level of support by congressional leaders for, 86–89; level of support among public for, 61, 71–76, 217, 222, 255–256; level of support between public and Congress compared for, 92–93; see also Aid to Families with Dependent Children